FROZEN
IN TIME

FROZEN IN TIME

CLARENCE BIRDSEYE'S OUTRAGEOUS IDEA ABOUT FROZEN FOOD

MARK KURLANSKY

DELACORTE PRESS

Library of Congress Cataloging-in-Publication Data
Kurlansky, Mark.
Frozen in time : Clarence Birdseye's outrageous idea about frozen food /
Mark Kurlansky.
pages cm
Audience: Age 10 and up.
ISBN 978-0-385-74388-4 (hardback) —
ISBN 978-0-375-99135-6 (library binding) —
ISBN 978-0-385-37243-5 (ebook) — ISBN 978-0-385-37244-2 (pbk.)
1. Birdseye, Clarence, 1886–1956—Juvenile literature. 2. Frozen foods
industry—United States—History—Juvenile literature. 3. Inventors—United
States—Biography—Juvenile literature. 4. Businessmen—United States—
Biography—Juvenile literature. I. Title.
HD9217.U52B5753 2014
338.7'664—dc23
[B]
2014017840

The text of this book is set in 11.75-point Goudy Old Style.
Book design by Trish Parcell

Printed in the United States of America
10 9 8 7 6 5 4 3 2 1
First Edition

To the memory of the too-short but good life of

Cooper Dean Stock,

a boy of curiosity and laughter

CONTENTS

PROLOGUE

The Nerds of the Industrial Revolution

It's easy to take for granted the food we eat today. When you open the freezer to take out a pizza or a bag of peas or a box of waffles, you're probably not thinking about who "invented" frozen food. But someone did, and that man was Clarence Birdseye. Some people might say that this is a book about a nerd, but it is really a book about a man who started a food revolution.

Clarence Birdseye was one of those kids who don't quite fit in. He was intensely interested in things his peers were not thinking much about. He did not care about what was hip or fashionable, and he was sometimes ridiculed for his peculiar interests. He didn't have enough money to finish college and was forced to drop out, yet he ultimately made a fortune off one of his ideas.

Although this story isn't from the headlines of today, it might sound like it's happening now. A list of people who changed the world in our time would include Bill Gates, a man who got his start devising a computer program for tic-tac-toe in the eighth grade; spent most of high school and college creating other programs; dropped out of Harvard to start his own software company, Microsoft, at age twenty; and soon became the wealthiest man in the world. And Mark Zuckerberg, who started Facebook with a group of college friends. Like Gates, Zuckerberg didn't finish college and started his own business, which made him a billionaire by age twenty-three.

Twenty-first-century inventors achieve fame and fortune at a much earlier age than their nineteenth- and twentieth-century counterparts. In truth, there have always been life-changing inventions, and the inventors from a century ago were just like the young people of today. They were people who looked at what could be created and found innovative ways to make new projects happen.

When Clarence Birdseye was alive, from the late nineteenth to the mid-twentieth century, the rate at which original, life-changing inventions were being developed and sold was dazzling. These dramatic inventions included electric lights, automobiles, the phonograph, and even the airplane, as well as smaller ideas, such as portable cameras, drinking straws, Styrofoam, fountain pens, and barbed wire.

Birdseye's interest in industrial food is not surprising, as there were many before him who made their fortunes from products like flavored gelatin, dried cereal, processed cheese, or sliced bread. Making a fortune on developing a really melty fake cheese is no stranger than selling an app that takes photos of your dog in a hat for more than a billion dollars. The key to invention is simply imagining something.

CHAPTER ONE

A Fast-Changing World

If Clarence Birdseye hadn't been born in Brooklyn (which was not part of New York City in the 1880s) on December 9, 1886, his life might have been very different. Brooklyn was the third-largest city in the United States and one of the fastest growing. Between 1880 and 1890, the population of Brooklyn increased by more than a third, to 806,343. One of the factors that made such growth possible was refrigeration. When populations of a few hundred thousand people or more lived in a concentrated area that produced no food, it was difficult to supply and distribute the needed quantities of fresh and nutritious food every day. Once people were able to buy a few days' worth of groceries and refrigerate them, population density began to rise.

A critical component of refrigeration around the world was ice generated in winter on the frozen lakes of upstate New York and New England and stored year-round in icehouses along the Hudson River. There the ice was kept insulated with sawdust until it could be shipped to cities. The storehouses supplied New York City with more than one million tons of ice every year for food and drinks.

The pleasure of enjoying iced drinks on a hot day had been a luxury for the wealthy since Roman times, but in New York City in the late nineteenth century, it became commonplace. Almost half of Manhattanites and Brooklynites stored food in their homes inside insulated boxes chilled by blocks of ice. A few people even had artificially chilled refrigerators, though at that time they were dangerous and clumsy electric machines with unpredictable motors and leaky fluids.

Birdseye was born into this world of iced drinks and refrigeration. He and other New Yorkers lived in a city where ice was used more than anywhere else in the world.

Even though Birdseye lived most of his life in the twentieth century, he spent his formative years in the late 1800s and grew up to become a nineteenth-century man. He was born at the height of the Industrial Revolution, and though he worked in an age of electronic invention, all his inventions would be mechanical, never electronic.

When Birdseye was born, the popular heroes were the inventors of the Industrial Revolution, who created that great shift from products made by hand in workshops to products made by machines in factories. He grew up in a time when industry was admired and industrializing was considered an admirable feat, as creating new technological gadgets is today.

In Birdseye's age the world was rapidly becoming industrialized, yet the food industry lagged behind and was still mostly artisanal. Not everyone had an icebox, and the preservation of refrigerated food had not been perfected. People had to rely almost exclusively on fresh produce.

Yet the world had evolved, thanks to new inventions. In 1876, just ten years before Birdseye was born, Alexander Graham Bell invented the telephone. The following year Thomas Edison invented the phonograph. In 1878 Joseph Wilson Swan, a British inventor, patented the first incandescent lightbulb and lit his home with electric lights. The year before Birdseye was born, a German engineer named Karl Benz—perhaps as important in his day as Bill Gates is today—patented the first automobile for practical use: a three-wheeled vehicle powered by an internal combustion engine, the kind still used in cars today, which is fueled by periodically filling the tank with gasoline. Also in 1885, another German, Gottlieb Daimler, built the first gas-powered motorcycle; the following year he built the first four-wheeled automobile.

Among the other important inventors at the time of Birdseye's birth was George Eastman, who was to have a profound effect on Birdseye. In 1884 Eastman patented roll film, and in 1888 he produced a lightweight camera that used the film, naming it the Kodak camera. His company, the Eastman Kodak Company, was the first major supplier of photographic equipment and gave birth to amateur photography, a passionate hobby of the young Clarence Birdseye. These cameras were to him and his generation what the latest cell phones and tablets are to us today.

In 1884 the synthetic-cloth industry began when a French chemist, Louis-Marie-Hilaire Bernigaud, Comte de

Chardonnet, patented a process to make artificial silk, which a decade later became known as rayon. That same year Lewis Waterman, a Brooklyn insurance agent, frustrated with the inefficient pens of the day, invented the capillary-feeding fountain pen, the first practical alternative to a pen dipped in an inkwell. Also in 1879 James Ritty, an Ohio barkeeper, became the first manufacturer of cash registers, which he had invented. In 1885, the American inventor Hiram Maxim demonstrated the first machine gun to the British army. In 1886, Birdseye's birth year, in addition to Daimler's automobile, Coca-Cola and the first washing machine were invented. The following year barbed wire, which divided up the open range and changed the character of the American West, as well as contact lenses, were patented. In 1888 Marvin Stone, an Ohio-born inventor, came out with the first paper drinking straw. In 1892 Joshua Pusey, a cigar-smoking attorney from Pennsylvania, invented the matchbook. In 1891, when Birdseye was four years old, Jesse Reno invented the escalator. Typical for his generation, Reno was part inventor and part entrepreneur, creating a sensation in Birdseye's native Brooklyn when he showcased the escalator for two weeks as a ride at the Coney Island amusement park. It was then featured on the Manhattan side of the Brooklyn Bridge—itself still a sensation as the longest suspension bridge in the world, connecting Brooklyn and Manhattan for the first time in 1883.

EUROPEAN INVENTIONS

Birdseye grew up in a time when new devices seemed to be coming out every week, garnering a great deal of public attention with claims that they would change everyone's life. Young people in particular embraced the new devices. It was an exciting time to be growing up.

In the nineteenth century there was a notable difference between the culture of American inventors and that of European inventors. In America, when someone came up with a new industrial idea, he registered it with the government, which gave the inventor a patent to establish his authorship of the idea. Americans had a Puritanical belief that anyone who invented something had a moral obligation to put it to useful service, so they thought inventions were of little value without practical and commercial applications. While Europe had the same patent-registry procedure, European inventors worked on patents that were merely theoretical, lest they give the impression of harboring lowbrow commercial interests. They did not have a capitalist view; they did not want to use inventions to make money.

There were, of course, exceptions on both sides. One was Dr. John Gorrie, who ran a hospital for the US Navy in Apalachicola, Florida, that treated victims of yellow fever and malaria. He invented a primitive form of air conditioning in the 1840s that produced artificial ice by expanding compressed air. Gorrie cooled his hospital and his home with his device but was so attacked by religious conservatives for interfering with God's design that he published his ideas in the *Commercial Advertiser* under a pseudonym. Not realizing who the writer was, the editor of the publication criticized the author for failing to put his ideas into service. It would be sixty years before modern air conditioning was developed, at the beginning of the twentieth century.

Then there was Robert Fulton, the father of the steamboat, an American inventor who actually benefited from the European view. The steamboat had had a long development that had nothing to do with him. It was a European idea, as was the steam engine. A Frenchman, Denis Papin, invented a piston steam engine in 1690 and a man-powered paddlewheel steamboat in 1704 but failed to attract any interest in them. The Scottish engineer James Watt built a greatly improved steam engine at the time of the American Revolution. But although the French, the Germans, the British, and the Americans built various steam-powered vessels, there were no *commercially* successful steamboats until Fulton's. So the great inventor Robert Fulton did not exactly invent anything. Rather, he put the right kind of engine in the right kind of vessel and established a commercial run on the right route. Earlier lines existed, but they were established on less profitable routes or on routes that already had good land transportation.

Fulton established his line in 1807 on the East River in Manhattan, making trips up the Hudson to Albany, the state capital. It was successful, in part because there was no good land route for hauling freight between these two important centers. Fulton is today often erroneously remembered as the inventor of the steamboat—in much the same way that Birdseye is erroneously remembered as the inventor of fast freezing. The real reason we still know the name Fulton is that he launched an industry by showing that money could be made from steamboats and that it was a commercially important idea.

Birdseye grew up in a world where mere concepts and

ideas were not enough. Inventors were expected to solve a problem, form a company, and, hopefully, earn a fortune. Alexander Graham Bell, a Scot who moved to Canada and then to America, was fairly well known, not only as the inventor of the telephone but also as the founder of the first telephone company, the Bell Telephone Company, in 1877. By the time Birdseye was born, just nine years later, Bell Telephone had placed phones in 150,000 homes and offices.

In 1876 Thomas Edison came to the public's attention for selling his telegraph idea to Western Union for a surprising $10,000. Then in 1880 he created another industry, Edison Lampworks, which manufactured 50,000 lightbulbs annually. When Edison developed an idea, which he did with astounding regularity, he built a company. This was the model Birdseye and his American contemporaries would follow.

CHAPTER TWO

Bugs Begins

Clarence Birdseye understood that he had a funny name, so he quickly dropped the Clarence and went by Bob for the rest of his life. Even people today who know the frozen-food brand Birds Eye, with its descending bird as a symbol, are often surprised that there actually *was* someone with such an odd name. All his life people had trouble believing that Birdseye was really his name. One of his favorite stories was how he once found himself in San Francisco, short on money, and wanted to cash a check. He called the local branch of General Foods' Birds Eye Division, a company named after him, explained his problem, and gave his name. The man on the other end of the line told him if he stopped kidding and gave his real name, he would connect him with someone.

Birdseye, who loved to tell stories, had another favorite, about the origin of his name. According to him, it was originally two words—Bird's Eye. In his story the young page to an English queen saw a large hawk swoop down toward her majesty. "This page boy ancestor of mine, according to the records, took out his trusty bow and arrow and shot that bird right in the eye," Birdseye would explain. "The queen was so tickled, she gave him the name right on the spot." He never produced these records, so there is reason for suspicion.

However, Birdseye loved hunting and hyperbolic tales of improbable shots. A great influence of the nineteenth century that would never leave him was the romance of the American West, which combined those two loves. He was born in a time when people who did not adjust well to life on the East Coast often went west, hoping for better, only to live with great deprivation and often violence. There was a brutal war of extermination against the native tribes throughout the territories. In 1886, Birdseye's birth year, the US Army, having failed to capture Chiricahua Apache leader Geronimo in Arizona, negotiated a treaty with him, which was never honored. The last action of the US Army against the native tribes took place when Birdseye was four years old. It was the shooting of three hundred mostly unarmed Lakota Sioux men, women, and children at their Pine Ridge, South Dakota, reservation by the Wounded Knee Creek on December 29, 1890.

Once the bloodshed ended, the western romance began, both on the East Coast and in Europe. Western landscapes became popular, as did rugs and other Indian artifacts. Romantic novels of western adventure were widely read; lacking massacres and broken treaties, the battles were represented as gripping but fair fights. Birdseye loved these spirited tales as a boy, and in fact all his life, and cowboys, hunters, and trappers fascinated him. His favorite writer was George Alfred Henty, a nineteenth-century English war correspondent turned popular novelist who wrote adventure stories, usually for boys. The lead characters were always highly intelligent, extremely resourceful, and courageous. He wrote 122 novels before he died, in 1902. Birdseye's favorite Henty novel was his 1891 *Redskin and Cowboy*. It is the tale of an English boy who is forced to leave the safety and quiet of his uncle's home and journey to the American West, where he meets such characters as Straight Charley, Bronco Harry, and Lightning Hugh. Although most Henty novels are thought of as children's books, Birdseye read them and other westerns his entire life, rereading his favorites.

As a kid growing up in Brooklyn, Birdseye dreamed of being a smart, capable young hero of a Henty novel. During his childhood, in the 1880s and '90s, several historians named Buffalo Bill Cody the most famous person in the world. He had earned his nickname after having been hired by the Kansas Pacific Railroad to keep the rail workers supplied with buffalo meat. According to legend, in eight months between 1867 and 1868 he killed 4,280 buffalo (actually bison). This kind of killing was another nineteenth-century American reality that strongly influenced Birdseye.

Historians have labeled the second half of the nineteenth century the age of extermination. The American bison herd, the largest land animal herd ever recorded, was by the late nineteenth century reduced from the tens of millions that once roamed the plains to only a few hundred. Today about 200,000 live on preserves and ranches. Passenger pigeons, which were thought to number five billion when Europeans started coming to North America and may have represented as much as 40 percent of the continent's bird population, were killed for cheap food. The last passenger pigeon passed away in a Cincinnati zoo in the early twentieth century.

In the nineteenth century four hundred thousand skunks, five hundred thousand raccoons, and two million muskrats were killed in a typical year. Beaver, seal, and sea otters were all victims. Gradually, led by such writers as Ralph Waldo Emerson, Henry David Thoreau, and John Muir, Americans started to grow concerned about the slaughter, and the government began regulating hunting. At several points in his youth Birdseye came into conflict with the new regulations.

Bob Birdseye wanted to be a colorful character, and in 1951 he wrote, "The public customarily thinks of me as an inventor . . . but inventing is only one of my lines. I am also a bank director, a president of companies, a fisherman, an author, an engineer, a cook, a naturalist, a stockholder, a consultant, and a dock-walloper." Clarence Frank Birdseye, Bob's father, for whom he was named, did not pursue a life of adventure. Born in 1854, he attended an elite Brooklyn school, graduated from Amherst College in 1874 and Columbia Law School in 1877, and, like his father and grandfather, became a prominent attorney. He wrote numerous books, often on education, such as *The Reorganization of Our Colleges* and *Individual Training in Our Colleges*, as well as a number of legal textbooks, including his 1879 revision of New York State code and statutory law, which became a standard legal textbook.

Clarence Senior married Ada Jane Underwood, Bob's mother, who was born in Brooklyn a year after he was, in 1855. If the urge toward industrial invention has a genetic strain, Bob did not inherit it from the legalistic Birdseyes but from his mother's side. Ada's father, Henry Underwood, was a belt manufacturer. The machines of the Industrial Revolution ran on belts that connected motors to working parts through pulleys. Henry Underwood reasoned that the belts would stop slipping if they had more surfaces on the pulleys. So rather than a flat or rounded belt, he built a trapezoidal one to run through pulleys with angular grooves. His invention did not have the impact of electric lightbulbs, or even frozen food, but it improved many machines, and when Underwood patented his idea, it merited mention in the April 1860 edition of *Scientific American* in their roundup of new inventions. Ada's father was the first American manufacturer of leather belts, which he later improved, creating cotton-leather belts in the 1890s. Underwood's belts, and those inspired by his inventions, were critical to the growth of industrial machine technology and were a small but essential part of the development of refrigeration machines.

Clarence and Ada had nine children, but one of the twin girls born two years before Bob died before she was a year old. Bob was their sixth child. There is not a great deal known about Bob's relationship with his seven siblings. His older brothers Kellogg and Henry became businessmen, to whom he often turned for advice, and he seemed particularly fond of his brother Roger Williams Birdseye, born four years after him. In Bob's letters and journals his siblings are only occasionally mentioned, but he did name his two sons after Kellogg and Henry. The Birdseyes were a large family in which relatives were available for advice and connections. In the forty years when young, restless Bob was rummaging through opportunities looking for his career, relatives constantly aided him.

Young Bob showed few signs—or at least few were recorded—of being the garrulous social person he became as an adult. He disliked organized sports and other activities most boys were expected to participate in. It is not known if he had close friends. Most descriptions of the boy have him alone in nature. At an early age he had decided that what was important in life was to find his own way.

When he was about eight years old, the family bought a farm in Orient, New York, at the end of the North Fork of Long Island. The farm was named Wyndiecote, and Bob so loved it that he would use the name repeatedly for his homes as an adult, since he viewed it as his ideal home. He claimed to like "nothing better . . . than to tramp alone through fields or along the seashore studying the birds and other wildlife which I encountered." It was his mother, Ada, who first noticed that the boy was at heart a naturalist, which is defined as a keen observer of nature.

When Bob was ten years old, he became fixated, in that way ten-year-olds do, on something he had to have. In his case he just had to have a shotgun, which his parents weren't willing to buy for him. In his young mind hunting was not only an essential part of enjoying nature but also a way of profiting from the natural resources available to him. In his walks through the marshes around the sprawling Birdseye farm, he had noticed a great number of muskrats—large, homely, awkward, two-foot-long bundles of fur. Bob wondered where there would be a market for these large rodents. He wrote to Dr. William T. Hornaday, the director of the Bronx Zoo, and asked him if he would be interested in acquiring some muskrats. Hornaday wrote back, explaining that he already had all the muskrats he could use, but he referred him to an English aristocrat who was stocking an estate. The ten-year-old went into the marshes and set traps until he had twelve live muskrats, which he shipped to England. Nine of the muskrats survived the trip, and the Englishman paid him $1 for each. With that $9 Bob bought a single-barrel shotgun. Making a profit from ideas was always a fundamental belief of Birdseye's.

The following year, in the winter of 1897, after learning how to preserve and stuff animals by reading books and asking questions at taxidermy shops, Bob placed an ad in a sports magazine for "the American School of Taxidermy," offering courses at modest rates. It is easy to imagine the comical scene ensuing when someone wishing to learn more from the ad discovered that not only the professor but the entire school consisted of an eleven-year-old boy. Unfortunately there is no record of anyone responding to the advertisement.

When Bob was entering high school, the family moved to Montclair, New Jersey. Life in the new suburban town was still not one of adventure. In high school, although his interests lay primarily in science, he also took a cooking class. At the time progressive women wanted to help the female population have careers outside the home, so there was an increase in the number of cooking classes, which taught women to prepare food quickly so they would have time to keep a job but still have dinner on the table when their husbands returned home. Such classes grew out of a mid-nineteenth-century movement to educate women on home management. (Men were not taught to be concerned with such matters.) Eventually those classes would be called home economics and would cover the process of cooking and the science of nutrition.

By the time Birdseye was in high school, frugal, scientific, pragmatic, nutritious cooking was the established approach. His older sister Miriam, who graduated from Smith College in 1901 and earned a graduate degree in domestic science from Pratt Institute in 1907, may also have influenced Bob. She started as a home economics teacher in New York City and later became a prominent nutritionist. Another sister, Katherine, two years older than Bob and the surviving twin, would later marry one John Lang, divorce him, settle in Atlantic City, New Jersey, and become president and general manager of Mrs. Lang's Candy Kitchen, which sold candy in stores along the boardwalk. Little is known about life in the Ada and Clarence Senior household that would have led two of their children toward distinguished careers in food and a third to open a specialty food store.

The summer after high school Bob moved to New York City but did not find a lot of opportunities for a young man seeking an original life. He worked first as an inspector for the city sanitation department and then as a $3-a-week office boy in a Wall Street financial firm. In the fall his parents sent him off to Amherst College, in Massachusetts.

Amherst was the Birdseye family school. But Bob's interests were different from those of his father and brothers.

Amherst was a liberal arts college with no emphasis on science, Bob's major. Science majors were awarded bachelor of arts degrees, like literature majors. There was no bachelor of science degree.

In his first year Bob was an honors student in science but only average in everything else, including physical education. He did particularly badly in Spanish, a language for which he saw no use until much later in his life. However, Birdseye studied under respected professors of the day. His professor of biology, his favorite subject, was John Mason Tyler, who had graduated from Amherst in 1873, when the writings of Charles Darwin that were to be the foundation of modern biology were fresh off the press and not yet part of the accepted teachings in the field. Benjamin Kendall Emerson, with whom Bob hoped to study geology, graduated from Amherst in 1865, the year the Civil War ended. Edward Hitchcock, a doctor who taught physiology and anatomy and was a pioneer in the physical education program with which Bob struggled, was born in the town of Amherst in 1828, the year construction began on the first passenger railroad in the United States and Noah Webster's dictionary of the American language was published.

There was not much opportunity for western-style adventure at Amherst. Birdseye wrote in later life that he used to spend free time at Amherst wandering the fields with his shotgun on his shoulder. His fellow classmates called him Bugs because he was forever examining some bug or rodent in the countryside.

While out on one of his walks, Birdseye "suddenly . . .

came upon an open spring-hole where thousands of small frogs were congregating—layers and layers of them came to hibernate for the winter. 'What are those frogs good for?' I asked myself." And though seven years had passed, Birdseye thought he would try the Bronx Zoo again, since they had previously helped him sell the muskrats. He knew that the zoo had frog-eating reptiles that needed to be fed, and they said yes, they did want the frogs. They asked that he ship them alive, since reptiles eat only live prey, so Birdseye wrapped them in wet burlap and sent them to the zoo. For this he earned $115, which was more than the $110 annual tuition at Amherst.

On another occasion Birdseye wandered behind the town butcher shop and discovered an infestation of rodents. What would have been just a horrible black rat to most people, Bob recognized as a nearly extinct species, and he found a geneticist at Columbia University who was willing to pay $135 for a shipment of them.

He avoided talking about catching the frogs and rats and other such activities because they led to mockery, and he felt isolated at Amherst. He did not like being called Bugs, but for Bob happiness always came from answering his own calling, being who he was. Writing about his college days later, Bob said, "I did not realize at the time, as I have discovered since, that anyone who attempts anything original in this world must expect a bit of ridicule." In fact, he would come to understand that accepting ridicule was one of the keys to success.

• • •

After spending the summer between his freshman and sophomore years going west at last, to the New Mexico Territory, to work with the US Biological Survey, Birdseye returned to Amherst in the fall. He seemed to find his rhythm in school that year. Although he played no sports, he learned to do well in gym. He also joined a fraternity. (His father was a great believer in fraternities and had even written a book on the subject.) By spring 1908 young Bugs scored 96 percent in biology and had almost a 90 average. In those less competitive days, it was perfectly acceptable to be a C student; an A student was an unusual phenomenon. Bob was well on his way to being a brilliant student. He applied to take special advanced biology and geology classes.

But that year, for reasons that are not clear, the Birdseyes suffered a financial crisis, and there was no more money for schooling. On December 31, 1908, Bob wrote the school registrar, "It will almost certainly be necessary for me to go through the rest of this year without any financial aid from home; and to this I must borrow about $300—$150 or $200 at once. Is there a student loan fund at Amherst and if there is can I secure the necessary money at not more than six percent interest and for one or two years."

Apparently, he was not given a loan, because after spring 1909 he dropped out of college. This was the end of his formal education.

What was he to do with only two years of college? Without a college degree, he could not become the fourth generation of distinguished Birdseye attorneys, but he was not likely to have done that anyway. He had wanted to go to school to learn, not to launch a career. He could have returned to Wall

Street and tried to make his mark in business. New York was full of possibilities. But that was not what Birdseye was inclined to do. When he was in his sixties, he said, "Any youth who makes security his goal shackles himself at the very start of life's race." Birdseye was not looking for financial security. He was looking for adventure. And where did you find adventure in 1909? Out west.

CHAPTER THREE

Bob Goes West

After Bob left college, he resumed his job from the previous summer with the US Biological Survey in the New Mexico and Arizona territories. Both territories were still considered a part of the western frontier, even though in 1901 a railroad line extended to the Grand Canyon and a tourist village was built there, stimulating the birth of southwestern tourism. With the primary mode of transportation still horses and the territories lacking the necessary infrastructure to apply for statehood, it wasn't until 1912 that New Mexico and Arizona would become the forty-seventh and forty-eighth states.

The primary function of the US Biological Survey—a branch of the Department of Agriculture—was to ask farmers and ranchers which animals bothered them and then to set up campaigns to eradicate those species. At the top of the list were wolves and coyotes, predators hated by ranchers because they ate livestock. The survey hired hunters and trappers to get rid of them. In 1907 alone the program killed

544 coyotes in New Mexico and 1,424 more in Arizona. There was considerable controversy about the vicious steel traps that would hold an animal by the leg until it starved to death. In the 1920s the survey began poisoning the animals with carcasses injected with strychnine, producing a slow and agonizing but certain death. Contemporary attitudes regarding the treatment of wildlife have changed and practices deemed cruel have been banned, but in Birdseye's time the big predators—wolves, coyotes, bobcats, and mountain lions—were hunted or trapped.

According to Birdseye, the US Biological Survey originally hired him as an "assistant naturalist . . . [part of a] scientific party, which was studying birds and mammals in New Mexico and Arizona." At the time the survey sent naturalists throughout the territories by horseback estimating animal populations and studying their habits, especially what the large predators preyed on. The survey largely discredited ranchers' claim that the wild predators were destroying livestock: while this did happen, livestock were not the primary or preferred prey of any of these animals. In the case of coyotes, the survey found that they largely ate mice, yet this did not stop the campaign against them.

Wandering the western frontier on horseback with a rifle, shooting wildlife, Bob was living a childhood dream. Again he thought of a business opportunity. Bob knew that Indian trading posts offered only 25 cents for a coyote or bobcat fur, but he felt sure that they were worth more than that. When he returned to New York at the end of the summer, finding first a job with an insurance company and later one with the city's Department of Sanitation as a "snow checker"—the man who maintains records on the amount of snow removed from city streets after a blizzard—he discovered that furriers in New York would pay $1.25 each for bobcat and coyote pelts. Bob wrote to the traders to whom he had spoken in the Southwest and offered them 50 cents for pelts, double the trading posts' rate, and sold the pelts in New York himself for a 75-cent profit. He earned $600 on his fur trading that winter and decided to return to the Southwest the next summer.

Living in the Southwest, Bob acquired some exotic food habits that remained with him all his life. When he found something in nature, Birdseye always wondered what it would taste like and what would be the best way to cook it. He liked his rattlesnake cut in slices, dusted with flour, and then fried in salt pork. While camped on one of the then-undeveloped rims of the Grand Canyon, the naturalists discovered that their only provision, pork belly, had gone rancid. Bob Birdseye wasn't worried and went off to find dinner. He gathered field mice, chipmunks, gophers, and even a few pack rats, which he carefully skinned and gutted before wrapping them all in cheesecloth. Finally he simmered the meat in a pot of boiling water. He praised the resulting stew, though there is no record of anyone else sharing his enthusiasm.

Birdseye's colleagues rarely partook of his specialties, preferring canned food—typically beans, corn, and tomatoes—carried by packhorse as they traveled the countryside. Bob was struck by the extent to which westerners lived on food from a can and noticed that there seemed to be a great need for preserved food. As he traveled by horse, he would often see something sparkling in the sun on the horizon, only to realize that he was approaching a ranch or a town, both of which were always marked by piles of discarded cans. He regarded canning as an inferior way of preserving food, because the food had to be reheated and was no longer in its fresh state. Even so, he had a great fondness for it. "He just loved canned food," said Gypsy, the wife of his oldest son, Kellogg. It reminded Birdseye of his youth, when he rode in the West, though he played a major role in the decline of canned food in the American diet.

As winter approached in 1910, Birdseye decided to go to Washington, D.C., to work for the Department of Agriculture. At the time, the capital was a genteel Southern town of 331,000 people with horse-drawn carriages and hitching posts, but it was growing fast in both population and building construction. Washington could have become a high-rise megalopolis like Manhattan, but in that year a law was passed restricting building heights to the width of the adjacent street plus twenty feet, so they have remained the same as they were when Bob moved there.

While in Washington, Bob met the adventurous men of the National Geographic Society, including C. Hart Merriam, one of its thirty-three founding members and the head of the US Biological Survey. When the society was formed, in 1888, it was led by Gardiner Hubbard, a Boston lawyer who had financed Alexander Graham Bell's development of the telephone and had been the first president of the Bell Telephone Company. He declared, "The more we know, the greater we find is our ignorance. Because we know so little, we have formed this society for the increase and diffusion of Geographic knowledge."

This was Birdseye's kind of language, and the society's magazine spoke to that, too. At the time, there was nothing more exciting to Bob and other adventurous young men of his generation than *National Geographic* magazine. By 1910 it had distinguished itself for exploration, investigating new ideas, and photography—all passions of young Birdseye. Part of what made the magazine exciting was the use of new photographic technology. To people who grew up in the late nineteenth and early twentieth centuries, portable cameras with film that had to be developed generated the excitement. *National Geographic* was said to publish the best photography of the day. In 1907 it had created a sensation with Edward S. Curtis's portraits of American Indians. Bob, like many others of his generation, was enthralled with the possibilities of photography, and among his dreams he envisioned becoming a photographer, traveling to exotic places to record the landscape and customs.

Henry Gannett, another of the society's thirty-three founders, was chief geographer for the US Geological Survey, an organization whose topographical maps of the American West in the late nineteenth century set a new standard for mapmaking. Henry's younger cousin Samuel was also among the founders, and was a geographer with the US Geological Survey. As a surveyor, he defined the borders of several new western states. The West still had uncharted territory. To young people like Bob who longed to wander the American West, the maps were treasures.

Bob was meeting men who to him were legends, and he found their tales of exploration spellbinding. One of the most exciting adventures at the time was the exploration of the frozen lands of the north. When Bob arrived in Washington in 1909, Admiral Robert E. Peary, whom Birdseye admired, had announced that he was the first to reach the North Pole. Members of Peary's expedition had shot color photos, with a process invented in 1907, which the magazine published, along with an article detailing his trip.

Prior to his 1909 expedition, Peary was already a famous explorer, having led expeditions in Greenland and the Arctic. He traveled by dogsled and was famously photographed wearing Arctic furs, as he was known for learning Inuit ways of dress and survival. His wife sometimes accompanied him on his remarkable trips.

While reading about Peary's life was exciting, Birdseye became even more intrigued with the people living in Washington—especially Samuel Gannett's daughter, Eleanor. When they met, she was finishing her degree at George Washington University. She was a well-educated woman for her generation, as were Bob's sisters. Bob and Eleanor dated for five years, though for most of that time they didn't see each other, because he was constantly off on his adventures.

He didn't talk about being an inventor with Eleanor; even after he became one, he seldom used the word to describe himself. She could see that he had an insatiable curiosity and a great sense of adventure. Despite her quiet ways, Bob could see that Eleanor did not come from the kind of conventional home he'd had and was not looking for the kind of man who would become a prominent lawyer or work on Wall Street.

So she was not perturbed when he left on an adventure

in the spring of 1910, when the Department of Agriculture needed a field researcher for an important medical mission. Just as he'd had no qualifications for his work with the US Biological Survey, Birdseye had no qualifications for the medical mission, but his willingness to take on a difficult and dangerous job secured him the post.

CHAPTER FOUR

Real Bugs

In the early twentieth century, a man like Clarence Birdseye, with a love of science and adventure, would inevitably stumble into one of the great medical expeditions. Bob had been born into an exciting age of medical pioneers whose defeat of dreaded diseases made them into larger-than-life heroes. Some researchers in fact died from exposure to the illnesses they were trying to conquer.

In 1910 the US government decided to send a team of medical crusaders to the Bitterroot Mountains of Montana to combat a deadly strain of what became known as Rocky Mountain spotted fever. Few would be willing to accept the hardship, risk, and uncertainty of this project. According to legend, when the US Biological Survey was asked for volunteers, the response was "Why not ask Birdseye?" Bob was one of only two volunteers from the survey, drawn to this project by the same traits that would eventually earn him fame and fortune: boundless curiosity, fascination with the latest scientific ideas, and a thirst for adventure.

Rocky Mountain spotted fever is a life-threatening disease. Much is still unknown about how it spreads and how it acts on the human body. But in 1910 even less was understood about it. It was a uniquely American disease, occurring only in the Western Hemisphere. Its name comes from the place where it was first identified; elsewhere it had other labels, such as São Paulo fever, New World spotted fever, and American spotted fever.

There are tremendous differences in the number of people who die from the disease in different areas: in one it may kill 5 percent of victims; in another 70 percent. The reason for this remains a mystery. In 1910 the mortality rate was typically high enough that an outbreak would terrify an entire population.

A victim can have the disease for as long as two weeks without exhibiting any symptoms. Eventually he gets a sickish feeling for a few days that suggests an oncoming cold or flu. Then he may be afflicted with an extremely severe headache and painful joints, light begins to hurt his eyes, his neck becomes stiff, and he develops a dangerously high fever. At that point doctors sometimes suspect meningitis. The patient cannot sleep and at times becomes delirious. After several days of those symptoms, slightly raised red spots appear on the skin that are easily confused with measles. (Recent science has revealed that the disease organisms in the cells lining the capillaries swell and break, and blood seeps through the capillary walls.) Those tiny welts show up on the entire body, including the hands and feet. Without any treatment, many people will recover in a matter of weeks, but a significant number, especially over the age of forty, will die.

In the nineteenth century the disease was not fully understood. Records exist of an outbreak of the fever, then called black measles, in Idaho in 1896, and there are accounts of diseases with similar names among westward-moving pioneers. But until the US government began researching the outbreak in the Bitterroot Valley of western Montana in 1910, there had been no scientific study of the disease soon to be known as Rocky Mountain spotted fever.

Pathology—the study of the causes of diseases and how they spread—did not exist until Birdseye's time. Little was understood about diseases.

The exciting new age of medicine that was part of Bob Birdseye's time, an age when diseases could be identified and then conquered, began with Louis Pasteur. The French chemist demonstrated in the 1850s that fermentation was caused by the growth of organisms that were so small, they could be seen only with a microscope, and he proposed that microorganisms caused diseases.

Medical researchers armed with new knowledge and equipment began traveling the globe and conquering epidemics. Cholera was often eradicated, notably in New York City, by purifying drinking water. Bacteria were identified in outbreaks of numerous diseases, including bubonic plague, typhoid, leprosy, and tuberculosis. During the 1898 Spanish-American War, as yellow fever was decimating US troops, army physician Walter Reed went to Cuba and found that a microorganism carried by a specific species of mosquito caused yellow fever; eventually this discovery led to sanitation programs in Cuba and Panama, also hard-hit, that wiped out the disease in those areas. In 1906 construction of the Panama Canal—which shortened shipping routes between the Atlantic and the Pacific and was funded by huge investments from powerful nations, especially the United States—had been stopped by outbreaks of yellow fever among workers. Because of Reed's research, the project was able to be completed.

Montana's Bitterroot Valley was one hundred miles of wooded flatland that was previously a lakebed between the Bitterroot Mountains and the Sapphire range. The Bitterroot River runs through it, making the valley an agreeable setting sheltered by the mountain ranges. The native people were healthy, and the whites who started settling there in the mid-nineteenth century had no particular health problems until 1873, when spotted fever struck. The first documented case involved one of the few white men living in the valley, and he died from it. Later the widespread occurrence of a strange disease coincided with the spectacular expansion of the lumber industry; the west bank of the river, where the lumbering was prominent, was also where the disease was affecting people.

The advance of medicine at the turn of the century included a growth in public health institutions, and in 1901 Montana established a state board of health. A Ravalli County board of health had existed since 1896. Once there were agencies to monitor disease, they started noticing a large number of patients in the Bitterroot Valley with diagnoses such as black typhus fever, blue disease, and black fever. The spotted fever was not unique to the valley; outbreaks were also discovered in neighboring Idaho, in Colorado, Oregon, Wyoming, and possibly even earlier in California, Washington, Nevada, and Utah. However, it was a much more life-threatening disease in the Bitterroot than anywhere else. In Colorado the disease had a mortality rate of 23 percent, but in the spring of 1901 Montana had fourteen cases and all but four died, resulting in a mortality rate of 71 percent.

In Bitterroot the leading theory was that melting snow somehow caused the black measles. Though it may sound silly today, the fact was that every year there was an outbreak of the illness in the spring, just as the snow started melting, and there had been notable research suggesting that many epidemics, such as typhoid and cholera, were spread in water. In 1889 a particularly well-educated Montana physician who had studied the work on yellow fever noticed a tick on a patient and suggested that this might be significant.

SCIENCE

In 1902 a new crop of investigators arrived in the Bitterroot Valley in the spring, as the disease never struck before mid-March. Two of the scientists were pathologists from the University of Minnesota, Louis B. Wilson and William M. Chowning, who headed the team. Wilson and Chowning shocked both the public and the medical community by documenting eighty-eight cases that had occurred between 1895 and 1902, of which sixty-four had been fatal, establishing the terrifying mortality rate of 72.7 percent.

The pathologists explored all the newly discovered sources of disease, including water, insects, and arthropods, such as ticks and mites. Every afflicted person that Wilson and Chowning examined had been bitten by a wood tick two to eight days prior to the development of symptoms.

In 1904, with property values in the Bitterroot plummeting, the Montana State Board of Health obtained a commitment from the US surgeon general to sponsor research there until the nature of Rocky Mountain spotted fever was completely understood. But one of the effects of this commitment was to emphasize that the answers weren't known, and so, with plans for tourism, irrigation, and orchards in the works, the local press started to avoid mentioning the disease. There was humiliation and fear attached to it, so when someone died of Rocky Mountain spotted fever, the obituary writer avoided giving the cause of death, much as during the AIDS epidemic seventy years later.

The locals adopted the habit of examining their bodies nightly for ticks. Those who worked outdoors, especially on the infectious west bank of the river, also started carrying small bottles of carbolic acid with them. Carbolic acid was one of the modern miracles of the new age. The British surgeon Sir Joseph Lister, who had pioneered the idea of keeping surgery safe from dangerous microorganisms, developed carbolic acid as an antiseptic. However, if it was applied directly to the skin, which the Bitterroot people would do when they opened the bottle and held it upside down over the tick bite, a red acid welt appeared on the skin. Still, this was better than the killer fever. Not surprisingly, given the level of fear, many fraudulent medicines supposedly guaranteed to save you were sold as cures or preventatives in the Bitterroot, including sarsaparilla, an early version of root beer. This trade was much dampened in 1906 by the passage of the Pure Food and Drug Act, a piece of legislation Birdseye would one day play an important role in revising.

Also among the new fields of science was entomology, the study of insects. After 1890, when it was discovered that arthropods—eight-legged cousins of insects—could transmit disease-causing microorganisms, a wide range of doctors, public health officials, and veterinarians became interested in studying ticks. In 1909 the term *medical entomology* came into use for the specific study of the role of arthropods in disease. Therefore, the project in the Bitterroot represented the forefront of pioneering medical research, and the scientists who worked there were among the first pathologists in medical history.

Howard Taylor Ricketts, a pathologist at the University of Chicago, became interested in Rocky Mountain spotted fever, and in 1906 he went to the Bitterroot to conduct his investigations. He proved that the wood tick was the transmitter of the disease and successfully identified the organism that caused it, for which he won the dubious honor of having it named after him, *Rickettsia rickettsii*. In 1910 he went off to study an outbreak of typhus, a somewhat related disease, in Mexico and died while working on it. Field epidemiology was very dangerous work.

In February 1910 Robert Cooley, Montana's first official state entomologist, who was deeply committed to solving the Bitterroot spotted fever problem, went to Washington, D.C., to ask help from the US Biological Survey in studying the connection between wild animals and the life cycle of the tick. The survey and the US Bureau of Entomology were both housed in the same small brick building. Cooley left with three recruits: Willard V. King, a gifted entomology student from Montana who had delayed his senior year to work for the bureau; Arthur H. Howell, a thirty-eight-year-old zoologist from the survey who would publish 118 works on birds and mammals by the time he died in 1940; and Bob Birdseye, a twenty-four-year-old college dropout.

No one else had been willing to volunteer because there was no guarantee of anyone's safety. Howell was a married man with children, and he agreed to work in the field camp only on the condition that a younger volunteer, single with no children, would go trapping and shooting with him in the highly infested areas—a role that Birdseye was more than happy to assume.

To Bob's great joy, part of his job was unrestricted hunting. The age of extermination was over: A growing number of Americans believed that too many animals were being killed, and government agencies were modifying their outlook in order to manage wildlife populations and restrict the kill. However, Bob was exempt from the new restrictions, free to kill as he saw fit in the effort to collect a wide range of ticks and find a cure for spotted fever. Thrilled, he shot and trapped gophers, chipmunks, pine squirrels, woodchucks, ground squirrels, wood rats, snowshoe rabbits, cottontail rabbits, several species of mice, flying squirrels, badgers, weasels, muskrats, and bats. He also killed the large and dangerous brown bears, mountain sheep, coyotes, both mule and white-tailed deer, and elk. Most of what he killed he shot, but he also set traps. In the process he collected 4,495 ticks and killed 717 wild animals, though his goal was to get 1,000. He was Buffalo Bill at last.

The center for this science and adventure was a suitably rustic abandoned log cabin that had once been a farmhouse. Cooley, King, Birdseye, and a cook named Paul Stanton lived and did research in the cabin, which they named Camp Venustus, after the scientific name for the dangerous tick they were studying, *Dermacentor venustus*. When the men posed for a picture in front of the cabin, Stanton wore his cook's apron and the other three stood in their suits and ties. In a three-piece tweedy suit, a small man with already-thinning hair, and spectacles, Birdseye did not look that different from the famous inventor and entrepreneur he would become in his fifties. The photo gives no clue that this man risked his life every day, wandering into the canyons on horseback with his hunting rifle.

After Bob became famous, he said little about his significant contributions to the medical research or the historic significance of the project with which he had been associated. In interviews he was often asked about this period, and he always talked about how many animals he killed, sometimes pointing out that it was well over the usual limit. He would also reminisce about spending a lot of time out in the wilderness with his colleagues and playing practical jokes on one another.

Howell was often the target of pranks, as he would remain in the cabin writing a paper on their work on which only his name would appear. He'd made clear from the outset that he intended to avoid danger. Back in Washington, he'd reasoned that, since he was married with children, the job was too dangerous for him to do fieldwork. King and Birdseye had made arrangements with a nearby doctor in the event a tick infected one of them; Howell often stated that at any sign of a tick embedded on him he was packing for Washington. Bob and Willard could see that this was a young man's game out in their cabin in the foothills, where they would take all the risks, and therefore devised a clever plan.

In the cabin the three checked one another for ticks every morning and night. Bob proposed an idea to Willard that "if on one of the nightly inspections we could just discover a tick between Mr. Howell's shoulder blades where he could not possibly see that it was purely imaginary, he would be off for Washington and we could do the paper work as well as the field work." So one day, while skinning a coyote he had shot and putting the ticks he had found into vials, Bob put one tick, engorged with coyote blood, into a separate vial. At night while examining Howell, Bob claimed to find a tick between his shoulder blades. Howell was so upset, he insisted that Bob not only cut it out with a scalpel but also cauterize the wound, which Bob obligingly accomplished with a heated blade as Howell winced in pain. Then Bob handed him the vial with the tick from the coyote. It worked even better than the two young men had anticipated, for the next morning Howell was making arrangements to return to Washington.

Some weeks later Bob had a remarkable hunting trip in three days of pouring rain. He shot three wild mountain sheep, shy creatures found on inaccessible rocky ledges, and a brown bear and collected an enormous quantity of ticks from the bodies. He was so excited that he neglected to check himself for ticks, and when he finally did by an evening campfire, he found seven of them. Three were thoroughly swollen with his blood. For several days he had the aches and nausea that were well-known symptoms of spotted fever. He spent three terrified days before he realized that he simply had a grippe from being out for too many days in the rain. But it left him feeling that his joke on Howell was not as funny as he had thought it was.

Years later he told Howell what he had done, and according to Bob, Howell laughed. He had probably been relieved to return to Washington anyway.

Now the two young men, Bob and Willard, were on their own, along with the cook and occasional visits from Cooley. An unknown percentage of the tiny creatures they were gathering for study could deliver a fatal bite. A horse serum had been developed that might protect them from tick bites, but it was untested, and Bob and Willard thought the serum was as risky as facing the ticks.

While they were in the field, Josiah J. Moore, a University of Chicago pathologist, concluded from experiments that the minimum amount of time a tick needed to attach to a guinea pig in order to infect it was one hour and forty-five minutes, and that on the average it had to stay in place, feeding on the host, for ten hours. Cooley instructed Bob and Willard—in fact, it may have originally been Howell's idea—to stop their work every two hours to inspect each other's bodies for ticks. They did occasionally find a tick, but neither ever contracted spotted fever, possibly because of luck or because Moore was right about the necessary feeding time.

This procedure became standard in tick collecting for

spotted fever. So did their clothing. They wore high shoes with additional leggings tied onto the shoes and the pant legs so nothing could fly up a trouser leg. Their outer clothes, cotton for the summer weather, were soaked in kerosene, which at least for a short time served as a tick repellent. At night they left their clothes in an airtight closet with bisulfate of carbon, a common insecticide.

By day Willard went into the brush with his flag for flushing out ticks and vials for collecting them. He had a white wool flag, later replaced by lighter flannel, on a pole, and he waved it in the brush. Bob, with a hunting rifle on his shoulder and as many traps as he could carry, went out into the most infested canyons. Bob photographed the animals, and Willard photographed and studied the ticks. At night the two young men lay in their tent, having lively debates about the future of the spotted-fever campaign. Back at the cabin, Willard worked late into the night at his microscope. They wanted to document the complete life cycle of the tick and determine which animals served as hosts at which stages.

When Game Warden J. L. DeHart learned of the quantity of animals Bob had killed, he angrily referred to it as "wanton slaughter." It was perfectly legal, and the slaughter was not useless. The ticks that were collected led Willard to determine that they had a two-year life cycle, not one year, as Ricketts had thought. This was significant, because it enabled Bob to determine that the tick fed on small animals, such as mice, when it was young but as a mature adult moved to large animals. He showed that it was pointless to have a campaign against small rodents, including the gopher (correctly called Columbian ground squirrel), which had come to be regarded by the young men as the leading culprit. Bob and Willard concluded that spotted fever could be controlled only if a campaign against small rodents was combined with a program treating large animals, principally domestic livestock, with repellent.

It was an important breakthrough, but this was not what ranchers wanted to hear. They did not want the expense of treating their livestock; rather, they preferred blaming everything on the little gopher, which was, for them, a hated and destructive pest.

Cooley erected livestock dipping vats throughout the valley for ranchers to voluntarily run their cattle through. But the program was not really voluntary, because ranchers who did not dip their livestock could not move their animals. In a community that tended to be distrustful of any government programs, it only added to this one's unpopularity that it took some experimenting to get the right strength of arsenic in the dipping vats so it would kill the ticks but not hurt the livestock. Hides and udders got burned before the right formula was found. The ranchers had been much happier with Ricketts, who simply endorsed a program to exterminate gophers. In the long run, though, it became obvious that the new program was more effective.

Since there were no ticks in the winter, the project suspended activities then. In the winter of 1912 Bob was back in Washington, and he did not return to Montana. The spotted fever campaign continued without him and had its first fatality: Thomas McClintic of the US Public Health Service. In all, fourteen people died in the fight against spotted fever between 1912 and 1977. In the 1940s, with the discovery of antibiotics, a cure was found, and the crisis seemed to be over, except for another serious outbreak in the 1970s.

The research in which Birdseye participated has led to solving riddles about other serious illnesses, such as Legionnaires' disease, Lyme disease, and Potomac horse fever. It led to the opening of the second-largest government laboratory in the United States, in Hamilton, Montana, where World War II studies on insect-borne diseases helped save the lives of soldiers throughout the Pacific. If Birdseye had done nothing else, his fieldwork on spotted fever and ticks would have earned him a footnote in history, as it did Willard King, who went on to distinguish himself studying the mosquitoes that were plaguing World War II troops in New Guinea.

But Bob had a different destiny, though he had little notion of it at the time. He only knew that the century was still young and so was he, and there were opportunities for other adventures. All his life Birdseye was restless—eager to move on to the next thing. In 1912 the next thing was Labrador, a sparsely populated frozen wilderness that would give him his most famous idea.

CHAPTER FIVE

Labrador: A Frozen Land

Bob had not yet turned twenty-four when, in 1912, he was invited to spend six weeks along the Labrador coast on the hospital ship of the celebrated medical missionary Wilfred Grenfell. Bob knew he wanted to do something daring and original, and he wanted to make money doing it. And so he said good-bye again to Eleanor, the explorer's daughter, who understood his need to go, and he headed north.

Labrador was one of the most remote and undeveloped corners of the world. At the time it was a possession of Newfoundland, which was classified a dominion, a self-ruling non-nation of the British Commonwealth. Canada had a similar status but was separate from Newfoundland and its frozen northern possession.

Labrador and Newfoundland's first Europeans were fishermen, drawn there in the seventeenth century by the huge profits to be made back home selling dried and salted codfish, with which the American North Atlantic was teeming. Cod, like the buffalo and the passenger pigeon, thrived in the North American wilderness in extraordinary numbers, beyond anything Europeans had known.

Also beyond anything they'd known were the bitterly cold, long Labrador winters. Many Europeans thought the northern winters were so harsh as to make the region un-inhabitable for year-round settlement—an odd assessment, since there were indigenous people living there at the time. But New England was far milder and soon had year-round settlements and even a year-round cod fishery. In Newfound-land and Labrador, on the other hand, the harbors froze up in the winter and fishing was discontinued. While a few fisher-men would endure the Labrador winter, the rest would leave and return for the spring thaw. Once the harbor froze, there was no way in or out.

The European fishermen who settled in Labrador lived a life of hardship and poverty, which is why there was little in-terest from Labrador in separating from England in 1776; nor were Newfoundland and Labrador interested in 1849, when Canada gained self-government. When they finally did con-template self-rule, it was as their own country and not part of "Canady," which seemed a very far-off and different place from these cold and rugged colonies. In 1907 Newfoundland gained dominion status and Labrador went with it, becoming a kind of colony of Newfoundland without representation in the legislature. It wasn't until 1949 that the two finally joined Canada.

In 1912, when Bob went to Labrador, he was going to a place far wilder than the American Wild West. Most of the 250,000 combined population of Labrador and Newfoundland consisted of fishermen in the more southern island, Newfoundland. Few people lived in Labrador through the winter, and there were no towns or cities, only a few villages.

Most Labradoreans were fishermen, huddled in the rocky coves along the coast; fur breeders, trappers, and traders; the indigenous Inuit, referred to by Europeans as Eskimos; or Montagnais Indians, who lived in small groups in the interior, descendants of the Algonquians who had been pushed north. There were animals that could be shot for meat, hides, and furs, as well as salmon, halibut, herring, lobsters, and above all, cod to be caught and eaten in the summer. In March there were seals to be hunted. Berries were the only local fruit, and the only greens were the tops of turnips in the summer. Anything else that was to be eaten, including fruits, vegetables, and grains, had to be imported in the summer months before the harbors froze.

Dogsleds provided the only winter transportation except for snowshoes for hiking. There was no electricity or telephone service. Most people made their own soap from boiling spruce ashes with seal fat. The only doctors were those who worked in the two small hospitals built by Grenfell, which unfortunately were too far for most people to reach.

Wilfred Thomason Grenfell was born in 1865 in England and attended medical school in London; however, he soon became interested in the missionary movement and spreading Christianity. At that time (the time of Bob Birdseye's birth) the British Empire was losing its power in the world. Young men were no longer recruited to fight wars to gain control of far-off lands. Many young men, raised in a tradition of going off on far-flung adventures, became missionaries.

In 1892 Grenfell was sent to Newfoundland and Labrador to continue missionary work with fishermen. When he was studying Labrador, he found an old map that said, "Labrador was discovered by the English. There is nothing in it of any value." In fact, many Englishmen saw their countrymen making fortunes on cod and furs from there and viewed Labrador and Newfoundland as sources of great wealth. But the people in Labrador who produced the salt cod and fox furs for Europe were in fact pitifully poor. They traded their products to large companies like the Hudson Bay Company in exchange for supplies and ended up in perpetual debt.

The day Grenfell first arrived, a man took him to a hovel made of sod and showed him a man dying of pneumonia. Grenfell realized that he had found the place where he was most needed.

Most of the fishermen had never seen a doctor. Grenfell wrote:

> *Deformities went untreated. The crippled and blind halted through life, victims of what "the blessed Lord saw best for them." The torture of an ingrowing toenail, which could be relieved in a few minutes, had incapacitated one poor father for years. Tuberculosis and rickets carried on their evil work unchecked. Preventable poverty was the efficient handmaid of these two latter diseases.*

The following year he built Labrador's first hospital, in Battle Harbour, a community of a few dozen dark-roofed white buildings wedged between the frozen sea and the icebound cliffs on the Atlantic coast of southern Labrador, just north of the straits that led to the mouth of the St. Lawrence River. Then he built a second—they were little more than cottages—farther up the coast, at Indian Harbour. In 1894 he formed the Grenfell Medical Mission.

At first Grenfell spent his winters, when Labrador ports were frozen and inaccessible, raising money in Britain and the United States. In 1899 his new hospital ship, the coal-fired two-masted *Strathcona I*, was launched, and starting in 1902 he spent every other winter in Labrador. He learned to love the Labrador winter in the same way Bob Birdseye would learn to love it: for its stark beauty, the thrill and fun of dog-sledding, the simplicity of life without stores or crowds, and the warmth of the rare encounters with the few comrades who were spending the winter the same way. Grenfell wrote that, because of the absence of stores, "we are relieved of the constant suggestion that we need something."

Once spring came he was on his hospital ship, bringing medical help, sailing into the Labrador coast's deep unknown fjords and islands, some of which had never been charted on a map. It was such a six-week tour that Bob joined in the spring of 1912 as the harbors thawed and became navigable again. The older man had a huge impact on Bob. Though Grenfell never mentioned him in his 1919 autobiography, Birdseye frequently referred to Grenfell in his journals.

At the age of forty-nine, with his bushy mustache and smiling eyes, Grenfell was an adventurer, forever trying out new ideas. He experimented with bringing in reindeer from Lapland as domestic animals that could haul goods like sled dogs. He also started a cooperative so the local people could buy provisions at reasonable prices.

Grenfell understood that the root of the health problems there was poverty, and the root of that poverty was that the natives were being forced to trade what they produced to the big companies for the things they needed instead of earning money. He was constantly looking for more profitable ways of working in which the locals could earn cash. Instead of trapping foxes for their furs, which they then traded, he thought they could farm the foxes and sell their pups. It had never been done in Labrador, but Grenfell thought it not only had the potential of earning the locals a considerable amount of cash but was more humane than letting foxes starve to death with a leg in the steel jaw of a trap. He knew nothing about the breeding of foxes but was confident that it was feasible because he had seen a litter at the Washington zoo that had been born in captivity.

Grenfell established a farm in St. Anthony, a handful of scattered houses in northern Newfoundland. The village had one of the harshest climates in the region but was a convenient location because he had a hospital there. He brought the foxes in from Labrador on his ship, and a visiting Harvard scholar recalled the frisky pups playing on deck with dogs and people. The red foxes were particularly friendly and would run up to greet visitors. The white-and-silvers were shyer. But foxes were difficult to breed; it was hard to keep the young alive, and after a few years some that had become favorite pets died of a spreading disease. Grenfell closed down the project and turned the farm into a summer vegetable garden.

• • •

Where others saw only wilderness, Bob saw hidden opportunity. When Grenfell talked about fox farming, it caught his interest. Birdseye had made money in coyote furs in the Southwest, and animals were something with which he was experienced. He had decided, perhaps in the Bitterroot project, that, as he later put it, he "was not cut out for a career in pure science and wanted to get into some field where I could apply scientific knowledge to an economic opportunity."

A successful fox farm had been established in the interior of Labrador by the time Birdseye arrived. Fox farming had become the most important industry on Prince Edward Island, with high prices being paid for live foxes. At every port where the *Strathcona* landed, Bob talked to fur traders and other men involved with foxes, and he concluded that there was money to be made in trapping silver foxes and shipping them to the United States as breeding stock.

By July of 1912 Birdseye was back in New York, looking for an investor in his new scheme. According to his journal, his father wrote a letter to Harris Hammond, a wealthy contact in Gloucester, Massachusetts, which is the earliest record of a link between Birdseye and the New England city. The Hammond family spent part of their time there. Harris was the son of John Hays Hammond, a wealthy mining engineer who had worked in Mexico and South Africa. The elder Hammond was a close friend of the president of the United States and later Supreme Court Justice William Howard Taft and many other well-placed men. When John Hays Hammond Jr. said he wanted to be an inventor, his father had the boy sit down with Thomas Edison and Alexander Graham Bell to talk about his ideas. John's older brother Harris was more in the mold of his father. He understood about adventures.

Birdseye had a difficult time getting a meeting with Hammond. He tried visiting the businessman's office day after day. When finally they did meet, Bob explained his idea of fox farming in broad terms. Hammond asked few questions and sought no details. He agreed to give the venture some backing, handed Bob a check for $750—the equivalent of about $18,000 today—to get him started, and told Birdseye, "Keep me informed." This was the beginning of the Hammond and Birdseye Fur Company.

The next day Bob spent $350 on supplies and deposited the remaining $400 in a bank in St. John's, the Newfoundland capital. It would take thousands of dollars to buy enough animals to start breeding foxes. Birdseye later said that he also got backing from Grenfell's New York connections.

Bob bought an abandoned fur-trading outpost in Labrador 250 miles up the coast from Battle Harbour, where the ships came in from Newfoundland. That is a long way from town when the only transportation is dogsleds. In St. John's, learning that there was a proposal to ban the export of foxes, he met with legislators to try to dissuade them from the measure. He finally found his loophole, as there was to be no ban on the export of locally raised offspring.

But before he could raise foxes, he needed knowledge and skills. He studied the farms on Prince Edward Island and drew detailed diagrams. He then obtained a license to capture wild foxes for breeding. He also met with the fishing commissioner and other officials, went to shops, and visited a seal factory. On his crossing to Labrador he met fishermen and grilled them about their techniques and their problems. He operated like a journalist, constantly hunting down information.

He learned that foxes died easily, even from drinking too much milk, and puppies were even more fragile. They could eat cod heads, which were virtually free, and "moldy bread was good fox feed [too]. Fish in seal oil was cheap, kept well through the winter and was a good feed. Liver tends to loosen foxes' bowels. For breeding one male can serve two females although it took experience to accomplish this—that is, on the part of the breeder."

When Bob got to Prince Edward Island, breeding foxes were selling for as much as $8,000. He was able to find three pairs to begin with, which he bought for only $1,000 a pair. He seemed fond of the animals, describing some as playful, some, especially females, as gentle. They seemed almost like pets, if you didn't contemplate their fate. He wrote, "Considering that the foxes are supposed to be wild, they aren't at all bashful any longer." The problem was that they were constantly dying, especially new pups.

In addition to learning the intricacies of breeding and raising wild foxes, Bob had to learn how to survive a Labrador winter. Clothing, for example, had to be heavy enough to hold in his body heat and yet light enough to keep him from sweating; if he sweat, it would freeze, especially at night.

He also had to learn about sleds and sled dogs and managing a team. Birdseye was impressed with "the full-blood husky dog of northern Labrador," he wrote in his journal, and he referred to the huskies' howling as "canine music." After listening to them through a sleepless night, he wrote that it reminded him of the noise made by a large crowd on election night.

Labrador sled dogs were close to wolves in appearance and often in temperament. These were extremely strong dogs, fearless and ready to attack whatever threatened, even a polar bear or a man, both of which a real wolf would shy away from. They seemed impervious to cold, even when covered in ice. They could save a man's life, because they could always find their way, even when snow blindness or fog bewildered the human driver. They averaged about six miles an hour but were capable of traveling at two or three times that speed. Each dog had its unique personality and temperament, and a driver needed to know his dogs.

The sled, the *komatik*, was designed for hauling freight for scientific expeditions and for traders. It was very different from the Alaskan racing sled, with the perch in the back, that most people picture as a dogsled. A *komatik* was an eleven-foot-long platform on long runners, ideally made of light and durable black spruce, although there were many variations. There were even stories of drivers in an emergency breakdown finding whale ribs to use. The runners should be slightly more than two feet apart. Packing a *komatik* required skill. It was extremely important that the weight be right for the terrain and that the freight be well balanced.

Bob traveled all over Labrador by dogsled. On January 10, 1913, he averaged almost ten miles an hour, covering sixty-five miles in six and a half hours, which is the total amount of daylight in Labrador at that time of year. His journal shows him frequently gone for three or sometimes even six weeks, procuring foxes or provisions. He often wrote of six-hour journeys just to visit a neighbor. Surviving the weather was challenging. It was often well below zero degrees Fahrenheit, sometimes as low as −40 degrees. He later said that he regularly suffered from frostbite. "After a while you get used to it just like mosquito bites."

Provisioning a journey was important, since there was always a possibility of spending some extra time lost. The *komatik* traveler had to know what kind of provisions to take; that salted food, such as pork or cod, resisted freezing and was therefore better than canned food, which would quickly freeze up and would be very difficult to thaw and also had extra inedible weight. Grenfell liked to travel with "pork buns"—heavy dark buns laced with salt pork and molasses, so dense that one of them was as filling as a meal. Bob lived on these buns when traveling with his dog team.

More is known about Bob Birdseye in his five years in Labrador than at any other time in his life, partly because this was the time he most liked to talk about, but mainly because he filled long evenings alone by writing page after page of mail to his family, even though the mail-carrying ships could not get past the ice for the entire winter and much of the spring. In 1914 the ice did not melt enough for ships to arrive until July. But Bob kept writing and sent off a thick pile of pages when he had a chance. Despite his wanderlust, he felt close to his family and missed them.

• • •

Bob's journals show a lonely man who relished time spent with others, none more than Grenfell, whom he always referred to as Dr. Grenfell. "Golly it was so good to see him again," Birdseye wrote to his family after the Englishman visited him in the summer of 1914. "He is certainly a Prince, and it is one big life-size pleasure to meet him."

He also kept what he called field journals. It is not certain exactly why he kept them. The name implies a scientific purpose. It may have had something to do with his training as a biologist or his work with the US Biological Survey. But the style, tone, and even content of these journals (indices and accounting aside) were not very different from the letters he wrote home. They read as though he were chatting with someone.

The journals were handwritten in bound hardcover doeskin notebooks with lined pages. He started the first one during his last summer in Montana and continued the practice in Labrador until his final entry in the twelfth notebook in July 1916.

The letters and notebooks tell much about Bob Birdseye, even though he did not readily talk about emotions or matters of the heart. Descriptions of his visits to fox farmers on Prince Edward Island show that he made very quick assessments of other people. He wanted to learn from anyone he encountered and noted in his journal who was forthcoming and from whom he had to "wile" the information.

The journals show that he was an extremely methodical man and a tireless worker. In the early notebooks he numbered each page and used the last pages for a detailed index. In later notebooks the index was dropped and the final pages were devoted to a detailed accounting of his expenses. After his first winter he realized that he needed help, someone to run his fox farm while he was away on trips, and he brought in a recruit from his hometown of Montclair, Perry W. Terhune. The fact that one of Terhune's tasks while Birdseye was away was maintaining his field journal shows that he was keeping journals as more than just a personal record. The parts written by Terhune are in a much more careless script, with no descriptions, no index, and many days skipped or simply marked "No work done." Bob never had such days. He worked on writing or indexing the journals, checked accounts, or spent the day reading, but he always reported some profitable use of his time.

The writings show that he had a self-effacing, sometimes corny, but endearing sense of humor. He wrote to his family, "Wouldn't you folks welcome a rest from this long-winded journal, and a few weeks of 'I am well! I am warm!' 'I am sleepy,' 'I have a frozen toe,' 'I went to Cartwright and frost burned my nose'?"

Normally Bob liked to describe the food he was eating. In a letter to his parents he wrote about rabbit, "Mostly we had 'um fried! But there's a scattered pie, and an occasional stew. One of the favorite breakfasts is fried rabbit livers, the thinnest crispiest deliciousest bacon, hot cornbread, and powerful good coffee. Doesn't that sound good?"

If Bob were alive today, he would be called a foodie, someone who spent much of his time thinking about food, cooking food, and eating food. He seemed obsessed with the subject. Of course, food was, as he frequently pointed out, a matter of survival. "Weather and Grub!" he once wrote.

"Those are the two fundamental facts on which every other event hinges in this neck of the woods—or rather barrens."

In his journals and letters he frequently offered recipes, and these included not only local game and fish dishes but also desserts:

MOLASSES PIE

For dinner today we had my first molasses pie—and it was really mighty good. It was between two crusts. No other flavoring than molasses was used but Mrs. Lewis says that boiling the molasses and adding a few spices improves the flavor of the pie.

He would frequently end a recipe with an editorial comment such as "Yum! Yum!"

He often wrote in either his journal or his letters home what he ate for breakfast or dinner. The entry on October 13, 1914, was a typical one, when he sat down at his fox farm and began a letter to his family:

Well, folks, having just disposed of some toast and cocoa after a ten-mile ante breakfast walk from Cartwright in a roundabout way to Muddy Bay, I feel in good humor to inflict another chapter of this letter.

And as was always his style, the more exotic the food, the more enthusiastically he received it. His palate, like his mind, was endlessly curious. He wrote his parents that a porcupine he had eaten was "unexpectedly tender, in spite of the beast's age and sex." He described as the "pièce de résistance" of "one of the most scrumptious meals I ever ate" lynx that had marinated for an entire month in sherry and was then stewed and served with a sauce made from the marinade. He said he ate polar bear and professed a particular fondness for the front half of a skunk.

Birdseye loved seal meat, especially that of the ringed seal, which he correctly identified as *Phoca hispida*, except for old males. He wrote his family, "'orned Howl (horned-owl) for Sunday dinner—does that sound good? Well, it *was* good, no matter how it sounds." He also ate beaver and a variety of birds, including hawks. He explained to his family that he was able to eat fresh meat every day by having "no food prejudices" and eating "anything that tastes good." He was so enthusiastic about these foods that he threatened to can some of them and bring them back to New Jersey "so you folks could sample them."

He even studied local books to learn about food traditions and was very excited when a book at GM explained the English origin of the Labradorean tradition of eating pea soup on Saturday nights.

The writings also show that he was endlessly resourceful. He fashioned a berry harvester from a tin can and repaired engines. He had already become a professional hunter, but now he also became a skilled fisherman, catching salmon and trout on the fly, jigging for cod, netting capelin.

In October 1912 he went goose hunting with Grenfell, also an avid sportsman, and Grenfell laughed at what a voracious hunter Bob was, even drawing an ink illustration in Bob's journal of the bespectacled Birdseye stomping through the marsh with his shotgun stock held high, trying to club a fleeing bird. Some have attributed this drawing to Bob, since it was in his journal, but it bears Grenfell's initials, WTG, and matches the style of the doctor's other drawings. Bob also learned medical skills from assisting Grenfell. He described an operation where Grenfell successfully removed a second thumb from a six-month-old child's hand. Grenfell had enough confidence in his young friend that he left medicines with him, and apparently Birdseye did give medical assistance to locals during the winters. He recorded having treated some two dozen patients with such complaints as sore throats, toothaches, pain in the side, and hacking cough.

In Birdseye's Labrador writings are some early signs of the inventor. One day in early 1915 he was at a house with a tub and got to take a bath. He wrote that when he got back to New Jersey, he should invent a foldable rubber tub for traveling. There is no trace of his ever having built it.

From time to time, living in a frozen world, he turned his mind to reflecting on the nature of freezing itself. In December 1914 he made a simple observation that tortured and plagued his curiosity for years. He wrote his father:

> *Practically every morning throughout the winter the water in my pitcher is frozen—often so hard that it has to be thawed out with hot water. So a few mornings ago, after a cold night, I was much surprised to find, upon thrusting a hand into the pitcher, to find it filled with water instead of ice. When, however, I poured some of the water into my*

bowl and some more into a glass, and then scooped
up a handful I found that the bowl was full of a
spongy mass of ice crystals; and the same formation
had taken place in the glass and the water pitcher—
yet a few seconds before there had been no sign of
ice in the water. Evidently the water had been in a
state of equilibrium—at the freezing point, and all
ready to congeal, but needing some little stirring up
to start the crystallization. I seem to remember seeing
the same thing done in a physics lab experiment,
but certainly never ran across it before "in nature."
Did you?

Some days later he commented on the phenomenon to his family again, adding, "Some of you physics-sharks please give me an explanation of this happening." This is the earliest record of Bob contemplating the science of freezing and the laws of crystallization.

In Labrador he still seemed to be searching for his career, but he already was drawn to the idea of having numerous careers, something he took great pride in later. Toward the end of his life he liked to tell the story that a young man once asked him if he had it to do over, would he choose the same occupation. His answer was "Which occupation?"

Photography was one of the new fields he often considered. When he first arrived, after less than a week there, he shipped out his first six rolls of film. The locals loved to pose for pictures and would ask him, "Would you sketch off me?" (Would you take my picture?) That first year Bob had the idea of a book of photographs on Labrador. In July 1913, when in New York, he dropped off a proposal with photos at Scribner's. He never commented on the publisher's response, but no book deal was forthcoming. On September 5, in St. John's, Newfoundland, Bob sold twenty-five prints to a publisher to be used in a picture book on Labrador. He sold the prints for $1 each and retained all future rights. Bob was always smart about business agreements.

He also seemed interested in writing, perhaps influenced by Grenfell, who wrote and published engaging tales of the people he met in Labrador. Bob's father and his sister Miriam were regularly publishing books, though neither his father's legal books nor his sister's books on nutrition seemed destined for a wide audience. In November 1913 *Outing*, a sportsmen's magazine from Chicago, published an article by Birdseye titled "Camping in a Labrador-hole," about an incident that had happened a year earlier. The style was not unlike that of his journals, regularly stopping to tell readers what he ate. He described how difficult it was to manage a dog team and to travel by sled, and how they were trapped in a snow blizzard for three days with nothing to eat but raisins, prunes, rice, and the candy he always carried to give to children. The experience was nearly an early end to Bob Birdseye, and in fact five of his dogs did not survive. The writing lacked a strong storytelling narrative but was illustrated with his photos, his admiral-in-sealskins self-portrait, and shots of his sled and dog team.

A month later *Outing* came out with another article of his, titled "The Truth About Fox Farming." This was more like the Birdseye known in later years: everything you could know about fox farming, complete with his diagrams and, of course, a few photos taken by him of his and other fox farms. His photography was without artifice, intended purely to document. It was a new skill for him, but at this time there were not many amateur photographers, so he was a pioneer.

In 1913 Bob went back for a visit to Montclair. That summer, between lunches with his brother Kellogg, visits to his father's office, meetings with backer Harris Hammond, consultations with furriers, a visit to Scribner's with his book proposal, and even a visit to Amherst—all of which were mentioned in his journal—Bob probably managed to see Eleanor in Washington or New York, but he mentioned nothing of this in his journal. By August 28 he was back in Newfoundland, preparing for Labrador's early winter.

The following year he visited home again. It seemed almost certain that summer in 1914 that Europe was about to go to war, what history would later call World War I. This had huge implications for Birdseye's fox business. For one thing, he got his cash flow from British investors, possibly Grenfell connections. He wrote in his journal, "Because of the war possibly causing some of the pledged English underscriptions to be withdrawn we might get into serious straights [*sic*], for want of capital." The other reason a war would affect Bob's business was that the primary market for fox fur was Europe. American women seldom wore such furs. It was a European look, and Europe was about to be consumed with war. The principal fur centers, in London and Leipzig, were both shutting down. The Hudson Bay Company stopped buying fur.

After two years in which he traveled, by his estimate,

five thousand miles by dogsled gathering foxes, in 1914 Bob's business was shut down by the Newfoundland government, which finally banned the export of live foxes from Labrador and Newfoundland. The conventional wisdom of the time was that the high-quality-fur business was dying.

The fur market in New York was dismal. Top-quality ermines were selling for 15 cents each. But Bob saw opportunity. The United States, the one developed country that was not at war, was prospering. Surely this new prosperity would be reflected in fashionable women in furs, especially with pelts available for bargain prices. This was Bob's kind of gamble, and he had an advantage, as he was a great salesman. His obvious intelligence, his ability to articulate his idea, and his contagious enthusiasm almost always carried him through. He persuaded a New York furrier to stake him to $8,000.

Back in Labrador Bob began killing his foxes, freezing them by packing them in snow, and sending them to be skinned. He also started buying quality pelts wherever he could find them at cut-rate prices. He traveled thousands of miles by dogsled again, buying furs, offering low prices but paying in cash. The big fur buyers rarely offered cash, so he was able to make very good deals. Labradoreans were selling their furs for historically low prices. He wrote of how he bought one top-quality silver fox for $375 that a year before would have been worth $4,000.

He wrote that the people were so hard up, they would take "any price I see fit to give." He did express some remorse for exploiting poor and desperate people, even commenting on how badly dressed their children were, with leaky boots. But he didn't change his behavior, pointing out that he was still paying "twice what the Hudson Bay Company is giving." By the end of 1914 he had cornered the fur market and cleared $6,000 profit—almost $140,000 in today's money.

With these substantial earnings he felt ready to marry the woman he loved. In July 1915 Bob left Labrador, and in St. John's he wired home to say he was coming. According to his journal, he also "wired EG." That small notation was the first time he ever mentioned Eleanor Gannett in his journal.

On July 25, 1915, Bob was back in New Jersey. That night he sat down with his older brother Kellogg to discuss business and told him that he was engaged to marry Eleanor. In his journal he wrote that he told Kellogg about "EG"—it was almost as though he didn't want her to be identified by anyone except himself.

Then, for almost an entire month, there are no entries in his journal, but he was not lonely. On August 29 he returned with Eleanor by car from Berlin, New York. In his journal he described the Taconic Inn, where they stayed, the various people on the property, and who their families were. He included in the journal the torn upper half of two pieces of letterhead with a picture of the Taconic Inn, which boasted electric lights and steam heat. Saving these and pressing them in his journal was, for Bob, a rare sentimental gesture. But why not? Though he never mentioned it, this was his honeymoon. He also didn't mention that a week earlier, on August 21, they were married. But at least he now started referring to Eleanor in the journal by her name rather than EG.

Life had now changed, because he was married to Eleanor. Suddenly the preparations for returning to Labrador included not only the usual shopping for shotguns, ammunition, and equipment but a week of daily shopping at Wanamaker's, where day after day Eleanor and Bob's sister Miriam bought bedroom and dining room furniture, plus a great deal of aluminum and white agate kitchenware—all to be shipped to Labrador. However, New York was no longer just about business. They all went to the Museum of Natural History together and then to their first movie, *Birth of a Nation*.

Miriam seems the sibling with whom Bob had the most in common, as she was also fascinated with food. At the time she was lecturing at Cornell University on nutrition, particularly about meat. She seemed to become closer upon his marriage to Eleanor. They were both college-educated women and coincidentally would both later write about gardening.

Then Bob and Eleanor were off to Labrador by the usual route: a train to Boston; a second train to Maine; a boat to Halifax, Nova Scotia; a third train to Sydney, on Cape Breton Island; a second boat to the tiny seaport of Port aux Basques, Newfoundland; and a fourth train across the rock-bound, barely populated wild interior to St. John's before boarding one final boat to Labrador. One takes the same route today, except that the train from Port aux Basques to St. John's, which used to be called the *Newfie Bullet*, no longer runs. There is now a highway with signs warning of the perils of crossing moose.

The newlyweds had to wait two weeks at a hotel in St. John's for the boat to Labrador. Compared to anything in Labrador, St. John's was a big city, but in fact it was just a rugged fishing town, dating back to before 1620.

In October they got to Labrador and started building a new house he would name Wyndiecote, the old Long Island name that to Bob meant home. He wrote that he was spending all his time on this project. Perched on a rock ledge over Muddy Bay and reachable only by a long stairway that climbed the rocks, it was a simple house, though luxurious compared with the shacks most people lived in around the bay. Built by a local trapper, Charles Bird, it was only one story with just three rooms; windows looking out at the angry sea, the windblown sky, and distant woods surrounded the large living room. It was not an impressive structure, but it still stands today, though its location has changed. Not even Bob realized it at the time, but it is technically the birthplace of the modern frozen-food industry. It has not been preserved for its historic importance, however. It's lasted because houses are scarce in Labrador, and you don't throw away a solid one.

They finally moved in on December 9, which happened to be Bob's twenty-ninth birthday. They had hired a live-in maid—not uncommon at the time—back where they came from. Bob now took Sundays off, and he and Eleanor read and went for walks in snowshoes in −14-degree temperatures.

Eleanor, in some ways a prim and proper woman of her time, was also quite unusual, as she was ready for adventure at any time. She traveled with Bob on long journeys with a nine-dog sled, setting traps in subzero weather. Years later she liked to amuse her children with a story of the time she fell off the back of a *komatik*, and Bob, up front managing the dog team, didn't notice for about ten minutes, in which time he'd covered about a mile. He looked back and saw no Eleanor, then turned around and found her.

Eleanor adapted quickly to life on the frontier. They took

target practice together with .22 Colt revolvers, which they also used to shoot rabbits that were caught in their traps. At first, though she did well with targets, Eleanor couldn't hit the rabbits, but she soon caught on. She gradually found her place with the Hammond and Birdseye Fur Company, doing paperwork and looking after foxes, which they were still breeding, though they could export them only if they killed them. She also established a darkroom in the new house so they could develop film and make prints from Bob's photography.

In May fox pups were born. The journal, and apparently their lives, became consumed with caring for one struggling pup. Bob records when the pup gets his first teeth and when he has "a copious movement" due to the use of castor oil. Finally, on May 18, 1916, Bob reported that the pup died at 6:00 a.m. of acute indigestion.

Everyone in Labrador was eager for news of the war, which was scarce. They would not hear about it until the harbor thawed a month later. The Dominion of Newfoundland had given more than its share to the war effort: an entire regiment was slaughtered on the first day of the battle of the Somme in 1916.

In the meantime, Bob and Eleanor had foxes to worry about. Once the harbors thawed, they went back to New York. Eleanor was more than six months pregnant, but this was the soonest they could leave. Her pregnancy had not taken up nearly the space in the journal that the fox pup had. Once in New York, Birdseye simply noted, "Shortly after breakfast E and I went to Dr. Stern's office and made arrangements. I gave him carte blanche in making hospital and all other necessary arrangements." That taken care of, Bob tried to work on business in New York. After numerous attempts to meet with Hammond, who seemed always to be in Gloucester, Massachusetts, Birdseye was informed, "Mr. Hammond is no longer interested in Hammond and Birdseye." Bob's father tried to set him up with other prospective investors, and apparently something worked, because he went back to Labrador, where he awaited the arrival of Eleanor and their new baby.

On September 6, 1916, their son Kellogg was born. Five weeks later, Eleanor set off for Labrador with the baby. The ship she was to have sailed on from Newfoundland never arrived, because a German U-boat had sunk it. Finally she managed to get on the last boat for Labrador before ice shut the ports for the winter, and it had to sail through a storm to get there in time. To raise a baby in a subarctic wilderness with the closest medical facility, Grenfell's hospital in Battle Harbour, 250 miles away by dogsled seemed a risky decision. But Eleanor and Bob were not troubled by it. Years later the family would ask, "But what if Kellogg got sick?" and Eleanor would smile softly and say, "But he never did."

The first obvious change now that Bob was a father was that he stopped writing. He dropped his journals altogether and wrote far less to his family. The family would still hear from him whenever there was a mail ship, but the packets were much lighter. He urged his parents to keep writing back "the same number of good letters that you always sent me when I was a poor forlorn bachelor." Though he was always understated in his mentions of Eleanor, it was clear how much he enjoyed having her with him. He described her as "the only genuine Washingtonian north of the forty-nine." Eleanor began writing to Bob's parents, too.

FOOD IN LABRADOR

Typical of Birdseye, he did not worry a great deal about the proximity of a hospital, although he was concerned that Kellogg eat well. Ringing in his ears was Grenfell's constant admonition to the people of Labrador that it was poor diet that was causing widespread anemia, dyspepsia, beriberi, and scurvy. Fruits and vegetables had to be brought in on trips to Newfoundland. Livestock for meat or milk could not be kept, because the dogs would kill them. Sled dogs, the only means of transportation, were not optional. Now Bob thought a lot about food preservation because of the long winters. He had to have food for his family.

Fish was the cheapest, most plentiful food. One of the summer tasks was to preserve salted fish. In the winter fish was frozen by a technique called snow packing, in which food was buried in a barrel of snow and left outdoors. Since the temperature was below freezing all winter, it remained frozen until unpacked for use.

Birdseye asked himself many questions about food and survival in the subarctic. Why, he wondered, did people in Labrador eat lean food in the summer but a tremendous amount of fat in the winter? The ultimate winter survival dish was something called bruise, a combination of dried and salted food mixed with a tremendous amount of fat. Usually it was salt cod, hardtack, flour, and water, baked hard and mixed with cubed salt pork and then boiled and served like a hash with huge globs of melted pork fat. Bowls of melted fat were often placed on the table to spoon onto food. Bob laughed when he heard a host say, "Have some more grease on your bruise," but everyone then took a few spoonfuls. It was a Sunday-morning breakfast favorite. He remembered that people also ate a great deal of grease in the Southwest, where it was hot in the summer; they would open a can of corn and eat it with pork fat.

Bob reflected on such phenomena. He asked his parents in a letter why people in hot and cold climates eat more fat than those living in a temperate zone.

The constant diet of grease and preserved and conserved food gave him a longing for food that tasted fresh. "Good lord," he once wrote his family. "How fine gull gravy tastes when one hadn't had anything fresh for a long time." It was not only Bob who felt this yearning for fresh food. He told his parents that whenever people met in Labrador, the first thing they asked each other was whether they had seen any fresh food where they came from. He often described the excitement and relish with which neighbors would gather for a meal when they had gotten some fresh food. When he bought foxes, he also tried to buy beaver, lynx, martin, otter—whatever he could get. He wanted them with the furs on so he could stuff them and sell them as specimens. But also he wanted to eat the fresh meat. Everyone in Labrador craved fresh food in the winter. Although Birdseye loved irony, he was absolutely serious when he referred to a meal with fresh food as "today's big event."

His food concerns were immediate. He was not thinking

of ambitious plans to launch a new food industry; he was just trying to make sure his young son and his wife ate well. Making that task even more difficult, Bob was reluctant to travel and leave Eleanor and Kellogg alone. He wrote in a 1917 letter, "Pulling teeth would have been a mild process compared to running off and leaving E. and Sonny."

Bob and Eleanor had brought live hens with them from Newfoundland, along with a large supply of fresh potatoes, turnips, beets, carrots, parsnips, cabbages, onions, apples, and grapes. They'd also brought thirty dozen eggs, because they didn't think the Rhode Island Reds would start laying until spring. Finally, they'd brought two beef hindquarters and a whole lamb.

"So you see that our larder is going to be well-stocked," Bob wrote home to New Jersey, "and we needn't fear scurvy or rickets, or pip, or beriberi or any of those little ailments which come of a too salt diet!"

All he had to do now was figure out how to keep this trove in reasonably fresh condition throughout a long winter. In the event of failure, they also shipped a large supply of canned fruits and vegetables. The grapes froze on the way to Sandwich Bay, and the eggs spoiled quickly and could not even be fed to the foxes. But by the following spring the hens were producing. Bob had several hundred partridges frozen in the fall. Another reason that freezing, by packing snow into barrels, became more important with Eleanor's arrival was that she disliked gamey-tasting meat, so a wild goose or a partridge kept even a few days was too gamey for her.

All of this was driving Bob's lively mind to reflect on the

science of freezing. Freezing was not new. Frozen food had been available all his life. But when it thawed, it was mushy and less appealing than even canned food. Frozen food was a last resort. No one really wanted to eat it.

But to Birdseye's surprise, the frozen food in Labrador was not unpleasant. In fact, in his judgment it tasted just like fresh food. What accounted for the difference? The Inuit had traditionally enjoyed this high-quality frozen food. They fished in holes in the ice and pulled out a trout, and it instantly froze in the 30-degrees-below-zero air. When they cooked it, it tasted like fresh fish. In fact, sometimes they would put the frozen fish in water to thaw, and the fish would start swimming, still alive—according to Birdseye, sometimes after being frozen for months. Bob never understood the mystery of the live frozen fish, but he did learn to ice-fish, instantly freeze the fish in the air, store it outside in the cold, and thaw it in water when ready to cook it. And he learned to snow-pack fresh meat. Frozen game was so fresh when it thawed that it did not taste in the least aged, and even Eleanor liked it.

He noticed that the meat and fish were not as good when frozen in the early or late winter, and he wondered why. He would cut paper-thin slices of the frozen food and see that the food that had been frozen then did not have the same texture as the food frozen in the dead of winter. The spring and fall food had a grainier texture and leaked juices when thawed.

Birdseye thought about the difference between the frozen food in Labrador and commercially frozen food, with its grainy texture and leaking juices, and he realized that the ice crystals were too big. If food is frozen too slowly, the larger ice crystals will damage the cellular structure, even break down cells. Everyone knew that the height of winter was the best freezing season. Birdseye figured out why.

It was clear that in the dead of winter, when the air was −30 degrees Fahrenheit or even colder, the food froze instantly, whereas in warmer weather it took longer. This was not hard for Birdseye to understand when he thought about it: it had to do with the science of crystallization, of which everyone in Labrador had some knowledge, because preserving food with salt was a way of life there. Salting food and freezing food are opposites. For the best results, freezing needs small crystals and salting needs large ones. For centuries sea salt had been in great demand in places like Labrador that have a great deal of fish but not a sunny enough climate for evaporating seawater in the sun—the only economically viable way to produce sea salt, as the cost of fuel made cooking it down not feasible. The fish required sea salt, not because, like the fish, it came from the sea, but because of its large crystals. Solar evaporation is a very slow way to make salt, and so the crystals are very large. This is the rule with any kind of crystallization: The more slowly the crystals form, the larger they are.

He started experimenting with vegetables. He had bought a lot of cabbage in Newfoundland and had been storing it in the house. When the weather turned very cold, he took a large barrel and put an inch of seawater at the bottom. Then he put a thin layer of cabbage leaves. Once this was frozen, he added another layer of seawater and another layer of cabbage. He repeated this until he had a full barrel. When he wanted some cabbage for the family, he would lop off a chunk with an axe and cook it, and he found that it tasted exactly like cooked fresh cabbage.

Not all attempts were successful. Some caribou were butchered and frozen into blocks of ice, only to find out months later that it had not been frozen enough and the meat had rotted.

On April 6, 1917, the United States entered World War I, despite President Woodrow Wilson's election-campaign promise not to. Bob always said that he returned to the United States because of the war. But he did not clarify why.

Did they go home because of serious family problems? In May 1917 Bob's father, Clarence, and older brother Kellogg were arrested and charged with conspiracy to commit fraud. Bob had seldom taken an important step without consulting both of them. During the years he traded furs in Labrador, they had been his regular advisors and the two family members most often mentioned in his writings. And of course Bob and Eleanor had named their first son after Kellogg.

Accounts of the trial make clear that this was not a small oversight or a slight brush with the law but an elaborate conspiracy to steal a fortune. It appeared that Bob's father, a leading figure in New York State law, whose books were studied by law students and lawyers, was the ringleader in a scheme involving lying to and deceiving a considerable number of business associates, many of whom testified against him.

Whether or not this was a factor in Bob's return to the United States is not known. It may have just felt like the right time to go home. All his life Bob lost patience with a project once it succeeded, and he now had financial success as a fox breeder. It was time for a different kind of life. He was married and a father, and he intended to have more children. Their second child, Ruth, was born in 1918.

It is tempting to say that after years of contemplating freezing, making frozen food, and searching for commercial opportunities, Bob was ready to go home and start the frozen-food industry. But in fact, nothing was further from his thoughts. Back home no one liked frozen food or wanted it, and it seemed that in a temperate climate with year-round ports and a steady supply of fresh food most of the year, there was no need to freeze food. He thought his days of freezing food, just like his days of traveling by dogsled, were over. He later said of what he had learned about freezing, "I tucked this knowledge away in my subconscious mind, but its commercial possibilities did not dawn on me at that time."

CHAPTER SIX

A Very Big Idea

Bob and Eleanor and young Kellogg and Ruth, the new baby, did not settle in New York or New Jersey to be by the troubled relatives. Instead they went back to Washington, D.C., where Bob looked for a job that he would like. First he worked for Stone and Webster, a Massachusetts-based engineering and construction company with which Bob's Wall Street uncle, Henry Ebenezer, had a business involvement. Then, in 1919, Bob left this growing firm for a position as an assistant purchasing agent for the US Housing Corporation. For a time he also worked for a bottled-water producer. The life of adventure seemed well behind him in 1920, when he switched jobs again and became the assistant to the president of the US Fisheries Association, a lobbying group for commercial fishermen.

On March 5 Bob's father and brother were sentenced to two years in prison for insurance fraud. Their sentencing was covered in the *New York Times*. Clarence Frank Birds-eye Sr. was a powerful, well-respected man and patriarch of the family. On April 30, 1920, Bob's father, age sixty-five, was received at the Western State Penitentiary in Pittsburgh, and became prisoner no. 10849. His occupation was given as lawyer/author. He surrendered his gold cuff links, gold collar buttons, gold penknife, and gold ring and began his sentence.

His father's and brother's convictions must have been devastating to Bob. In fact, the incident is not well known among his descendants. His father served his two years and was released in 1922 but died five years later at the age of seventy-three—two years too soon to see his namesake son become wealthy and famous. Bob's mother, Ada, moved in with Miriam in Washington, D.C., where Miriam did nutritional studies for the US Department of Agriculture. But by then Bob and Eleanor had left Washington.

Those years while his father was in prison, 1920 to 1922, were formative years for Bob Birdseye. As assistant to the president of the Fisheries Association he was confronted with the full range of fishery issues, from sea to market. He was back with the two topics that always drove his interest, wildlife and food, and the big question was how to get fish to market in better condition.

Most fish lost much of its value while being transported. "The inefficiency and lack of sanitation in the distribution of whole fresh fish so disgusted me," Bob explained twenty years later, "that I set out to develop a method which would permit the removal of inedible waste from perishable foods at production points, packaging them in compact and convenient containers, and distributing them to the housewife with their intrinsic freshness intact."

This was the beginning of what grew into a very big idea. In most markets the fish that was being sold to consumers was greatly inferior to fish landed at the docks of fishing ports. This created two problems, both of which disturbed Bob: people were not eating fish at its best, and fish was losing value on its way to the market. Bob thought that if he could find a way to deliver it to the customer in the same condition it was in when it arrived at the docks, many more people would eat fish, and the fishing business could greatly expand. He developed an inexpensive container that would keep fish chilled until it got to market. With Birdseye's box, fish arrived in considerably better condition, but it was still not comparable to fresh fish, and a great deal of fish was still lost to spoilage. He knew there had to be a better solution.

Later in life Birdseye developed a pet theory that the subconscious resembled an electronic calculating machine. "If you feed the right information into it," he would say, "it will quietly go to work in mysterious ways of its own and, by-and-by, produce the answer to your problem." He kept thinking about his constant struggle for "fresh food" in Labrador. He remembered the quality of the frozen food, and he believed that was due to its freezing so quickly. How could that be accomplished artificially in climates that were not 40 degrees Fahrenheit below zero? After much reflection following the failure of his container device, Bob said, "my subconscious suddenly told me that perishable foods could be kept perfectly preserved in the same way I had kept them in Labrador—by quick freezing!"

If this could be done industrially, then "fresh" food would be available everywhere at any time of year. The more Bob thought about this, the more he thought this was an idea with huge potential. He left his job and moved to New Jersey, where he persuaded an ice cream company to lend him an area in their plant to conduct experiments in freezing. Eleanor was about to give birth to their third child and second daughter, who would share Eleanor's name. But Bob and Eleanor, after a quiet five years, were off on another adventure.

As with many inventors before him, Bob Birdseye made no scientific discoveries. His inventions were original ideas about how to use existing knowledge—creative thinking. To him, fast freezing was a traditional idea that came from the Inuits, the native inhabitants of Labrador. All his life he credited them. But freezing also has another story.

In human history, the use of fire and heat developed much faster than the harnessing of ice and cold. This may have been because heat, associated with life, is more appealing than cold, which is associated with death. Or it may simply be that it is much easier to learn how to make fire than to make ice. While human beings were relatively quick to heat their food, it took a long time before they learned to chill it, despite the fact that the untapped use of the cold meant that a great deal of food was spoiled and discarded. Spoilage was simply an accepted fact of life. Even in the twentieth century, after commercial freezing was developed, it was a struggle to convince stores that the money they spent on maintaining frozen food was less than the money they lost from spoilage.

For centuries the primary effort to reduce the spoilage

caused by warm temperatures was to bring food to market at night. Animals would be slaughtered at the market to avoid having the meat spoil in transport. Sometimes fish were brought to market live, in ships with tanks.

Frozen food had a sad, almost comical beginning with Sir Francis Bacon, lord chancellor of England, one of the first English scientists, if not the first. He developed theories and questioned their validity, which is the way a scientist works, yet he ended up being perhaps the only martyr to the frozen-food industry.

In March 1626 Bacon was riding in a coach through the Highgate area of North London with the physician of King Charles I. Through his window Bacon gazed at the winter snow still on the ground, which made the landscape look as if it were sprinkled with salt. Though remembered as the great champion of scientific method, Bacon rarely carried out actual experiments. But on this occasion, while speculating with the physician on whether snow could preserve meat the same way that salt did, he suddenly had an urge to try something. Stop the coach!

The two got out and went to a poor woman's house, where they bought a chicken, which she killed and cleaned for them. The men went outside, knelt on the ground, stuffed the bird with snow, and encased it in more snow—exactly the technique used by Bob Birdseye and his Labrador neighbors three centuries later. The cold affected not only the chicken but also Bacon, who became extremely ill. He was taken to a nearby house, where his condition grew worse. He wrote that the experiment of chilling the chicken "succeeded." Only hours after writing the note, Bacon died of pneumonia.

His chicken is often considered the first frozen food, and the reason it is often said that frozen food truly began in 1626.

The year after Bacon's death, Robert Boyle was born in Ireland to the very wealthy earl of Cork, who judged him too sickly for school and so had him taught by tutors at home. A poster child for homeschooling, Boyle became the first true chemist in the modern sense of the word: a researcher who broke the physical world down to basics and tested his theories about their composition through controlled experiments. Unusual for his time, Boyle was interested in understanding everything he could about the phenomenon of coldness. An issue of the day was the question of where cold came from. Heat came from fire, and there were all sorts of theories about the source of fire, but cold was a mystery.

For a long time many Europeans believed cold came from an uncharted island north of the British Isles known as Thule. Aristotle had written that it came from something called *primum frigidum*, but what was this? Aristotle said it was water, which Boyle refuted by showing that material that contained no water, such as metals, could be chilled.

Boyle also pointed out that the surface of water, the part exposed to the air, was the first to freeze. He challenged French philosopher René Descartes's widely held belief that cold was simply the absence of a drifting substance called heat. He also disproved the theory that earth, air, and saltpeter were the source of cold, though he did conduct experiments on how saltpeter and numerous other salts intensified cold.

Bacon before him had had the same idea but couldn't prove it. At the time, producing cold was a trick performed by magicians. Bacon speculated that a number of "magic" stunts that produced cold were done through the use of salts, either common table salt, sodium chloride, or saltpeter, potassium nitrate, to intensify the cold of snow or ice. The use of salts to lower temperature would be a key to the Birdseye freezing process.

Boyle also investigated the nature of ice, showing that it was water in an expanded form. He conducted numerous experiments to show that the volume of ice was greater than the volume of the water from which it was made. Filling the sections of an ice cube tray half full of water and freezing it easily demonstrates this phenomenon: the resulting ice cubes will fill more than half of each section. This is also why, when a bottle of wine freezes, expanding ice forces the cork out of the bottle.

America was to be the place where refrigeration and commercial freezing were developed, leading to rapid advances in the frozen-food industry. This is striking, because Europeans were in the forefront of preserving foods through smoking, salting, and canning. A French chef, Nicolas Appert, invented canning in the time of Napoleon by discovering that food that was heated and hermetically sealed in a jar would not rot. The French and later other Europeans had great enthusiasm for canned or jarred foods and even today feature them prominently in deluxe food shops.

Yet the American embrace of cold as a way to preserve food has also meant that Americans led the way in the manufacturing of refrigerators and freezers. The first refrigerator was a European invention: in 1748 William Cullen, professor of medicine at the University of Glasgow, built a refrigerator based on the fact that evaporating liquids cause a lowering of temperature. Cullen caused a container to lose not only its fluid but its air, becoming a complete vacuum, with the result that the water in a tank that surrounded the refrigerator froze. He wrote a paper on his work and had it published in a local Scottish journal but never attempted to promote the idea.

Nor did all Americans market their ideas. In 1758 Benjamin Franklin wrote a paper on his experiments showing that liquids that evaporate faster than water, such as alcohol, can cause water to freeze. But this did not lead him to build a refrigerator or an ice maker, either of which would have been landmark inventions in 1758.

It was another half century before an American built a refrigerator, but his approach was very different. The device was built in 1802 by a Maryland engineer, Thomas Moore, who, like Birdseye, was less interested in scientific theory than in solving the problem of getting fresh food to market. He built a metal box for butter surrounded by ice in a cedar container tightly insulated with rabbit fur. With this box he was able to carry butter from his farm to the Georgetown market, twenty miles away. Everyone wanted his hard butter rather than the unrefrigerated, coagulated grease of other producers and gladly paid his very high prices. Clearly Moore wanted to start an industry. He patented his box and published a pamphlet about "the newly invented machine called a refrigerator." Industry didn't follow, and Moore earned little money from his invention, but he was hugely influential.

The American dominance in freezers and refrigeration

started with making ice available to everyone, not just the wealthy. In the eighteenth century most European countries stored ice in icehouses, traded it commercially, and used it chiefly to chill drinks. But it was a luxury, sold to the privileged at a very high price. In Russia and France only the royal families were allowed to produce ice.

America started out the same way. The average colonial had no access to summer ice, but icehouses were a feature of the large Virginia slave plantations. George Washington, Thomas Jefferson, and James Madison all had icehouses for enjoying chilled drinks any time of year. In the North, harvesting ice was a low-status, low-wage job; in Philadelphia convicts in prisons were used to make it. Yet wealthy Southerners paid high prices for ice. Further hampering the ice market was the religious belief that using ice out of season was tampering with God's design. There was a similar attitude toward greenhouses.

But America had a revolution with a populist democratic ideology, a belief in the common man, and after that, even while being led by wealthy aristocrats who lived in luxury, the new country often shunned luxury products in favor of popular or inexpensive ones. Icehouses were popularized by a little-remembered but extremely influential man named Frederic Tudor, the son of a distinguished lawyer who had clerked for John Adams. Tudor's father sent three of his sons to Harvard, but not Frederic, who thought it was a waste of time and wanted to move on to making money. He started in a shipping office and, at age seventeen, invented an improved bilge pump for emptying seawater from the hull of a ship.

A few years later he started a business shipping ice to the

Caribbean, particularly Martinique and Cuba. He shipped it carefully insulated in hay but noticed that Caribbeans, understanding nothing of the nature of ice, walked through the streets with it in the midday sun and even attempted to store it in water, which, being warmer, melts the ice. Apparently the idea that water was the source of cold still lingered.

In the 1820s Tudor hired Nathaniel Jarvis Wyeth, another man who had shunned education for commerce. Wyeth revolutionized the ice business, first with a saw-toothed ice cutter that made the blocks more regular and produced them more cheaply, and then with the use of sawdust for insulation. Wyeth produced a series of inventions that by the 1830s made Tudor's the premier icehouse in America. Tudor's ice, much of it cut from Henry David Thoreau's Walden Pond, near Boston, was shipped all over the world.

By the 1830s ice had already transformed the diet of urban Americans. Fresh fruits, vegetables, meat, fish, and milk became increasingly popular. Farmers in upstate New York shipped their milk and other products on ice by train to New York City markets. Fresh fish was brought in on ice from New England. By the Civil War Tudor and his competitors were shipping New England ice to fifty ports and had ships leaving every day. New uses of ice were being contemplated. Couldn't it be used to ship meat? The United States had a surplus of meat, and there was great demand for it in Europe. Tudor became a multimillionaire, and his ice became a common international commodity.

Americans rapidly became the world's greatest consumers of ice, largely because Tudor's and Wyeth's innovations had greatly reduced the cost. Twelve and a half cents could buy one hundred pounds. Southerners became passionate about iced cocktails, the mint julep being one of the most famous. The Port of New Orleans became a major destination for ice, and New Orleans became known for its cocktails. By 1850 New Orleans was buying fifty thousand tons of ice every year, and even though the ice could sell as cheaply as $15 a ton, the volume of sales made ice an important trade. But nowhere was more ice consumed than in New York City, which used twice as much as New Orleans.

By the Civil War, ice in America was used not only for drinks, but also to store food and keep it fresh. Gradually icebox manufacturers understood that the flaw in the Moore model was that there was no circulating air, which helps to cool the ice. That was why, as Boyle had observed, ice froze first on the surface. After 1845 iceboxes had circulating air and were far more effective.

European scientists continued to develop important ideas and avoid their commercial application. In 1834 Charles Saint-Ange Thilorier, a chemist in the School of Pharmacy in Paris, was able to apply enough pressure to carbon dioxide to convert it to a solid carbonic acid. This was an arduous and dangerous undertaking that others had failed at, and Thilorier's assistant had lost both legs in an explosion caused by one of their experiments. He never attempted to commercialize his discovery, although many years later the same carbonic acid, now called dry ice, became an essential part of refrigeration. It is clear that Thilorier understood the potential of his discovery. He mixed dry ice with snow and ether and produced a temperature of −110 degrees Celsius (−166 degrees Fahrenheit), which at the time was by far the coldest temperature ever produced artificially. He simply was not interested in practical applications.

Great progress was made when, in 1859, a Frenchman, Ferdinand Carré, produced a machine that made artificial ice. Though it took some time for this technology to be accepted by industry, eventually it would mean that ice could be made anywhere; it did not have to be cut and stored in the North in winter. But despite this invention, the natural-ice trade prospered for the rest of the century. Maine became the leading exporter, shipping 3,092,400 tons out of state in its best year, 1890.

Some historians fix the date of the first commercial frozen food as 1875, but there may have been earlier attempts. The first US patent for a frozen-fish process was awarded to Enoch Piper of Camden, Maine, in 1862. He froze salmon by placing it on racks under pans of ice and salt, which lowered the air temperature. After the fish was frozen hard, which took about twenty-four hours, he dipped it in water to give it a glassy sheen. More patents followed, and small frozen-fish operations started around coastal New England.

Fish was the usual object of frozen-food experimenting because it was the product that had the greatest losses from spoilage. But it was also the most demanding. People could accept a berry that on thawing had gotten a bit soft and juicy, but it is very hard to sell soft and juicy fish.

In 1875 large-scale operations began freezing food in a room insulated with sawdust, the old Wyeth idea, using ice and salt, an even older idea. Bob saw this type of operation in use for frozen bait in Battle Harbour, Labrador, and described the operation: "In the upper room cracked natural ice and coarse solar [evaporated sea] salt were mixed and filled into rectangular metallic tubes which passed downwardly through the freezing and storage chamber on the ground floor."

Frozen-food production spread from New England to the Great Lakes region to the Pacific Northwest. In 1876 American frozen meat was shipped to England, and by 1881 it was being shipped as far as Australia. By the last decade of the nineteenth century, British Columbia was shipping a million pounds of frozen fish to Europe every year, mostly salmon but also halibut and sturgeon. In 1902 H. A. Baker Sr. was freezing berries in barrels in Puyallup, Washington, and selling them.

But this frozen food had an unenthusiastic public, principally attracted by low prices. Food critics and nutritionists gave it poor ratings, especially the fish. This was an age when prime fish, such as salmon and halibut, were caught in enormous quantities and sold at low prices. But only the fish that had not sold when it was fresh was sold to the freezing companies, so frozen fish started out with very poor quality.

By the 1890s mechanically made ice was increasing frozen-food production. The concept is simple: An object can be chilled by putting it next to something cold. The cold removes warmth from the object next to it, making it also cold. Even before the issue of fast versus slow freezing, there was the issue of direct versus indirect—whether or not the food would have direct contact with the refrigerant, which was usually salt in some form. Direct contact was a problem, since the whole purpose of freezing food was so that it could be conserved without being salted.

Though salt acts by natural laws, it can do so many different and seemingly contradictory things that it appears to operate by magic. A key to understanding salt lies in the common phenomenon of salt melting ice. In many countries more salt by far is used for deicing roads than for any other purpose. In the United States 8 percent of salt production is used for seasoning food and 51 percent for deicing roads.

Anyone who has spent a winter in a place that has ice and snow has seen salt shoveled or spread on roads and sidewalks, with the result that the ice melts. How is it possible that salt melts ice, yet can be used as an agent for freezing? The answer is that salt does not melt ice by raising the temperature but by lowering the freezing point. Water freezes into ice at 32 degrees Fahrenheit, but this is not cold enough to freeze salt. So if water has salt in it, it can be considerably colder than 32 degrees and still be liquid—a liquid as cold as ice.

This can be easily demonstrated with two bowls and a thermometer. Take two identical small bowls, and place five ice cubes in each. In one bowl cover the ice with a quarter cup of table salt. After twenty minutes the unsalted ice won't have melted, but liquid will be forming in the bowl with the salted ice. The salted ice will appear to be melting, but if you measure the temperature of the liquid, it will be 29 degrees, three degrees *below* freezing. After thirty minutes the ice in the other bowl will start to melt. This liquid will be 41 degrees; it will melt because the temperature is above freezing.

Camp Venustus, Birdseye's log cabin in the Bitterroot, in 1910.
Pictured left to right: Willard V. King, Paul Stanton, Clarence Birdseye
wearing his three-piece suit, and Robert Cooley.

Above: Wilfred Grenfell's 1912
sketch poking fun at Birdseye's
hunting skills, found pasted into
Birdseye's diary for October 10, 1912.

Left: A smiling Birdseye in fur
in Labrador, circa 1912.

Clarence and Eleanor's first home, which they had built in Muddy Bay, Labrador.

A stock certificate from May 1923 in Clarence Birdseye's name, for Birdseye Seafoods, his original company in New York.

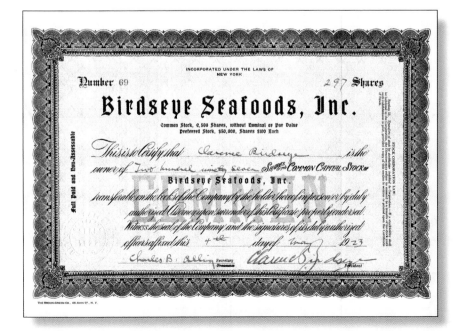

Birdseye with Eleanor and Henry, the two youngest of his four children, circa 1929.

Marjorie Merriweather Post, whose company, General Foods, bought Birdseye Seafoods in 1929.

An ad for Birdseye Frosted Foods promoting the miraculous quick-freezing process. It ran in the March 2, 1930, issue of the *Springfield Sunday Union and Republican*.

Birdseye in a 1930s home movie, chasing finback whales off of Gloucester Harbor with a tagging harpoon he invented.

Birdseye at work in his office, 1943.

The Birdseye Seafoods building in Gloucester Harbor, circa 1930.

Dehydrating carrots in the laboratory on the second floor of the Birdseye building in Gloucester Harbor in the summer of 1943. Pictured left to right: A. Pothier, Clarence Birdseye, and Helen Josephson Schuster.

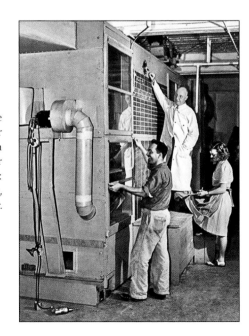

The Birdseyes' dining room in their home on Eastern Point, Gloucester, in 1942 or '43. Eleanor is facing the camera; Clarence is opposite her, with his back to the camera. On his left is their elder daughter, Ruth, and on the right their younger son, Henry.

Birdseye in 1947 excitedly serving lobster in his Eastern Point home, which he loved to cook for guests at his "lobster feeds."

Above left: Clarence and Eleanor Birdseye in their home in Peru during the winter of 1954. *Above right:* Birdseye feeding ocelots in Peru.

Birdseye at work in 1955 or '56, upon returning from Peru.

The liquid in the salted bowl will be 21 degrees. So now the salted liquid is eleven degrees below freezing and the melted unsalted ice is nine degrees above freezing. Furthermore, as time goes on, the unsalted melted ice remains at 41 degrees, while in the salted-ice bowl the temperature continues to drop as long as there is some unmelted ice. The salted water drops to 12 degrees, twenty degrees below the freezing point of water, but remains liquid.

Salt does not melt ice—it liquefies it, but the liquid is as cold as ice. It can be carried in coils, it can be sprayed to chill objects, or, as Bob did, it can be pumped inside metal plates, and contact with these plates will cause freezing. Or the brine can be directly applied to food and it will freeze it.

This is important, because a liquid is a much more efficient vehicle for freezing than a solid or a gas. A human without clothes can survive for more than an hour in an air temperature of 35 degrees Fahrenheit without any great difficulty because the cold air is gas. But in water of the same temperature, a liquid, the person will die in minutes. This is also why traditional ice cream makers turn the canister in ice that is liquefied by salt. If you just used solid ice, it would take far longer to freeze the ice cream.

For Bob Birdseye, who was trying to freeze food as quickly as possible in that room in the ice cream factory, a liquid refrigerant was essential. This was why, when he had snow-packed cabbage in barrels in Labrador, he added seawater.

Three hundred years before Bob, Bacon had written about these ideas, though he clearly did not completely understand them. But he was right. In the twentieth century, with more science available, using salt became the standard method of freezing.

The first industrial freezer in the United States was the Ottoson brine freezer. Food was submerged in a brine solution at freezing point. The brine had the same percentage of salt as the cellular composition of the food, which was supposed to keep the salt from being absorbed by the food. But this equilibrium was nearly impossible to maintain, and often the food became unbearably salty.

In 1921 Paul W. Peterson built the first "indirect freezer"—a machine in which the refrigerant and the food never come into contact. The food was packed in containers and immersed in a liquid refrigerant. In 1923, the year Bob started his first frozen-food company, Gordon F. Taylor developed a new kind of direct-contact freezer in which a whole fish moved on a conveyor belt under a spray of cold water and then was frozen with brine. The frozen fish was then sprayed with water again to wash off the brine and give it a crystalline glaze of ice. From Bob's point of view, the interesting idea in Taylor's machine was the use of a conveyor belt for mass production.

By the 1920s, when Bob started thinking about commercially freezing food, fast freezing was well known in science, and even industry had experimented with it. The earliest commercial fast-frozen food, which was whole fish in salt and ice, had been produced in 1915 while Bob was in Labrador and not noticing. Also by the 1920s European scientists had expounded on fast freezing and the principals of crystallization, but in reality most frozen food was still slow frozen and made from the cheapest, poorest-quality fresh food. State laws tried to protect consumers from the terrible frozen food. In the state of New York slow-frozen food could not be sold unless a store posted a sign over its entrance in letters a minimum of eight inches tall stating FROZEN FOOD SOLD HERE. New York State also banned the serving of frozen food in its prisons.

Perhaps Birdseye didn't arrive at the idea of freezing sooner because of how bad frozen food's reputation was. At the 1883 International Fisheries Exhibition, a highly influential gathering in London of all the North Atlantic fishing nations, which influenced attitudes about everything from eating fish to managing fisheries, frozen fish had been presented and received horrible reviews. The press described its smell as a "stink" and its look as "withered." Forty years later this was still the prevailing image of frozen food.

There was a minor breakthrough in its acceptance during World War I, when the US Army bought small quantities of frozen fish and chicken to feed soldiers. This led to a considerable amount of talk about frozen food after the war, though few people actually ate it.

By the time Bob began his experiments with freezing food in 1923, frozen food had been around for fifty years, and all the technology he needed for the kind of production he envisioned was available. But, by his own confession, he knew almost nothing of it. He did not know about Ottoson's machine, or Peterson's, or most of the studies and debates. He knew only what he had learned about freezing in Labrador. But this had taught him something no one else seemed to understand: he could piece together the techniques that other people had developed and make a product that would be astoundingly good. This was his belief, and it didn't matter that when he told people he would make frozen fish "as good as fresh," almost everyone would scrunch up their nose or roll their eyes.

In 1923 Bob set out to start his own frozen-fish company, Birdseye Seafood, in New York City by selling $20,000 in stock. He looked everywhere for investors in his big idea. Henry Ford had expressed interest in frozen food, so Birdseye made an effort to get his backing, but he got no response. Then the Clothel Refrigerating Company, which produced refrigerators for the navy, became interested in Bob's venture and provided him a space on White Street, a short distance from the Fulton Street Market, where wholesale fresh fish was bought and sold.

What was new about Bob's work was as much in the packaging as in the preparation of food. He was still primarily interested in figuring out how to get the product from wholesaler to retailer to consumer in a sanitary, efficient, convenient package. If his boxes had worked better, he might not have gone into freezing.

Perhaps the most famous Birdseye myth is that Bob went to a store, spent $7 on salt, ice, and an electric fan, and with these reproduced the Labrador winter and froze a fish. There is an element of truth to this, which is that this was how Bob worked: he found a few banal household items and solved a problem.

The problem with frozen food was not only that it didn't

freeze quickly enough but also that it wasn't cold enough. Birdseye estimated that a piece of meat was not truly frozen until it reached −96 degrees Fahrenheit. Existing commercial freezing was done at about 25 degrees, only a few degrees below the freezing point.

Bob always chose low technology over high, and so in his home in Yorktown Heights, in New York's Westchester County, he experimented with various salts and even dry ice. His salts had to drop the temperature very low and very quickly. Years later Bob would recall, "Production of perishable foods, dressed at the point of production and quick frozen in consumer packages, was initiated, so far as I am aware, in the kitchen of my own home late in 1923 when I experimentally packaged rabbit meat and fish fillets in candy boxes and froze the packages with dry ice."

He discovered that all that was necessary for quick freezing was that the temperature pass very quickly out of the first freezing temperature, which is from 33 degrees to 23 degrees Fahrenheit. He eventually settled on calcium chloride in a solution he could maintain at −45 degrees, which was the temperature of some of the coldest days in Labrador. Below that point, crystallization is rapid and crystals become very small. To speed up freezing, he had to freeze smaller amounts. Freezing at the time was an entirely wholesale business, and huge blocks of food, including whole sides of beef, were frozen. Fruits were frozen into blocks of as much as four hundred pounds. The food was placed in a barely freezing environment and frozen over a number of days. Not only were these quantities too massive to be frozen quickly, they also had no retail market, because what could a family do with a frozen side of beef or four hundred pounds of strawberries?

He developed his own machine for packing and freezing fish fillets. The machine weighed twenty tons, considerably larger and heavier than Clothel's two-ton refrigerator. In 1924 Bob was awarded his first patent for this fish-freezing process. In his patent application dated April 18, 1924, he made the following claim: "It is well known that fish like many other dietary articles has been frozen for the purpose of suspending, or preventing, decomposition through oxidation, bacteriological or other action, but the present invention goes much further than that and accomplishes results heretofore unknown in the seafood industry."

If Bob didn't pioneer actual freezing, he had to pioneer most everything else in his process. He experimented with the different heat-insulating properties of fiberboard, cardboard, cork, and wood. His ideas were so new that the National Bureau of Standards could not furnish him with any information on the insulating properties of fiberboard. No one had tested it, so he did. His first patent makes clear that his concern was as much with packaging as with freezing itself. The patent goes into elaborate diagrams and explanation of the packaging—insulated fiberboard boxes—and was the first of many patents Birdseye was awarded for packaging.

One of Bob's first true innovations was packing fish in corrugated cardboard, fiberboard, and eventually waxed cardboard, rather than the traditional balsa wood boxes used for salted fish. Balsa wood worked well enough, but his quality frozen fish was going to cost more than people were accustomed to paying for frozen food. He wanted to produce it as inexpensively as he could without sacrificing quality. The wooden boxes cost $1 for every pound they held. They were supposed to be returnable, but customers seldom bothered. Later in 1924 Bob patented his second, improved box. He was very concerned with eliminating all air pockets within the package of fish, because bacteria, which led to decomposition and illness, could grow in these spaces.

Bob, like Gordon Taylor with his conveyor-belt freezer, froze one fish at a time. Whole fish went through the extra steps of being skinned and filleted. The fillet not only froze faster but was easier to thaw and use. His quick-frozen fish went on the market in 1924. Birdseye Seafood was broke within a year. New Yorkers didn't want to eat frozen food. What had gone wrong? Was it his idea? As Bob later in life would tell young people, the key to success is not just having an idea and believing in it, but being willing to gamble. What had gone wrong with his seafood company was not the idea or that he'd been overly ambitious. It was just the opposite. He had not thought big enough. If he wanted to sell frozen food in a world where people didn't eat frozen food or even have freezers, he had to create more than a company; he had to create a whole new industry. This was a gigantic undertaking. But he believed he was on the path to an important innovation. He had solved a few of the problems, but he needed more time and more money to solve the others.

Though they had three small children to raise, Bob and Eleanor gambled everything on this big idea to make it work and sold their life insurance policy of $2,500 or, according to some, $2,250. The gamble was a testament to Eleanor's faith in Bob throughout their marriage. She also used to explain to their children, "Dad was born ahead of his time. There is so much going on in his head, the world can't even catch up." Their daughter-in-law, Kellogg's wife, Gypsy, said of her, "I call her Saint Eleanor. He was just the most fortunate man to have had her for a wife."

Bob and Eleanor sold their house in Westchester and, with their three children and a fourth expected, moved to Gloucester, Massachusetts, the oldest fishing town in the United States, to start anew.

CHAPTER SEVEN

A Very Big Deal

When the Birdseyes arrived in Gloucester, the city had just celebrated its three hundredth birthday. Founded in 1623 as an English fishing station, it remained, and still is today, one of the leading fishing ports of the United States. Its deep and extensive harbor, on the headlands of a peninsula but in the sheltered lee of the wind, makes it the ideal port for New England's richest fishing grounds.

In 1873 the population had grown to 15,397, making it the most populous town in Massachusetts, and so a new charter designated that it was now a city. When the Birdseyes arrived, in the mid-1920s, most of the population directly or indirectly made their living from the fishery. In addition to the fishermen and their families, there were the "lumpers," or dockworkers, and the ancillary trades that repaired ships, made iron fittings, and manufactured oilskins for the fisherman to wear. Glue was made from fish skins and, in the 1880s, sold worldwide by William LePage.

The people in Gloucester lived a hard and tradition-bound life. A close-knit community of skilled blue-collar workers was an ideal place for starting a new industry. It was a hardworking town with a tough waterfront of bars and merchants. The harbor was crammed with the masts and canvas sails of some 150 fishing schooners, as well as fat-hulled square-rigged barks that arrived with sea salt from Trapani, Sicily. The Gloucester fish industry used enormous quantities of salt—one of the things Bob was about to change.

At the time, there was already an inventor in town, John Hays Hammond Jr., the brother of Bob's former backer in the fur trade, Harris Hammond. Only two years younger than Bob, John was known for inventing the remote control. He also came up with a radio-controlled gyroscope system that allowed him to pilot an unmanned yacht on a 120-mile round-trip between Gloucester harbor and Boston in 1914. Fishermen encountering the ghost ship at sea were disconcerted.

During World War I Hammond invented a system to protect the remote control from enemy interference and then an electronic guidance system for targeting warheads. In addition, he worked on the first radio-guided torpedo and invented, among other things, an eye wash, a harmonic organ, an altitude-measuring system for airplanes, a magnetic bottle cap remover, and a meat baster.

Like other eager young inventors of the time, Hammond was constantly coming up with ideas for whatever problems confronted him. By the end of his life, his more than four hundred patents would outdo even Birdseye by about a hundred patents. Perhaps most telling of the disparity between their lives was that when Bob and Eleanor were settling in Gloucester, Hammond was building a castle on the west side of the harbor.

By the summer of 1925 the Birdseyes were living in a comfortable house with a wide porch at 1 Beach Road, near an exclusive golf club. It was not a particularly deluxe neighborhood, but the neighborhoods away from the harbor were considered somewhat better, because they were away from the harbor's smell. The house was an easy walk to what is known as the backshore, the part of Gloucester that is on the open Atlantic, with rough and majestic granite boulders and long sand beaches.

Bob loved the historic industrial fishing port and spent more years in Gloucester than in any other place in his life. The city itself is a confusing series of inlets, coves, and peninsulas, but to find the town center, one had only to sniff. The final stop on the Cape Ann peninsula after the picturesque Manchester-by-the-Sea was often called Gloucester-by-the-Smell. Lining most of Gloucester harbor, which includes the downtown, were fish flakes (rough-hewn wooden drying racks for salt cod), many of them owned by the Gorton-Pew Fisheries, a merger of the city's two largest seafood companies. Salt cod was Gloucester's biggest product, and it had to spend weeks drying in the sun—and giving off a rich, fishy odor. For people who grew up in Gloucester it was just the smell of home, but it made a strong impression on visitors.

• • •

With his infectious enthusiasm Birdseye was able to secure investors for a new venture, the General Seafoods Corporation. He brought in Wall Streeter Wetmore Hodges, and Hodges brought in two colleagues from J. P. Morgan, Isaac L. Rice and Bassett Jones. Together the three invested $375,000, which had the spending power of almost $5 million in today's economy.

Though Hodges was a young man, bringing him in was an important step. He knew many powerful New York financial people, and his father was Charles Hodges, a vice president of the American Radiator Company. Bob managed to interest the company in the future manufacturing of freezer units and was beginning to lay the foundations of the frozen-food industry. His new company was small, but he had numerous investors and backers interested in taking a chance on his ideas. Bob made his brother Kellogg a vice president of General Seafoods, and Kellogg moved to Gloucester with his wife, May, who was from Massachusetts, and their two children.

In 1926 Birdseye bought a building on a peninsula in the downtown harborfront area known as the Fort, one of the oldest neighborhoods in Gloucester. The first floor was used to develop frozen-food experiments, the second-floor offices for developing and planning the company's future.

Despite the modest size of the building, Bob's ambitions for General Seafoods were large. He chose that name because he imagined his company would have the esteem in the fish industry that General Electric and General Motors did in energy and transportation.

In fact, it was never his plan to just sell frozen fish. Most of the top people he hired were either financiers or engineers. His goal was to develop a frozen-food process, design new machinery, patent his ideas, and then either license them to other companies or sell his own company. Most important were the patents for equipment that could enable a large company that had the money to make frozen food a national or even international industry. The new company, Birdseye imagined, could go far beyond seafood and be called General Foods. In 1960 Joe Guinane, Bob's first manager and an engineer who worked on the design of new machinery, remarked that "there was not a frozen-food item that I do not recall Birdseye experimenting with at one time or another in the early days. He tried all kinds of things—not only seafood, meats, and vegetables, but baked and unbaked goods, as well as cooked foods." Birdseye envisioned the entire future of frozen food.

General Seafoods first produced thousands of pounds of haddock fillets frozen in rectangular cardboard boxes. Bob, who had once wanted to taste every food possible, now wanted to freeze any edible cuisine, an obsession that would stay with him the rest of his life. He prowled the docks for anything unusual that he could try freezing and let the Gloucester dragger captains know of his peculiar interest. Because of that, Birdseye froze whale, shark, porpoise, and, according to one account, an alligator.

Birdseye's inquisitiveness also led him to examine packaging and many other devices, in addition to freezing machinery. His colleague J. J. Barry developed an electronic machine for trimming fish. Birdseye invented a new brining and fish-scaling machine, which would dramatically cut manual labor. Although other electronic fish scalers existed, those would stall out when hitting a fin; Birdseye's did not. It was able to pick up fillets, wash them, and then brine them.

Bob was so excited about his machine that in July 1925 he wrote to Rice that it filleted 23½ haddock per minute, and he was anticipating a newer, better motor that might do as many as 50 per minute. Filleting machines would become the big thing of the 1920s seafood business, and by the 1930s both fresh and frozen fillets would dominate the seafood market. Filleting operations from the Boston Fish Pier and Nova Scotia came to Gloucester to look at Bob's work. The men from Boston told him that in the next twelve months they planned to produce and sell ten million pounds of haddock fillets.

The real game changer was Birdseye's freezing process. Of his more than two hundred inventions, the most important was one he applied for a patent for on June 18, 1927: patent 1,773,079, which began the frozen-food industry. Bob begins the application by asserting:

> *My invention relates to methods of treating food*
> *products by refrigerating the same, preferably by*
> *"quick" freezing the product into a frozen block,*
> *in which the pristine qualities and flavors of the*
> *product are retained for a substantial period after*
> *the block has been thawed.*

His invention description included every step of the process, including how to pack fish fillets in a box. Among the advantages he claimed for his method was that it was "indirect"—the product had no contact with the refrigerant—and that the frozen food came out in a package suitable for marketing to the consumer. He then claimed to have invented, for the first time ever, a way of producing frozen food "as a practical, commercial article of commerce."

He accomplished the quick-freeze process by eliminating air and packing food very tightly into cartons holding a two-inch-thick block, then pressing those cartons between two plates that were kept between –20 and –50 degrees Fahrenheit. The carton was held between the freezing plates for seventy-five minutes. The blocks not only froze the food solid but compacted it into a tight, regular rectangle, assuring complete freezing in a short period of time and no spaces for bacteria to enter.

Without making a scientific breakthrough, Bob had developed a process for freezing food on which an entirely new industry was founded. It was called multiplate freezing. His basic commercial freezing system remained the standard in the industry for decades to come, and in 1946 the *New Yorker* magazine stated that the only change in freezing since Birdseye's invention was that the plates were now hollow. Hollowing the plates and putting an ammonia-based refrigerant inside was, in fact, only one of Bob's improvements after the initial invention was created.

However, the breakthrough did not immediately clear the way of obstacles for General Seafoods to become the General Motors of food. In the world of inventing, inventers were often too far ahead of their time. They produced cars before there were paved roads or constructed telephones before there was telephone wiring. The classic example was

Thomas Edison, who developed a lightbulb that would have been commercially viable if only there had been an electric grid to hook it up to. Birdseye's problem was that the necessary infrastructure had not yet been built.

Bob first faced the issue in the summer of 1927, when he froze 1,666,033 pounds of seafood and wanted to ship it to the Midwest, where consumers had no fresh seafood. At the time there were no trucks or train cars capable of transporting frozen food, and no warehouses cold enough to ship the food to. Birdseye's company lacked the distribution network necessary for frozen foods. In addition, retail stores did not have equipment cold enough for holding or displaying top-quality quick-frozen food.

Then, too, there was the daunting problem of getting the consumer to accept the product. People laughed at the idea of frozen food. Most people thought that if meat was frozen, it was a whole side or the entire body of an animal. Frozen vegetables were unheard of, and the only frozen fruit people knew of was strawberries, most of which were purchased industrially for making ice cream or jam and jelly. Fish in fillets was still a new idea. They placed white notices inside each box of fish that stated, in red lettering, THE PRODUCT IN THIS CONTAINER IS FROZEN HARD AS MARBLE BY A MARVELOUS NEW PROCESS WHICH SEALS IN EVERY BIT OF JUST-FROM-THE-OCEAN FLAVOR.

To complicate matters, Birdseye had also drifted into the middle of a major debate of his time about whether industry was destroying the livelihoods of artisans and craftsmen. Labor unions that represented butchers, seafood processors, and poultry workers came out early and emphatically against frozen food. They believed that if this new idea caught on, food would all be processed in frozen-food factories and their workers would be out of business. At the time, Bob denied this. Sadly, they were right, although frozen food has not hurt them nearly as much as supermarket chains, which in turn are now being threatened by online food-delivery services. The canning industry also feared frozen food, and after Bob established the idea that frozen food would come in cartons rather than cans, can makers turned against him as well.

New ideas generate a great deal of distrust. Railroads were unenthusiastic about getting into the transport of frozen food, because they imagined huge liability for shipments that accidentally thawed. Public health officials and even some scientists at the US Department of Agriculture, where Birdseye believed he had friends, opposed frozen foods. The scientific community reasoned that if fast freezing preserved everything in its natural state, then pests and diseases would be preserved in the freezing process as well and contaminate food that would be shipped around the country. Bob bitterly complained that every time he launched a new product, he was forced to spend a great deal of research-and-development money at the Massachusetts Institute of Technology proving that it was safe to eat. He had to prove that his freezing process killed trichinae (which cause trichinosis) in pork and corn borers in corn before he could get approval to sell those foods as frozen products. Vegetables in particular were held in high suspicion by health authorities, because unlike the heating process in canning, freezing offers no sterilization.

• • •

In spite of public opinion, Birdseye solved most of the problems that he had pondered for multiple freezing. Now he could quickly produce a large amount of frozen food with indirect freezing, a limited air space, and a final boxed product in a convenient form suitable for marketing to home consumers.

His packaging invention came ten years before plastic was invented, when there wasn't another readily available strong, waterproof wrapping material. Wax paper gave little protection from moisture and completely deteriorated during thawing. Vegetable parchment wasn't waterproof and stuck to the box. The company had to get creative. They were able to coat the parchment with paraffin, which kept it from sticking while thawing, but that dried out in the freezer. They bought cellophane from France, but that disintegrated when it came into contact with wet fish. Exasperated, they persuaded the DuPont Company, which made cellophane, to add a waterproof coating to its product. The French chemical company saw the commercial potential and went into production, even though, at the start, General Seafoods of Gloucester was its only customer for it. New kinds of ink and glue also had to be developed, because frozen-food cartons became soggy as soon as they began thawing.

Bob was still focused on his central task of changing the freezing process. He developed an improved freezing machine: the continuous-belt freezer. Instead of plates, this machine had two two-inch-thick metal belts; a calcium chloride spray at −45 degrees Fahrenheit chilled the belts, which were adjusted so the packages would be pressed between them, freezing them from the bottom and the top so that the product in the box froze quickly. This was intended not only for greater production but for a future freezing all kinds of foods in different-sized boxes. The space between the belts was adjustable so packages would always fit tightly.

It was at first difficult to find the right belts. Birdseye started with Swedish belts made of watch-spring steel. He then tried copper, bronze, and Monel, a corrosion-resistant nickel alloy. The solution was stainless steel, a steel alloy with chromium to resist corrosion. Stainless steel had been in development for more than a decade but was not widely available until the 1930s. When Birdseye first explained the machine to investor Isaac Rice, Rice called it a "Goldberg contraption." Rube Goldberg was an engineer famous for cartoons in which he invented absurdly complicated machines to accomplish simple tasks.

Bob had built a contraption with a future, an improvement on multiplate freezing that was good enough to be the basis of a new industry. The drawback, the Goldberg aspect, was that his machine was fifty yards long, weighed twenty tons, and could be operated only in a cold, insulated room. The company bought a neighboring building in 1928 to house the huge machine.

Yet for all this innovation, General Seafoods still lacked a suitable transportation system and warehouses. Even if the company did manage to get its frozen food to retail stores, the stores had no way of keeping the food frozen. As a result, General Seafoods sometimes sold directly to large families, and stores that bought the frozen food often thawed it out to sell as fresh food. In 1928 the first retail-store freezer became available and, according to Bob, it cost as much as the entire rest of the store.

All these new ideas out at the Fort in Gloucester were not happening in a vacuum. Great innovations often feed off other visions, eventually creating a critical mass of thought that makes something happen. While the Birdseye group was struggling to invent a new food industry, so were many other companies. It was the dawn of many emerging food industries, which were putting new foods on the market and packaging them in new ways. In 1928, the year of the new freezer, both the slicing machine and bubble gum were invented. The following year 7UP soda debuted and Harland Sanders opened his first fried chicken restaurant in a gas station in Corbin, Kentucky.

The year the commercial freezer was invented, Kraft put Velveeta cheese on the market. Before 1928 cheese was sold from a wheel or block under unrefrigerated glass domes, and slices were cut as needed. Exposure caused the cut end to dry up, discolor, and crack, so retailers had to cut the dried end off every time they served a new customer, wasting a large part of the block. If better refrigeration and a good airtight wrapper like the one Birdseye worked on had been available, processed cheese might never have been invented. Chicago cheese merchant James Lewis Kraft began experimenting with a cheese-based factory blend. He made a fortune selling canned processed cheese to the army during World War I and continued developing the product and the company after the war was over. In part he combated spoilage by packaging cheese in small amounts. Velveeta, wrapped in tinfoil and packed in individual wooden boxes, was his crowning achievement: it melted so smoothly, it seemed like velvet. Kraft was not originally trying to make cheese melt well, but the "meltiness" of his processed cheese changed the way Americans ate and became a staple of the American diet, used in macaroni and cheese, cheeseburgers, grilled cheese sandwiches, and au gratin everything.

And Birdseye and Kraft were not the only innovators of food packaging at the time. In 1929 milk was first sold in cartons, and a British scientist, E. A. Murphy, whipped latex rubber with a kitchen mixer and created foam rubber.

By 1928 most of General Seafoods' impressive production of frozen food had not been sold, unlike Velveeta. Birdseye and his coworkers were learning to freeze meats, fruits, and vegetables, yet they could not develop the market. Advertising and marketing cost money, which the Birdseye company did not have enough of. Bob had an idea for an improved freezer but didn't have the money to develop it. The bottom line was that General Seafoods needed more capital; without that money it could never grow into a major industry.

Banks would not finance the new frozen-food industry. They would finance the old bulk freezing operations, but this new packaged frozen-food business seemed too risky. Birdseye once remarked that "a bank would no more loan on our inventory than on ice stacked in Death Valley!" Therefore, Birdseye had to seek another investor.

• • •

Eventually, Clarence Birdseye found someone interested in the future of frozen foods, and her name was Marjorie Merriweather Post. She was the daughter and heiress of Charles William Post, who had made a fortune in Battle Creek, Michigan, building the Postum Cereal Company. When she died, in 1973, her estimated wealth was $200 million—more than $1 billion today.

According to Birdseye legend, while Post was vacationing on her yacht in 1926, she sailed into Gloucester harbor. Her cook went into town for provisions and that night served her a goose. She was shocked to learn that this delicious goose, so tender, so—well, fresh-tasting—had been frozen. Who froze this goose? How did they do it? She wanted to know. Supposedly Marjorie, in her elegant dress, went down to the fishy, rough-and-tumble Fort and toured the General Seafoods plant. She then spent the next three years trying to persuade her husband or, in some versions of the story, her father to buy the Birdseye company. Eventually Postum secured the company for a record $22 million. The fabled story has been told in most Birdseye accounts and in obituaries for Marjorie Post that appeared in both the *Washington Post* and the *New York Times*. Yet there is little concrete evidence, and problematic parts of the story make its truth questionable.

Regardless, it is a fact that Marjorie sailed into Gloucester around 1926, as there is a photograph of her huge four-masted bark in the harbor.

The story overlooked what an accomplished woman Post was in her own right. She definitely did not go to her father. He died in 1914 and left her in charge of the company, which, as principal shareholder, she ran successfully for eight years.

Edward Francis Hutton, the second of her four husbands, an aggressive financial tycoon who had founded the E. F. Hutton brokerage house before the marriage, took over the company in 1922. Marjorie, who had been trained by her father, worked with her husband, and together they acquired a dozen food companies. They rarely disagreed, at least publicly. The goose story described Marjorie Post as a self-indulgent heiress who, because she enjoyed her dinner, was prepared to spend millions on a whim—unless a male figure reined her in. But the truth was completely different.

Marjorie Post's father, Charles Post, was born in Springfield, Illinois. He had a high-strung, restless nature and was given to depression, but he had a history of starting up new enterprises from ideas that excited him. Like Bob Birdseye, once successful, he was eager to move on to the next idea. In 1890 he traveled with his wife and three-year-old Marjorie to Michigan, where he checked into the Battle Creek Sanitarium, under the direction of Dr. John Harvey Kellogg, famous for a treatment of "inspirational talks" and a grain-based vegetarian diet. Kellogg and his brother, Will K. Kellogg, had concocted a line of health foods for their sanitarium, including "caramel coffee," a caffeine-free hot drink made from bread crusts, bran, and molasses. Charles emerged weak and emaciated—he restored his health with the Christian Scientists, who included a little meat in his diet—but he had gleaned a lot from his experience.

Post was so taken with Dr. Kellogg's operation that in 1892 he opened his own sanitarium, on a ten-acre farm outside Battle Creek, and called it La Vita Inn. He was clearly imitating Kellogg, with a similar treatment and a special diet, even including his own version of a caramel coffee that was also made with molasses and bran, as well as wheat berries. In 1894 he published a book, *I Am Well*, which promoted "mind-cure," a trendy idea among new American business-men that illness was not real and the human mind could cure all. Dr. Kellogg had been successful with several books on his health and diet ideas.

Neither Post's book nor his inn caught on. But he had an idea that he might be able to sell his coffee substitute. He started with mail order and in 1895 began selling it to gro-cers, branding the beverage Postum.

The first year Post lost $800 on Postum. That was when he realized that his real talent was writing advertising copy. He launched a national advertising campaign that offered to save people from the evils of coffee, which he claimed caused heart attacks, laziness, blindness, cowardice, and stupidity. Does coffee, he asked, "neutralize all of your ef-forts to make money and fame?" Soon Post was becoming wealthy from Postum sales. In 1897 he came out with a ce-real called Grape-Nuts. In the baking process, this concoc-tion of whole wheat, yeast, and malted barley flour turned starch into dextrose, the sugar found in grapes, and so the nuggets were "grape nuts." Always an aggressive and inven-tive copywriter, Post claimed that his products sent people "on the road to Wellville." Combined earnings from Postum and Grape-Nuts were more than $1 million in 1903. By the time Post died, eleven years later, he was one of the five larg-est advertisers in the country, with an annual ad budget of $1 million. Post eventually lost interest in most of the company's operations but had continued to insist on writing all the advertising copy himself.

The Kelloggs followed Post's example. Will, the underpaid, mistreated kid brother with no medical degree, had the job of boiling wheat dough and pressing it into thin sheets through rollers. One morning in 1894 the dough was too dry and flaked off as it came out of the rollers. From that he developed a process called tempering, which produced flakes, and the concept of cereal flakes was born. He began experimenting with other grains. Corn was particularly popular. Will wanted to do what Post had done, but his brother was a man of science who felt that selling cereal would be beneath him. Finally, in 1906, Will broke away from his brother and formed his own cereal company, which, like Post's, distinguished itself by its large and successful advertising campaigns.

Kellogg and Post were the beginning of modern marketing, paving the way for businessmen who liked to be in touch with all areas of their companies. While Kellogg stuck close to his original cereal products, Post wanted a huge company with many new food products and ideas, as he believed that any good idea would sell to the public if the right advertising campaign were supplied. By acquiring small, promising food companies, Marjorie Post made the company much bigger, and with her husband's connections it grew into a food giant. In 1925 Post bought Jell-O, an ambitious company that had expanded the market in flavored gelatin through advertising innovations, such as distributing Jell-O recipe books. In 1926 Post bought Baker's chocolate, which was one of America's oldest and biggest chocolate companies, and in 1928 it bought Maxwell House coffee. The Post company, with its skill, funding for marketing, and taste for new food ideas, was the perfect investor for Birdseye's General Seafoods.

In considering the acquisition of the Gloucester-based food company, Marjorie Merriweather Post would have done more than just visit the plant; she would have found out everything she could about Birdseye's business and ideas and the value of the company and its patents. Marjorie would have considered the potential for marketing and advertising. She would have talked it over with her husband, not to get permission but because he had financial expertise. And together they would have gone to Wall Street to raise the money for the deal.

Bob's company was of obvious appeal to the Postum Cereal Company. General Seafoods had developed the ideas and technology for an entirely new food industry, but it lacked capital and had a huge image problem that would require skilled marketing and advertising. Each company had what the other lacked. In addition, Bob always said that he and his partners had been trying to sell the company for some time, partly because they did not have the capital to develop their ideas and partly because the original plan had always been to make money by selling the company. Wetmore Hodges decided to go to people he knew at the Wall Street investment firm Goldman Sachs.

Bob always liked to call the deal to buy out his company the most money ever paid for a patent—an impressive victory, considering the fact that most of the important patents had not yet been granted and wouldn't come through until 1930. The total $23.5 million price was for the names, patents, patent applications, and all assets, but Postum actually bought all the patents for $20 million and the rest of the company for the remainder. Birdseye's personal share was about $1 million.

The acquisition was announced on May 7, 1929, with Postum as the majority owner. On July 27 its stockholders approved the purchase. Post's company reorganized as General Foods, going on the New York Stock Exchange on July 25 for the first time under its new name. It liked the Birdseye name (preserving it in the title of General Foods' new Birds Eye Frosted Food Division) as well as the Birdseye idea of becoming the leading food company.

For Clarence Birdseye, the timing was remarkable, as the deal would have been canceled had negotiations continued a few months longer. On October 29, 1929, known as Black Tuesday, the stock market took the greatest fall in history, and companies disappeared, along with millions of jobs and many people's fortunes. The Great Depression, an economic crisis that continued for ten years, had begun. In that climate it is unlikely that $23 million would have been spent to start a new industry, but the deal had already been made.

CHAPTER EIGHT

Magic

While millions of people began the 1930s in financial ruin, Birdseye went into the Depression with an extra $1 million, the equivalent of more than $13 million today. Taxes at the time were low, and a man with $1 million was very rich. Bob and his family were able to live comfortably during the worst years of the Depression, and he continued his frozen-food experiments with a good salary as the director of research for General Foods' new Gloucester-based frozen-food division, since the Birdseye mind was part of the deal.

Bob had a few ideas about how to spend his windfall, but he did not have the eccentricity of a Hammond to build himself a medieval castle. To him a baronial mansion seemed more appropriate. He had his seventeen-room mansion built in the Eastern Point peninsula on the tip of Gloucester harbor, in an astounding seven months, between December 1930 and the end of June 1931. When completed, it was valued at $200,000 ($3 million today), an impressive expenditure for the Depression.

Birdseye imported delicate floral wallpaper from France for the dining room. There was a screened porch, a pine-paneled study, a sunporch with a wall fountain. The five spacious bedrooms upstairs afforded stunning views of Gloucester harbor and out to the open bay and the Atlantic. Artwork wasn't of interest—notable since in Gloucester many people collected the excellent locally produced art in that period, as they do today. There was a shooting range in the basement, though Bob ended up using the basement more as a laboratory for his experiments.

The Birdseyes did not have a trendsetting style. The closest the house came to it was, not surprisingly, the kitchen. Stainless steel was a new idea that rarely made it into home kitchens. Don Wonson, who grew up next door to the Birdseyes, recalled that "the kitchen was all stainless steel. He was very meticulous about the kitchen, wiping it down with towels—stainless-steel sinks, big refrigerators, big stainless-steel with double doors. A big freezer in the kitchen. More refrigerators downstairs. Stainless-steel counters, even the drain boards were stainless steel."

Bob handpicked every detail. In an age when there were no blacktop driveways, he put in an innovative tar-and-crushed-granite pavement. The garage, which housed the Birdseyes' three cars, was very large, with a spacious apartment on the top floor. The huge wooden garage doors with massive iron strap hinges resembled gates to a castle.

For people who were known for their simplicity and

straightforwardness, it was an imposing mansion on a hill. Four tall white pillars announced the front entrance. Bob named the house Wyndiecote and finally had a home worthy of the name. It resembled the grand bourgeois look of his first home in Cobble Hill, Brooklyn, yet Bob was almost always seen in his little Ford.

What was Bob to do now that he had achieved his goal? His manager, Joe Guinane, said, "He was an impatient man and had little interest in the routine affairs involved in running the business. Once the problem was solved, he was eager to turn to something new." Some suggested that he retire. After all, he was in his mid-forties and had made his fortune. But Bob just said, "Following one's curiosity is much more fun than taking things easy."

He was not yet through with frozen food. After all, it's one thing to conceive of an idea and build the equipment to make it, but it is a very different problem to make the idea take hold in society. Frozen food was still a long way from being a real industry and an accepted part of American shopping and eating. All he had accomplished was getting the right people and money behind the project.

Bob continued his work, only now as an executive for the Birds Eye Frosted Food Division. One of the early marketing decisions, along with changing Birdseye to Birds Eye, was calling the food "frosted food" to emphasize that it was something completely different from the frozen food that people knew.

Bob later wrote, "Quick freezing was conceived, born, and nourished on a strange combination of ingenuity, stick-to-itiveness, sweat, and good luck." By the fall of 1929 the new Birds Eye division was operating at capacity, stockpiling frozen food for its launch. On March 6, 1930, the Springfield, Massachusetts, newspaper ran an advertisement with the headline "The Most Revolutionary Idea in the History of Food Will Be Revealed in Springfield Today."

The vaunted marketing and advertising experts of the former Postum Cereal Company had chosen Springfield as their site for launching twenty-seven frozen items, including porterhouse steaks, spring lamb chops, sliced ham, pork sausages, June peas, spinach, Oregon cherries, loganberries, red raspberries, fillets of haddock and sole, and bluepoint oysters. Twelve "demonstrators" were sent to ten participating stores. The demonstrators—all of whom were women, as were most of the shoppers—and the store employees had undergone a three-day training program, largely focused on how to explain the difference between slow and fast freezing. Each store was given a display freezer worth $1,500, which was far more expensive than most of these small family stores could have afforded. The frozen foods were sold on consignment.

The freezers were far from flawless, however, and a team of mechanics assigned to the ten stores was constantly checking temperatures and making repairs and adjustments, because it would have made a calamitous first impression if any of the food was less than top quality.

The owners of those first stores were people who believed that frozen food was the future and were willing to proselytize to a wary public. Paul G. Seyler, who worked for Thrift Stores in Springfield, one of the first self-service chains, said, "I clearly recall that it took five minutes of fast talking to sell a reluctant housewife a thirty-five-cent package of Birds Eye frozen peas." According to him, "The consumer just couldn't understand how anything frozen could possibly be safe, let alone good to eat." One of the store owners, Joshua Davidson, who had taken over his father's business, was interviewed by *Quick Frozen Foods* magazine thirty years later and recalled, "I could see this as a sound venture, a progressive step in the food industry, and I wanted to be in step. That's why I agreed to be one of the first ten dealers." General Foods tried to make the venture as risk-free as possible. It supplied the freezer and the food, and the store owner had to pay General Foods only for what they sold. "Frankly," said Davidson, "I couldn't afford not to be, the way Birds Eye offered to start me."

Davidson said he was constantly answering questions about how the food was made and how to cook it. One woman asked whether the company would start packaging meat and vegetables together. Davidson dismissed the idea, pointing out that people would prefer to choose their menu themselves. It was twenty years before complete frozen dinners would become popular. Mostly people wanted to know whether the frozen food had any taste. Many people asked questions but would not buy. But after a month of answering questions, the amount of frozen food sold in Davidson's store doubled.

If you sell only one and then you sell two, you have doubled sales. In truth, frozen food was slow to catch on. One of the problems was that fresh food was relatively inexpensive. A top-quality steak often sold for less than 30 cents. It was inevitable that frozen food had to cost a few cents more than the fresh food it was made from, because of the labor and other costs that went into freezing it. The consumer was not accustomed to this idea, because in the past frozen food was made from the cheapest, rejected fresh food and so was cheaper than good fresh food. But to freeze top-quality fresh food with modern equipment was expensive.

The ad in the Springfield paper, which featured the new label—an upside-down bird and the name Birds Eye Frosted Foods—claimed the company's "frosted food" was "little short of magic." The haddock, it claimed, was "as fresh flavored as the day the fish was drawn from the cold blue waters of the North Atlantic." And "here is the most wondrous magic of all! June peas, as gloriously green as any you will see next summer. Red raspberries, plump and tender and deliciously flavored. Big, smiling pie cherries—and loganberries. Imagine having them all Summer-fresh in March!"

This kind of hyperbole continued for many years, not only by Birds Eye but by major newspapers and magazines. In February 1932 the *New York Times* called frozen food a "scientific miracle in home management." It reported on peaches, strawberries, and oysters becoming available out of season as though the frozen item and a fresh one were indistinguishable. *Popular Science Monthly* claimed outright that frozen food and fresh food were "exactly the same." Today's discerning palate knows that frozen and fresh are considerably different, but for people who were accustomed to canned food or slow-frozen food, the new frosted food did seem miraculous. Consumers who had the courage to try it were pleased with how much better it was than they had expected. When frozen fillets were test-marketed in New England, where people were accustomed to fresh fish, three out of four purchasers returned to buy more.

One of the major advantages of frozen food was that you could buy it immediately but use it whenever you wanted. The drawback, of course, was that few people had adequate home freezers to take advantage of the new phenomenon.

For the first decade of the Depression, food purchases went something like this: canned food was for the poor, and out-of-season frozen food was a high-quality luxury for the wealthy. It wasn't until the 1940s, when Birds Eye started getting competitors, that prices came down and frozen food became more widely popular. Finding a way to produce at an acceptable price was one of the keys to commercial success.

When Bob invented a portable multiplate freezer, a typical low-technology Birdseye invention, in 1930, it was built from scraps of corrugated metal, with steel plates and coils carrying refrigerant. It could be brought out to fields to freeze produce as it was harvested. This brought the farmer and the farm one step closer to industry, which for Bob and his generation was considered a very good move, since they thought of industry as an improvement. (Many of today's advocates of food quality think just the reverse.) Devices such as the portable freezer increased production capacity and even brought the price slightly lower on some vegetables—expensive vegetables in any form are difficult to sell.

By 1933 there were still only 516 retail stores in America carrying "frosted food." When the company questioned store owners, the chief complaint was about the store freezer units.

Though they were given to the stores, they used a great deal of electricity and were expensive to operate. Bob was not happy about the freezer either, as the Frosted Food Division was losing money and General Foods was growing impatient. Giving away a $1,500 freezer to any store that would have it was a losing proposition in a very bad economy.

From the beginning Bob had seen better freezers as a key to launching frozen food. He had wanted Wetmore Hodges as a partner in part because his father was with the American Radiator Company, which was interested in developing freezers. Bob wanted a more affordable and more attractive store freezer. He persuaded General Foods to back the development of a new American Radiator Company freezer that turned out to be a huge step forward for frozen food. It put the food on display, with a slanted window in the front; more important, a freezer cost just $300. This was a freezer that stores could afford. The monthly running cost was about $3.50, instead of the $16 to $20 of the old freezers. The new freezers were rented to stores for $10 to $12.50 per month. In 1934 they were tried out in Syracuse, New York. Stores bought them, and the frozen food sold well there. Another test was launched in Rochester; from there the refrigerators spread throughout the Northeast into the Midwest, well on their way to national distribution.

Bob used his own talent for persuasion, traveling to stores to sell his product in person. "He was one of the most articulate and persuasive men I have ever known," Joe Guinane said. Bob had also become a minor celebrity and was booked for events that advertised "see[ing] a demonstration of quick frosting by Mr. Clarence Birdseye, the inventor of the famous quick freezing process." Sometimes the public was also invited to "meet Mrs. Clarence Birdseye." Mostly women attended these demonstrations, but at one event in a Boston hotel Bob's old friend from Labrador Sir Wilfred Grenfell, the man who by chance introduced Bob to freezing, went to see the Birdseye demonstration.

While the Frosted Food Division was struggling to make a profit, there seemed no limit to the exaggerated praise that journalists, politicians, and businessmen were willing to bestow on the "Birdseye invention." In 1931 Boston mayor James Michael Curley hosted a dinner to honor Birdseye, calling him a genius "whose contribution to the welfare of mankind gives promise of being the greatest in volume and value in a half century of American history." After Birdseye gave a demonstration, freezing a steak with dry ice, the mayor stated that Birdseye's invention "will probably be a greater contributing factor in preventing wars in the future than battleships or any other agency because, after all, wars are caused by starvation."

As though he were still living in Labrador, struggling for fresh food, Bob ate whatever wildlife he found in Gloucester, including birds he trapped. He would freeze these catches to see if they froze well. He was particularly fond of coot, a variety of waterfowl. He also liked to investigate more abstract concepts of freezing. How long would frozen meat keep? Scientists believed there was no expiration date to frozen meat if it remained unexposed to air, though some speculated that frozen animal fat would deteriorate after a few centuries.

Bob reflected on the moose Eleanor shot in 1929, which was butchered and frozen, and portions of which would frequently be thawed out and served for dinner. A moose is a very large animal, but by 1933 there was nothing left except for the neck. Even Bob, who ate everything, did not like moose neck. It was tough and gamey. Would four years of freezing change it? He had to find out, so he thawed it and cooked it and, to his surprise, found it to be quite tender.

He hired a chemist experienced in food issues, Donald Tressler, to head the research team and arranged for Tressler and his family to move into his old home with the long shady porch on Beach Road. Birdseye and Tressler conducted experiments, measuring meat tenderness with a tire pressure gauge and a laboratory instrument called a penetrometer. They demonstrated that meat was more tender after a week of quick freezing than before it was frozen.

Bob still wanted to find out how the Inuit fish that had frozen in the air were alive months later when thawed. Could a living organism survive freezing? The question was more than a century old. When Bob would catch pickerel in nearby Niles Pond, he would try to freeze them and keep them alive. His oldest son, Kellogg, always remembered his patient mother's irritation at constantly finding fish flipping around in the bathtub or floating dead. Bob would explain to children in the neighborhood what he was trying to do, and it was generally assumed that it could not be done, that Mr. Birdseye was brilliant but a bit eccentric, though some thought that if Birdseye thought it was possible, it was.

Around that time, between 1934 and 1936, scientists in the Soviet Union were wondering about the same thing. They concluded that freezing did kill animals, but they noted the exception with fish. The scientists then demonstrated that when ice formed around the skin and the subcutaneous tissue directly under it, the fish would become hard and appear to be frozen, but the living organs inside would not freeze and could continue to function. In 1934 N. A. Borodin, in his study "The Anabiosis or Phenomenon of Resuscitation of Fishes after Being Frozen," concluded that it could be done and that Arctic species were particularly suited to survive freezing. The fish Birdseye had observed in Labrador were pulled into −40-degree air, and the water on them instantly froze, possibly leaving the interior of the fish unfrozen and unharmed.

Some of Bob's ideas seemed to be great successes even though they were never used, such as a machine he built to freeze vegetables individually rather than in a block. A pea would come down a chute and land on one of a series of revolving freezing plates. Though his laboratory was small and employed only twenty-two chemists and assistants, Bob was fondly remembered in Gloucester as someone who offered work through the Depression. In a 1980 article in the *Gloucester Daily Times*, Bill Nickerson, a former Birdseye worker, said, "There was nothing as far as jobs go then. Mr. Birdseye gave me a job right out of high school, when I couldn't find another one." He worked as a 30-cents-an-hour laboratory assistant.

In this laboratory the team worked out the problems of freezing vegetables, fruit, and prepared foods. They learned that vegetables degenerated due to an enzyme that could be removed by blanching them—plunging them quickly into boiling water. Then they were rapidly cooled, quick-frozen, and packed in watertight cellophane. This left the vegetables with a bright color. Frozen peas became one of the most successful Birds Eye foods, because they were such a brilliant green.

The laboratory also solved the problem of frozen sliced onions, which always turned black with freezing. They found that if the onions were first plunged into boiling water for just the right number of seconds, they would remain white. Fruits were difficult, because they softened and turned brown with freezing. The color change, caused by oxidation, was solved by adding a small amount of sulfur dioxide or ascorbic acid (vitamin C), but the lab was not able to completely solve the problem of texture. An expert from Cornell University, Lucy Kimball, was brought in to develop techniques for cooking prepared foods so that they would maintain their quality after being thawed and reheated.

Retailers complained that there was not a wide enough variety of products, so Bob established a partnership with a large farm in southern New Jersey, Seabrook Farms, to supply a greater variety of vegetables. While he tried to encourage farms to modernize and become more efficient, Seabrook was already an agro-industrial operation, supplying produce for canneries. In 1911 Charles Seabrook had started Seabrook Farms as a model of modern agro-industry. Birds Eye was able to have them wash, blanch, and cool produce for freezing in the new portable freezers. Lima beans, which had been a mainstay of Seabrook's cannery business, were one of their early frozen-vegetable successes.

However, certain foods were problem products and never conquered. Birdseye could not freeze lettuce without wilting it or tomatoes without ruining their texture, and frozen bananas were an utter disaster. But between 1932 and 1934 more than one hundred types of frozen foods, many of them processed, were developed. Most of them were not put on the market until the 1940s because of a lack of interest from the public. But Bob was always sure that the day would come for frozen food, and when it did, they needed to be ready. In the neighborhood around the Fort, one of Gloucester's poorest, which also included the broad, sandy Pavilion Beach, Bob would occasionally distribute samples of new products to children and ask for their opinions.

Tressler wrote of 1929, when the laboratory began its work, "This was the beginning of the depression but we did not realize it." By 1933 General Foods realized it. They still believed in the future of frozen food and continued to aggressively market it, but they had to cut their losses. They closed down Birdseye's Gloucester operation, worked out of Boston, and did not return to Gloucester until the 1940s.

Bob Birdseye went from president of the division to consultant. He continued to take an interest in the progress of frozen food and to promote it whenever he got a chance, sometimes without even being asked. But his restless mind moved on to other ideas.

CHAPTER NINE

The Crazy Guy Down the Street

Unaffected by the Depression, unlike most people, the Birdseyes had found the good life in their Eastern Point Wyndiecote. Bob enjoyed entertaining guests in his home and was extremely open and casual, while Eleanor was a little more formal and reserved. Bob loved to cook, and they had dinner parties in their large formal dining room with thrilling sea views. He specialized in what he liked to call "lobster feeds," in which he would triumphantly emerge from the kitchen sporting an apron and a chef's hat, carrying an enormous platter of steamed lobsters.

The Birdseyes owned five hundred acres of land in West Gloucester, a more rural area on the mainland (Gloucester was built on an island) where the wealthy retreated from the smell of drying fish in the hot summer months. There they built an elegant two-story riding stable with a long arcade. They kept fine Thoroughbred horses and rode with slim English saddles. Birdseye, who had lived on horseback in the

Southwest and in the Bitterroot, was an expert horseman, and he taught his children to ride.

Bob was still an outdoorsman and took his dogs duck hunting in South Dakota every year. He taught the whole family to shoot and sometimes took them with him on those trips. Based on the amount of film he shot of sunsets behind Gloucester harbor and whitecaps spraying over the dark crests of the granite boulders, Bob must have loved these views. He seemed to love Gloucester. He cooked seawater down to salt and carried that salt in a vial wherever he traveled. Despite the stiffness of his writing, Bob was a sentimental man.

He tried to take care of Eastern Point, preserving its bird habitat. He persuaded the government to build a seawall in a nearby cove to protect Niles Pond from storms. Behind his house he had chicken coops with long runs for Rhode Island Reds, the same species he and Eleanor had raised in Labrador. They also raised big, fluffy chinchillas. Bob remained relatively unchanged from his youth and continued to sell the pelts and freeze the meat.

His interest in the arts expanded, although he kept up past traditions. Buffalo Bill's Wild West was never a forgotten romance, and he was still an avid reader of Henty adventure novels, rereading his favorite, *Redskin and Cowboy*. He also read the western novels of Owen Wister, famous for his 1902 *The Virginian*, and the western stories of Bret Harte. He also enjoyed going to movies to see westerns or staying home to play Chinese checkers, a game for which he had a near-fanatical passion.

Bob was a curious figure in Gloucester, a famously inventive genius who did odd things that regular people would not understand. When rats invaded his melon patch, he stood on the terrace and shot them with a handgun. He was always trapping or shooting or freezing something as though he were surviving on the frontier. Children would ask him what he was doing, and he would always eagerly explain.

He often involved his family in his experiments and was eager for them to learn. Sometimes there was no particular purpose other than to satisfy his own curiosity, such as when he got an idea for a new way to make potato chips and enlisted the children in his kitchen experiments, along with his wife, Eleanor, when she did not run out of patience. His daughter Eleanor recalled a moment during her early childhood with her dad, learning how to dissect animals in the Persian-carpeted living room. He also taught her how to skin mice and cure skins.

When Josephine Swift Boyer was a child in California, her family spent summers at their home on Eastern Point. Like a number of girls in the neighborhood, she took up an interest in birds. When she found a dead rail, a wading bird rare for Gloucester, she wanted to keep it, and not knowing what to do with it, she went to curious Mr. Birdseye. Not surprisingly, he turned out to be a skilled taxidermist. He showed her how to open the bird up, rub it with chemicals, and stuff it. Josephine's sister, Lila, said that her clearest memory of him was of his fine hands. A reporter from the *New York Post*, interviewing him in 1945, wrote that he had "powerful hands," a surprising feature for such a small man.

"He was a character," Lila said. "You couldn't help being fascinated by him." This was true, as he was always building strange things in his large, high-ceilinged basement or in the kitchen or even on the lawn. Lila, who loved birds and even in her old age nursed wounded ones back to health, remembered a strange contraption on Mr. Birdseye's lawn. "It was for capturing starlings. We always thought he was going to eat them, probably fast frozen, taste-tested for some experiment. In any case, we knew they were goners."

The neighbors were further amused when, amid much discussion of food shortages during World War II, Bob reminded people that there was lots of food out there to shoot and eat and that "food tastes are principally psychological," as muskrats, crows, squirrels, and even *starlings* were delicious.

Bob was fascinated with processes and how to improve them. Writing about his curiosity, he explained:

> *If I see a man skinning a fish, for example, a host of questions pop into my mind. Why is he skinning the fish? Why is he doing it by hand? Is the skin good for anything? If I am in a restaurant and get biscuits, which I like, I ask the chef how he made them: what did he put in the dough? How did he mix it? How long did the biscuits bake? At what temperature? When I visit a strange city, I go through the local industrial plants to see how they make things. I don't care what the product is. I am just as much interested in the manufacture of chewing gum as of steel.*

While his kids were learning to be yachtsmen at the Eastern Point Yacht Club, he preferred to go fishing on his rugged, forty-foot, wooden-hulled, open-deck power launch, the *Sealoafer*. If he caught something interesting, he would do what he did with all the other animals he encountered: try freezing it. After trying to freeze whales and dolphins, he started to become interested in studying them. As was the family tradition, he had someone film him at sea. There was the small bald man with glasses, dressed in a sweater and dress shirt and tie, walking out on a narrow plank over the bow of his boat with an enormous harpoon, which, like Queequeg in *Moby-Dick*, he would raise up and hurl into the side of a six-foot shark or a porpoise or a whale.

Caught in 16-millimeter black and white is the same Bob Birdseye of the Bitterroot, a relentless predator. In one sequence he is harpooning porpoises (in the 1930s hunting marine mammals was still legal). He invented and patented the kickless, handheld whale harpoon to allow single-handed planting of the harpoon—much more efficient than throwing it himself, although Birdseye seemed effective enough with the old technique. Typical of Birdseye, it combines medieval technology with pragmatic inventiveness to solve a problem. The invention has an aluminum rifle stock and a thick tube of black rubber to propel the harpoons. The rubber is stretched back by the turning of a large steel cogwheel with a hand crank, and a trigger releases it to fire the harpoon. The tool was limited in its application and never caught on, but it served Bob well at sea for four years. According to him, he harpooned fifty-two finback whales, the second-largest animals to have ever lived on Earth.

Another time Bob got creative was when he watched commercial fishermen landing red snapper one winter in Galveston, Texas. The fishermen were hand lining, dropping a baited and weighted line many fathoms to the coral reefs on the ocean bottom. When they got a bite, they quickly reeled the line up on their circling two thumbs, the way hand liners have been fishing for centuries. Bob thought that there must be an easier way to do this, but when he talked to fishermen, they told him they had always fished this way and, since it worked, were not interested in changing.

This was absolutely contrary to the Birdseye creed. Bob always said, "Just because something has always been done in a certain way is never a sufficient reason for continuing to do it in that way." Birdseye believed in change, believed in the constant updating and improvement of ideas. He said, "Change is the very essence of American life" and frequently stated, "There is always a better way of doing almost everything. Today anything which is twenty years old is, or should be, apt to be obsolete."

Despite the protests of fishermen, Birdseye worked on the automatic reel: a device installed on the side of a boat that lowered a baited steel cable to depths greater than one hundred fathoms. When a fish bit, the reel set the hook and hauled it up to the surface. It could even land the fish on the deck. Birdseye felt he was onto the next big idea and boasted, "The gadget does everything, in fact, except mix a mint julep for the fisherman." He truly thought it would revolutionize commercial fishing, because in one day the device could catch as many fish as three fishermen. He predicted that it would "make more sea food available, and increase fishermen's earnings." Like many people in the 1930s, Birdseye was not thinking about the concept of overfishing, the idea that the survival of a fish population could be at risk if too many fish were caught. He never ended up developing the device. Had it become a tool of commercial fishing, it would have revolutionized the industry, but its destructive power would be unacceptable in today's overfished oceans, and it would likely be banned.

Bob's work with lightbulbs had greater success and far more impact. He noticed that reflectors were placed behind lightbulbs to illuminate displays in shopwindows. "I didn't know the difference between an ohm and a kilowatt," said Bob, "but it seemed to me there was no reason why the bulb and the reflector should be separate units. Wouldn't it be simpler and cheaper to build a lamp which would contain its own reflector?"

To answer his own question, he formed the Birdseye Electric Company, which provided even more jobs in Gloucester. His 1935 patent 2,219,510 for a reflecting electric lamp was one of his most important. Designed for working areas and window displays, his lightbulb with the built-in reflector is a component still in common use today. He designed more intensely glowing filaments for more efficient lighting and heat lamps for keeping food warm, another idea of his still used today. He also manufactured neon bulbs with a decorative figure inside that would light up, displaying flowers, animals, religious symbols, and occasional advertising logos, such as his RCA bulbs, all of which are rare and collectible today.

Birdseye developed ideas and used them to create a company, which he then would sell, as he had done with frozen food earlier. In 1939 Bob sold the Birdseye Electric Company to Wabash Appliance Corporation of Brooklyn, on the condition that Birdseye Electric would keep its own name and personnel. In 1945 the Sylvania Company bought Birdseye and Wabash out and continued producing Birdseye bulbs.

Despite the earlier troubles, Birdseye's frozen food became a popular commodity. In 1930 eighty thousand pounds of it were sold, and by the mid-1940s ten times that amount was being sold every year. Frozen food grew, as Birdseye had always said it would, from a mere curiosity to a major industry. Still, there were problems that did not involve consumers. For instance, the frozen-food industry was struggling to get enough well-insulated refrigerator trucks for shipping to their growing market. Birdseye and other advocates of frozen food were a major force in pushing Congress into its 1938 revision of the Pure Food and Drug Act. The 1906 act was considered a huge step forward in consumer safety, as it established rules for food and pharmaceuticals, including truth in labeling, but Bob felt that its standards were not nearly stringent enough for the frozen-food industry. Birds Eye had introduced high standards, and it was thought that the only way the industry could grow, as new companies were being created, was to make sure that all frozen food was held to those standards, so the public would start associating "frozen" with "quality."

Birds Eye now had competing frozen-food companies, and there was pressure to lower prices, but Bob always understood the risk of lowering quality to lower prices. Increased regulations were needed to stop producers from cutting corners on quality. The 1938 Food, Drug, and Cosmetic Act, which replaced the 1906 act, increased penalties, had a longer list of harmful commodities, had tougher rules about mislabeling and adulterating, and required a list of ingredients on every product's label. It remains the underpinning of product safety in the United States.

In the early 1940s, World War II changed the way Americans ate. A scarcity of metals led to a decline in canning, which led many people to try frozen food for the first time. But the biggest difference in Americans' eating habits was that women were allowed to leave their domestic roles to work wartime jobs while men were abroad. Many women would not return to the kitchen, or at least not full-time, so a trend of looking for quicker and easier ways to prepare meals began and has continued ever since. A 1951 survey in *Science Digest* found that 41 percent of US housewives preferred frozen food to either fresh or canned because of its convenience. In addition, there was a surge in the number of US supermarkets, which chose to give a great deal of their ample space to frozen foods. By 1950, according to the American Frozen Food Institute, 64 percent of US retail food stores carried some frozen food.

Despite the positive developments, it was not enough for Bob to be the guru of the last big food idea. He wanted to be master of the next. Birdseye was convinced that the next important food idea was dehydration, and he wondered whether a process that extracted the water from food more rapidly—quick-drying—would be the same kind of improvement as quick-freezing.

He began his work on dehydration in his kitchen, with a coffee hot plate hung upside down from the ceiling and a plate of bread cubes placed a few inches below. Then he brought in a favorite piece of Birdseye equipment, an electric fan, to blow on the bread. With both the heat and the air blowing, he stirred the bread with a spoon. Bob concluded that this process dehydrated faster than the standard technique of just blowing hot air. There were other techniques. Pouring milk on a heated stainless-steel drum dried it, and placing beef inside the heated drum produced dried beef for World War II soldiers. Yet all these techniques resulted in the loss of flavor and nutrients, so Bob analyzed the problem.

He knew there were three ways of transferring heat. Traditional dehydration relied solely on convection, the transfer of heat by moving warmed matter, which in this case was air. But there was also conduction, the movement of heat from atom to atom, thereby moving heat through the matter that is being warmed; and radiation, heating by means of heat waves, like those given off by the sun or, in Birdseye's case, by an infrared bulb he designed himself, drawing on his experience as a lamp manufacturer. Bob thought that the drying process could be greatly sped up and the quality better preserved if all three techniques were applied at once. It took him six years to find a way to substantially reduce the drying time, but when he accomplished it, he called the food he produced anhydrous, as opposed to dehydrated, just as his frozen food was called frosted. Food that had once taken eighteen hours to dehydrate took ninety minutes with Birdseye's process. He claimed that the food did not have time to deteriorate and could be restored to a fresh state in four to ten minutes. He gave demonstrations using his infrared lamp and at times held up a beaker of water he had extracted from an anhydrous carrot, a great crowd-pleasing trick, though that shortcut demonstration required that the carrot be previously heated and have air blown on it.

Understanding the age he lived in, Birdseye promised that his anhydrous food process would save the housewife time, because the food was already partially cooked. It would also save kitchen space, because a package the size of two cigarette packs would contain food for a family, and the small packets could be stored without the risk of spoilage, saving trips to the supermarket. He claimed tremendous savings for wholesalers when "five truckloads of farm produce can be processed into one truck load." The grocer, he promised, could save 80 percent of his shelf space.

With the outbreak of World War II, Bob thought his moment had come, because lightweight, portable, nonspoiling food seemed ideal for soldiers in the field. He therefore intensified his research, installing machinery in his basement, with trays of vegetables along the wall awaiting processing. By his own account, during the war he traveled thousands of miles to gather information and ideas about dehydration.

In November 1945, after World War II ended, Bob officially launched his anhydrous food line. The army had used a great deal of dehydrated soups, vegetables, and stews during the war, but the soldiers weren't happy about that. No one really liked the taste of dehydrated food, even if it was anhydrous—a word that no one understood. Bob was not deterred, as he had been ridiculed and doubted before, and now, since the name Birdseye was taken seriously in the food industry, the *New York Times* ran a story with the headline "A New Page Is Turned in the History of Food." Bob established another Gloucester business, called Process Incorporated, to produce his anhydrous foods, and a number of companies signed on to distribute them. He invited two hundred food experts to lunch at the Waldorf Astoria in New York, and not until the meal was over did he reveal that the broccoli, carrot, mashed potatoes, and apple tarts were all anhydrous. The diners were truly surprised.

Anhydrous food was granted a patent in May 1947, but it was not a huge success. Soon all the new companies dealing in anhydrous food had closed.

While Birdseye had predicted "unprecedented growth" for both frozen and dehydrated food after the war, he admitted that for dehydrated food to keep up with frozen, the products would have to be improved.

Americans bought 800 million pounds of frozen food in 1945 and 1946. The *New Yorker* ran an article on the future of frozen food that began:

> *Not since the appearance of the first glacier, a few eons ago, has there been any phenomenon to compare with the frigid giant that is now looming on the horizon of the American housewife in the shape of the frozen food industry.*

The article excitedly pointed out that there were now forty retail stores in Manhattan that sold nothing but frozen food and that twenty-two of them had opened in the past six months, with more of those retail stores "popping up" all over the United States. Freezer manufacturing was booming, and more and more people were buying freezers for their homes.

Once frozen orange juice came onto the market, in 1950, US annual frozen-food sales shot up to $1 billion and were projected to reach $50 billion by 1957. Frozen foods now came in an endless variety, although some were widely recognized as being inferior to fresh, like eggs, cheese, and certain fish, and other foods still could not be successfully frozen, such as cantaloupe, grapes, lettuce, and onions. Once the recipients of farms' castoff foods, frozen-food companies were now the customer of choice for many farmers, because they paid well, bought with regularity, and gave guidance on soil and other technical issues.

With the heightened demand for frozen food, other companies entered the marketplace, and Birds Eye had stiff competition. There were more than five hundred brands of frozen food. A leading competitor was William L. Maxson, a New Yorker who made frozen meals and sold them to the Naval Air Transport Service. The navy continued to use his frozen meals after the war, serving them on navy flights. By 1950 Maxson had competition of his own: Frigid Dinners, Inc., of Philadelphia. But like Birdseye, Maxson saw an opportunity and the need for new technology, leading to his invention called the Maxson Whirlwind, an oven that thawed and cooked meals quickly.

Maxson's new oven was the beginning of a new age. It started with an accidental discovery in 1945, when an engineer at Raytheon, working on radar, found that his equipment produced unusually short radio waves, or microwaves, that rotated molecules and produced heat. This type of heat could be easily produced and, among other potential uses, could cook food rapidly. Bell Laboratories had done work on the idea in the 1930s. Now, with frozen food becoming commonplace, it was understood that microwaves could thaw a package of frozen food and cook it quickly. Frozen food could now be cooked and on the dinner table mere minutes after it had been removed from the freezer. This was the fastest food ever seen.

In another harbinger of the future, after the war the United States became interested in importing frozen seafood on a large scale from its new friend, Japan. Small amounts had been imported before the war from both Japan and India. Today frozen Asian seafood is a major component of the US fish market.

To deal with the increased competition, Birds Eye advertised innovatively and aggressively. It was one of the first to advertise in color in *Life* magazine, in 1940, and went on to become a pioneer television advertiser in the 1950s. It even sponsored its own situation comedy, *Our Miss Brooks*, in which Eve Arden played a schoolteacher—one of the first TV hits when it was launched in 1952.

Bob always believed in the central concept of agro-industry, through which technology would one day eliminate hunger in the world. He followed new industrial food ideas with great excitement. He was well aware of progress in microwaves and often mentioned it as one of the ideas of the future. He also believed in hydroponic farming, by which plants are provided nutrients in the water they are given, cutting out the need for soil and fields to grow crops. Hydroponic farming was not a new idea—Sir Francis Bacon wrote about it in the seventeenth century. But Bob envisioned a New York City whose produce needs were locally met, thanks to rooftop hydroponic farming. He predicted that "eventually we shall learn to manufacture food from sunlight, as plants do." And he also believed in the increasing use of antibiotics in food to prevent its decay, a practice that became widespread and is today often criticized as unhealthy.

CHAPTER TEN

The Last Idea

Often, when adventurous people start glimpsing old age and death, they are consumed with the urge to stave off time with one last adventure.

Bob and Eleanor were such people. Perhaps they recalled the words of Bob's old friend Wilfred Grenfell, who more than thirty years before had advised, "If you are reasonably resistant, and want to get tough and young again, you can do far worse than come and winter on 'the lonely Labrador.'"

Grenfell's words rang true for Bob and Eleanor. They wanted to go on an adventure, as they had when they went to Labrador. They wanted to leave their house and garden and push off one last time, especially since their children were grown and on their own.

Bob and Eleanor had always been sentimental about Labrador, perhaps in the way other couples are nostalgic about their first years of marriage, and they frequently spoke of their time up north. Throughout the years in Gloucester, with lobster dinners, evenings of home movies, and games of Chinese checkers, a pair of Labrador snowshoes always hung on a wall of their home.

The opportunity to go abroad showed up unexpectedly, like an intriguing uninvited guest. Still interested in food processing, Bob was visiting a lard-rendering plant in the 1940s, and something about the process started him thinking about a better way of converting wood chips into paper pulp. He did what he had always done: brought together some financial backers and some technical people and invented something new—in this case, a process for making paper.

Throughout history, many materials, including stone, clay, bamboo, Egyptian papyrus reeds, and dried animal skins were used for writing. But the most practical material was paper, invented by the Chinese possibly as long ago as 200 BC. Paper is made from the random weaving of fibers suspended in water. For many centuries the leading source of these fibers was old rags. Many other fibers were tried, including grasses, rhubarb, straw, and even animal excrement. In the mid-nineteenth century, ground wood pulp was settled on as the cheapest and most efficient source of paper fibers.

Perhaps because of the success with wood pulp, there was not a great deal of interest in Bob's ideas. But there were always a few papermakers interested in alternatives to grinding up trees. The New York–based W. R. Grace & Co. was one of a number of companies in the mid-twentieth century interested in using sugarcane for paper, and they were drawn to the Birdseye paper process.

Grace was a large old international company founded by an Irish immigrant in Peru, William Russell Grace. He became involved in the export of guano (bird droppings). This material may not seem like much, but it is rich in nitrogen and phosphorous, making it valuable in the manufacture of gunpowder and fertilizer. Even today guano remains a prospering South American trade. A steamship company called the Grace Line was created to ship the product, and that itself became a success. Thanks to shipments of guano, sugar, and fertilizer, by the 1950s W. R. Grace had operations in New York, London, Peru, Chile, and other places and owned the Grace National Bank, the Grace Chemical Company, and other businesses around the world.

Grace hoped to apply Birdseye's process to the production of paper from sugarcane scrap in Peru. A number of countries were suffering from acute paper shortages and had more cane than wood pulp. Peru was one of them. Grace found other potential markets for the paper process in Puerto Rico, Venezuela, Argentina, and Egypt.

Since Grace's Peruvian sugar fields produced a half million tons of sugar annually, as well as molasses and industrial-grade alcohol, mountains of crushed cane stalks and bagasse, or leftover crushed cane, were left behind. Bagasse was a fibrous substance perfectly suited to papermaking, and Grace already made paper with it, but his process was slow and inefficient, since it took six months to dry the bagasse enough to render it useful. With Birdseye's process, the useful cellulose fibers could be separated quickly from bagasse, and it might be possible to use the bagasse immediately. Grace thought Birdseye could greatly improve the company's paper process and built a large-output factory for it that would be a model to sell to other countries.

Bob loved the challenge, and he loved the idea of taking off for "the wilds" of South America. In 1953 he and Eleanor left their Wyndiecote by the sea in Gloucester and moved to Paramonga, the mountainous, cactus-studded desert of southern Peru. He quickly proved he was the same old Bob Birdseye, always thinking of adventure or food and writing home to report on it all to the family.

Bob was cooking, he was shooting birds with the shotgun he managed to bring in from the United States, and he started riding horses again, something he hadn't done since 1934 in West Gloucester. The terrain in Peru reminded him of the American Southwest, where he'd ridden almost a half century earlier. He also was doing a lot of fishing, and one day, while fishing in about forty feet of water, he felt a powerful tug on his line. He fought for thirty minutes to bring up what he thought would be an enormous fish, but it turned out to be a penguin. Once on the boat, the penguin continued to fight until they tied its feet and rubber-banded its sharp beak. Billy the penguin became a household pet.

Billy was not the only pet. The Birdseyes later adopted a deer and a redheaded parrot they named Pancho, which couldn't fly because Bob had accidentally clipped its wing while hunting. The Birdseyes resumed their old habit of raising Rhode Island Reds for their egg supply, and there were geese, ducks, squab, and guinea pigs around the house, though most of them ended up being eaten. The Birdseyes had a fifteen-cubic-foot General Electric freezer to keep a supply of meat for entertaining. Appropriately, they had the first freezer ever used in Paramonga, where most people didn't have refrigerators yet.

In the spring of 1954 Bob and Eleanor went back to the United States for almost two months, as Bob had patents to register. He and Eleanor also had the Gloucester home to check in on, children and grandchildren to see, and Henry and Ernestine's wedding in Albuquerque to attend. It was like one of those trips home from Labrador: a little business, a little shopping, and family gatherings. While in New York, Bob even phoned contacts at the American Museum of Natural History whom he hadn't used since 1910 and arranged for them to ship him taxidermy equipment and materials so he could send them bird specimens, similar to what he'd done in Labrador. When he returned to Paramonga, he killed four types of doves and several other birds and froze them until the package arrived from the museum. Over the next six months he killed and preserved specimens of sixty bird species and preserved forty mammal hides.

His inherent enthusiasm continued to drive him, even though at age sixty-eight he looked thin and uncharacteristically frail. During his two years in Peru he had learned how to reduce what had been a nine-hour papermaking process to only twelve minutes. Now he was eager to market it around the world, so in 1955 the Birdseyes left Paramonga again, abandoning Susie the fox, Billy the penguin, and Pancho the parrot. They might have preferred to go home to Gloucester, but Bob had work in New York City with the Grace company, so they rented an ample, well-furnished apartment at the Gramercy Park Hotel, opposite the leafy park.

From New York he assured *Time* magazine that "still

other ventures are afoot, and the days are not long enough for me to take advantage of all the opportunities I see." Doctors advised him to slow down, but he always insisted that "enthusiasm and hard work are also indispensable ingredients of achievement."

On October 9, 1956, at the age of sixty-nine, Clarence Birdseye died in his apartment in the Gramercy Park Hotel. He had asked that, rather than sending flowers to his funeral, people contribute to an Amherst College scholarship fund. He'd never forgotten how it felt to abandon his college education because of a lack of money. He didn't want other young men and women to go through that hardship. He asked to be cremated and have his ashes scattered in the sea off Gloucester, the place he so loved.

When Bob Birdseye passed away in 1956, frozen food had already become a multibillion-dollar international industry. It had been developing in Great Britain since the end of World War II, and eleven years after Bob Birdseye's death he became a fictitious British character called Captain Birdseye, a respectable, white-bearded old salt in a naval uniform who promoted frozen food. Few British people knew that there was a real Clarence Birdseye who had started the industry. The year Bob died, Giovanni Buitoni started the Italian frozen-food industry with frozen lasagna and ravioli. The ice cream industry was completely revolutionized by Bob's ideas on creating an entire frozen-food infrastructure, from factories to warehouses to trucks to stores.

Today frozen food is a major international business very similar to what Birdseye in the 1920s imagined it would become. Frozen Asian seafood exports alone account for billions of dollars in sales. Every country that has a food-export business exports frozen-food products. Many of Birdseye's ideas about industrialized food are not universally beloved today, but in many ways he would find this a world he had not only imagined but helped build. It is, as he predicted, a world in which food transcends geography and climate—any food, anywhere, at any time of year. Frozen food is an essential part of modern living—what modern home is complete without a freezer?

Birdseye's improbable ideas about frozen food changed our world, and that is what he is most remembered for.

Perhaps the more important thing about Clarence Birdseye was his ability to live life as an adventure. Curiosity is the one essential ingredient to an adventurous life.

acknowledgments

A warm thanks to all of my friends in Gloucester, and a special thanks to the Birdseye family for their kindness, generosity, and openness—Michael, Kelly, Gypsy, and Henry, thank you so very much. And great thanks to the American Museum of Natural History for science advice. Thanks to my agent, Charlotte Sheedy, and to my patient and wise editor, Beverly Horowitz, for guiding this book through publication.

CReDITS

Frontispiece: Courtesy of the Birdseye family. Birds Eye® is a registered trademark of Pinnacle Foods Group LLC.

INSERT
Page 1
Top: Courtesy of Rocky Mountain Laboratories, NIAID.
Middle: Amherst College Archives and Special Collections, Clarence Birdseye (AC 1910) Journals [vol. 3], pp. 42–43. Used with permission of the Birdseye family.
Bottom: Courtesy of the Birdseye family.

Page 2
Top: The Rooms Provincial Archive Division, VA 16–21. *The Bungalow, Muddy Bay*/Rev. Henry C. Gordon, [1921–1922], Henry Cartwright Gordon fonds.
Bottom: Courtesy of the Birdseye family.

Page 3
Top: Courtesy of the Birdseye family.
Bottom: World-Telegram Photo/C.M. Stieglitz. The *New York World-Telegram* and the *Sun Newspaper* Photograph Collection (Library of Congress).

Page 4
From the *Springfield Sunday Union and Republican*, March 2, 1930; p. 20 A. Birds Eye® is a registered trademark of Pinnacle Foods Group LLC.

Page 5
Top: Courtesy of the Birdseye family.
Bottom: Courtesy of the Birdseye family. Birds Eye® is a registered trademark of Pinnacle Foods Group LLC.

Page 6
Top: Cape Ann Museum, Gloucester, MA, USA.
Bottom: Cape Ann Museum, Gloucester, MA, USA. Birds Eye® is a registered trademark of Pinnacle Foods Group LLC.

Page 7
Top: Courtesy of the Birdseye family.
Bottom: Courtesy of the Birdseye family.

Page 8
Top left: Courtesy of the Birdseye family.
Top right: Courtesy of the Birdseye family.
Bottom: Cape Ann Museum, Gloucester, MA, USA.

BIBLIOGRAPHY

BOOKS

Carlton, Harry. *The Frozen Food Industry.* Knoxville: University of Tennessee Press, 1941.

Dolin, Eric Jay. *Fur, Fortune, and Empire: The Epic History of the Fur Trade in America.* New York: W. W. Norton, 2010.

Evans, Harold. *They Made America: From the Steam Engine to the Search Engine: Two Centuries of Innovators.* With Gail Buckland and David Lefer. New York: Little, Brown, 2004.

Foley, John. *The Food Makers: A History of General Foods Ltd.* Banbury, Oxfordshire: General Foods, 1972.

Freidberg, Susanne. *Fresh: A Perishable History.* Cambridge, Mass.: Belknap Press of Harvard University Press, 2009.

Fucini, Joseph, and Suzy Fucini. *Entrepreneurs: The Men and Women Behind Famous Brand Names and How They Made It.* Boston: G. K. Hall, 1985.

Grenfell, Wilfred Thomason. *Adrift on an Ice-Pan.* Boston: Houghton Mifflin, 1909.

_____. *A Labrador Doctor: The Autobiography of Wilfred Thomason Grenfell.* Boston: Houghton Mifflin, 1919.

_____. *Tales of the Labrador.* Boston: Houghton Mifflin, 1916.

Tressler, Donald, and Norman W. Desrosier, eds. *Fundamentals of Food Freezing.* Westport, Conn.: Avi, 1977.

Tressler, Donald, and Clifford F. Evers. *The Freezing and Preservation of Foods*. 2 vols. Westport, Conn.: Avi, 1957.

U.S. Patent Office. *Selected Patents of Clarence Birdseye.*

Williams, E. W. *Frozen Foods: Biography of an Industry*. Boston: Cahner's, 1968.

NEWSPAPER, MAGAZINE, AND JOURNAL ARTICLES

Birdseye, Clarence. "Looking Backward at Frozen Foods." *Refrigerating Engineering*, November 1953.

_____. "Postwar Problems of the Frozen Food Industry." *Meals for Millions*. Final Report of the New York State Joint Legislative Committee on Nutrition, 1947.

Burton, L. V. "Birdseye Demonstrates New Twenty-Plate Froster." *Food Industries*, November 1941.

Farrell, Morgan. "Quick Food Freezing Process Devised to Aid the Housewife." *New York Times*, February 14, 1932.

Harris, Herbert. "The Amazing Frozen-Foods Industry." *Science Digest*, February 1951.

Kahn, F. J., Jr. "The Coming of the Big Freeze." *The New Yorker*, September 14, 1946.

Kenyon, Paul. "About the Birdseyes . . . and More." *Gloucester Daily Times*, April 14, 1978.

CHRONOLOGY OF UNSIGNED ARTICLES

"For the First Time Anywhere! The Most Revolutionary Idea in the History of Food Will Be Revealed in Springfield Today." *Springfield Union*, March 6, 1930.

"Mayor Praises Clarence Birdseye for Work in Refrigeration Field." *Boston Globe*, July 8, 1931.

"Continuous Quick Freezer Developed by Birdseye." *Food Industries*, September 1940.

"Dinner, Frozen or Dried." *Newsweek*, November 19, 1945.

"Meet Mr. Birdseye—He Had a $22,000,000 Idea." *Look,* April
    30, 1946.

"Birdseye Changes Pace, Now Raises Wildflowers." *Cape Ann
    Summer Sun,* August 17, 1950.

"Father of Frozen Foods Dies: Clarence Birdseye Dead at 69."
    Gloucester Daily Times, October 8, 1956, 1.

"Clarence Birdseye Is Dead at 69; Inventor of Frozen Food
    Process." *New York Times,* October 9, 1956.

WEBSITES

The Internet is full of inaccurate information on Birdseye, most
of it feeding off each other. But there are a few useful sites:

amherst.edu (for information about the Birdseyes at Amherst)
foodreference.com (for a food time line)
library.hbs.edu (for a list of deals involving General Foods)

Index

ABOUT THE AUTHOR

MARK KURLANSKY is the *New York Times* bestselling author of *Ready for a Brand New Beat: How "Dancing in the Street" Became the Anthem for a Changing America; The Food of a Younger Land; Cod: A Biography of the Fish That Changed the World; Salt: A World History; 1968: The Year That Rocked the World;* and *The Big Oyster: History on the Half Shell,* among other books. He lives in New York City.

Praise for Shirley Russak Wachtel

"*A Castle in Brooklyn* is a story about love and endurance. It follows Jacob and Zalman as they survive 1944 Poland and make their way to America, to a dreamlike life that is shattered too soon. With deep empathy, Wachtel lays bare an incredible resilience and desire to live that will inspire readers and keep them turning the page. Magnificent."

—Rachel Barenbaum, author of *A Bend in the Stars* and *Atomic Anna*

"An enchanting, lively, and heartbreaking novel—all at once—*A Castle in Brooklyn* evokes such a tantalizing yet improbable image, especially for Holocaust survivors. Survival rendered them royalty, but could a fortress keep them safe from memories and destinies that could cross any moat? Wachtel delivers a most worthy debut."

—Thane Rosenbaum, author of *The Golems of Gotham*,
Second Hand Smoke, and *Elijah Visible*

A
Castle
in
Brooklyn

A Castle in Brooklyn

A Novel

SHIRLEY RUSSAK WACHTEL

Little
a

This is a work of fiction. Names, characters, organizations, places, events, and incidents are either products of the author's imagination or are used fictitiously.

Published by Little A, New York

www.apub.com

Amazon, the Amazon logo, and Little A are trademarks of Amazon.com, Inc., or its affiliates.

ISBN-13: 9781662508745 (hardcover)
ISBN-10: 1662508743 (hardcover)

ISBN-13: 9781662508752 (paperback)
ISBN-10: 1662508751 (paperback)

Cover design by Kathleen Lynch/Black Kat Design

Printed in the United States of America

First edition

For Arthur

PROLOGUE

Blueprint

There it was. Looking just like a gingerbread house from a fairy tale. Constructed of sturdy wooden beams, studs, crossbeams, and braces, the home was designed to withstand even the most turbulent of winters.

Situated in the heart of Brooklyn, the structure had shingles painted a mint green, windows adorned with stately black shutters, the home's roof pitched, the color a brick red. The pleasant cross gable with its exposed half-timbers, stone, and brick detailing all added a note of whimsy to the picture. Over the door, right beneath a green arch, a plain lantern cast a single golden ray of light on nights when the sky was moonless.

Once the sun was up, guests, of which there were always plenty, marveled at the soap-scrubbed concrete steps that led to the front of the home, the small, white metal mailbox adjacent to the door, but especially the front lawn. Like court attendants before the queen stood a tiny myrtle tree; shrubs of purple and green; a spray of yellow forsythia; and patches of sprightly pink azaleas, blue geraniums, and lavender. The tallest tree, an oak, could be seen craning its hoary head way beyond the roof, hinting of backyard pleasures.

Those lucky enough to set foot inside were greeted with light-filled rooms, made only more so by the buttery-yellow color of the walls, each stroke painted by Jacob himself. There was hardly a wall without a black-and-white photograph in a gilded frame. An elderly uncle sitting in an armchair, or a wide-eyed child throwing a ball, all greeting the visitor with an air that said, "Welcome. You are welcome here." No fussy oils of flowers in elegant vases or dancing ballerinas, and certainly not a preposterous family crest. No, Jacob's home was, beyond all things, a family home where love and acceptance echoed from the braided green-and-yellow rug in the living room to the stout chimney overhead.

The parlor, or as Americans like to call it, the living room, boasted an upholstered sofa decorated with blooming red roses scattered throughout, and of course, a Bakelite tube radio that sat on a small wooden side table with curved legs and dominated the wall between the windows.

The kitchen had all of the newest General Electric appliances, naturally: a range, and not an icebox, but a full standing refrigerator that blasted an icy wind each time Jacob would open the door as he hunted for a leftover drumstick or an extra slice of cake with chocolate frosting. Sometimes as his wife stood on the shiny linoleum with its yellow-and-white checkerboard pattern, he would surprise her. Sneaking up from behind her as she washed the lunch dishes while gazing out at the children—a boy and a girl—playing in the backyard, he would encircle her waist and plant a soft kiss on her cheek. Her gingham cotton apron felt cool to the touch as she turned her head ever so slightly to meet his lips in a kiss.

All in all, it was a sweet little home that was always, it seemed, filled with laughter and warmth and light. Not a big ostentatious home with ornate crystal bowls and fancy engravings, and, in fact, not really very big at all.

But for Jacob, it was everything—a castle. He sighed then, perhaps a bit too loudly, hoping no one would hear. Such a beautiful home with its gabled roof and buttery-yellow walls.

Jacob wished with all his heart that someday he could build it.

PART I

DIRT

ONE

Jacob, 1944

Jacob waited, swallowed hard, and listened to the silence. He thought about the house and how everything both inside and out was always full of light, a light that reflected the happiness of the family within. All too often, he had to admit to himself, his dreams had taken on more substance than his reality. Sadly, it was the only way he knew how to survive.

Before too long, he heard a soft chirping coming from the other end of the hayloft. It could be another cricket or even a mouse in hiding. Often, he would startle to a sudden noise, and fear would overtake him, a feeling that he was about to be strangled by some unknown force. Luckily, the source of the noise turned out to be a stray alley cat that had somehow wandered into the barn or a sudden wind that sliced past the fragile wooden doors. Still, he couldn't help worrying. And now, as the sound seemed to inch closer, once again, he felt his throat grip, his heartbeat quicken.

It wasn't until he heard a dull thud several feet away that he realized the source was not a cat or a sudden fluctuation of the wind. This sound was human. His mind raced. Fight or flight? And then, just as he was deciding on the best way to get his hands around the man's neck, the straw beneath crackled again, and he heard an urgent whisper.

"Hallo!" A child? How does a child suddenly appear here, in this damp pile of straw with walls that reeked of dung and wet fur? And yet Jacob, in the space of two years, had witnessed enough events where the impossible had been made possible.

Jacob placed his finger to his lips as the child edged his way toward him, the pupils of the child's eyes wide with terror. A shot of moonlight cascaded from a hole in the barn's roof, illuminating the pale face of the child, frightened, ghostlike. Before the intruder had a chance to ponder his next move, Jacob's arm reached out, catching the child at the elbow and pulling him forward. He was lighter than he seemed, the effort like lifting a bag of dead leaves.

"Please, I—" squealed the child, but before any other sound could emerge, Jacob clasped his hand over the stranger's lips. The blue eyes remained open, eyeballs twittering momentarily, until finally Jacob saw the eyebrows relax and the face resume composure. Releasing one breath, he removed his hand from the boy's face.

"Juden," Jacob mouthed, barely above a whisper, pointing to his own chest, then, *"Juden?"* pointing at the boy.

The child nodded, settling back in the straw.

Jacob felt his body go limp, and for the first time since he had heard the snap in the hay, he allowed the fear to leave him. After a while, the boy began to relax too. The two slept, neither having the strength to quell their curiosity just yet. When they awoke, flashes of sunlight had begun to seep through the hole in the roof.

Jacob eased his body against the wall, and when he spoke, his tongue was dry against his mouth.

"How did you get in here?" he asked, still in Polish. The boy sat back, too, hugging his bony knees against his chest, his eyes never leaving Jacob.

6

"The door to the barn was open, sir. I lifted the bar and had only to walk through."

Jacob was relieved that the boy's Polish was truly as impeccable as his own, nothing fake. He was not a German.

"Please don't call me *sir*," he said, a smile coming, to his surprise, across his face. "I'm only eighteen, and you have to be what, ten?"

"Twelve, sir!" the boy said, catching himself, then, "I mean I'm twelve, nearly the age of bar mitzvah!"

"Well, then, what's your name, nearly age of bar mitzvah?" Jacob asked, smiling.

"I'm Zalman. That's my name. Zalman Mendelson."

"Can't say that I've heard of the family. And how did you end up in this godforsaken place? You scared me. I thought you were one of the goddamn filthy krauts."

"I'm not that, sir. For sure I'm not that."

"Jacob—I answer to no other name."

"Sorry. But to answer your question about how I came here, to tell you the truth, I am not quite sure myself. I ran. Papa always said I was a good runner."

"So you ran all the way from town?"

"Well, when they came, I didn't know what else to do. I couldn't stay!"

Jacob looked at the boy for a beat, then began to feel dizzy. He put his head between his legs until the feeling passed.

On the surface, Zalman's story was too much like his own, he thought. But weren't they all the same, really? And yet he had to make sure there was not a shred of untruth in the tale. These days, even children were not to be trusted.

"Your town, the one that you escaped from? And your parents?"

"Raczki, Poland, sir . . . I mean I'm from Raczki, Poland," he said, catching himself. Jacob knew it well enough. It was his town too.

7

"My father? Why, Papa is an architect, and a good one too," Zalman added.

"A Jewish architect, really?"

The boy remained silent, lowering his head. Suddenly, a strange feeling began to overcome Jacob. It was a feeling something akin to shame. Had he become this boy's interrogator? After all, had fear such a stranglehold on him that he had become too much like those he detested?

"Zalman," he said, his voice softening, "you should be proud of your papa."

But before the child could acknowledge his words, a popping sound—*rat-a-tat-tat*—could be heard in the distance. Instinctively, the two buried themselves into the straw until, after several minutes, the gunfire ceased.

The most frightening of all was the silence that prevailed for the next twenty minutes. The morning grew late, though neither knew how many minutes or even hours had passed; neither had watches, but the hours were of little importance in times of war. Jacob stood up finally, feeling the muscles in his legs stretch painfully, never allowing his eyes to leave his companion as Zalman did the same.

"Monkey see, monkey do, eh?" said Jacob, and laughed. The boy looked at him curiously, then allowed a hint of a smile to cross his face.

"Well, then," said Jacob, sitting down again and bringing his knees up against his chin, "can you tell me, what were you running *from*?"

The boy plucked a piece of straw from the pile and turned it over in his hand.

"Running away? Weren't we all running away from the same thing? Running away from them?"

Jacob sighed. Until his conversation with the boy had begun, he hadn't realized how much he wanted, how much he *needed*, to speak with another person. It wasn't Mama. It wasn't Papa, or even Leon, but it was someone.

"Yes, that's true. What I mean is, before this, before you came here, were you at home with your parents, or were you in hiding?"

"Well, yes and no, and maybe both, because my parents had hidden me after Stefan left. And when the men came finally to our house, I knew just what to do. Did I tell you my father was an architect, and so I knew the place to go, a secret wall in the attic, that he had built when I was about five years old? It was a pirates' room with toy boats and costumes, even a treasure chest with money and its own lock. Stefan and I would go there on rainy days, but then Stefan had to work, because Papa said the family needed to eat since there were no more jobs in building houses. They—the Nazis—weren't building new homes or businesses; they were destroying them. So that's why Stefan had to go to work. I don't know exactly what he did. Maybe hauling boxes. He had wanted to become an architect like Papa—we both did—but one day Papa told us they had shut the schools, and later Mama sewed on the stars, such as we all have." Zalman pointed to the spot, continuing, "I tore mine off. You see there? Mama told me to do so as soon as I got to the pirates' place." The child shifted, throwing the blade of straw that had been in his hand into the hayloft.

"Mama had kept Stefan's soup warm all night. But when he hadn't come home that night, we knew that he had been taken. Papa said it had only been a matter of time, and sat down at the kitchen table, covering his face with his hands. Mama just went into her room and cried. After that, she was always crying."

Jacob caught sight of the boy's eyes, which were brimming with tears, and he envied him.

And then the story came fast, as if the child had tamped it down so long that the words exploded in a flurry. Stefan had, in fact, been put on the train, the event confirmed by Stefan's best friend, Sammy, who had managed to escape and stopped by the house the following morning. He, too, didn't know what would become of Sammy, perhaps flight into the woods like some of the others.

Zalman confessed that as he listened to Sammy's tale, he'd wanted to cover his ears, to stop it all, to go back in time when the world had been somewhat normal, but he'd known, even at his young age, that this was impossible. He became a voyeur of sorts, no longer a participant in his own life. Just like watching an old movie reel, not being a part of anything, not feeling. That was the only way to exist, to cope.

And that was what he did when the neighbors arrived with news that the Nazis were coming. House by house, taking them all; not a mouse, a bauble, or a speck of bread was to be spared. Zalman allowed himself to be hugged by each of his parents before going up to the pirates' place, where enough cans of vegetables, some baked potatoes, hard cheese, stale bread, and water had been stored. There were the books, too, even *Treasure Island*, which lay unopened on the floor along with a couple of broken toy boats and the useless treasure chest.

He heard them arrive the next day. And, like a moviegoer, he watched the corners of the room and listened to the sounds. The angry voices, the cries that made the walls tremble, a shot, then another, his mother's scream. And just as quickly, there was the silence. He listened to it for days as he ate some cheese and potatoes, peed into the enormous kettle in the corner. The books still lay unopened as Zalman crept downstairs, only to discover his father kneeling against the closet door as if he were praying, impaled by a single gunshot through his head. And then his eyes still dry, Zalman opened the door, and ran.

Zalman met Jacob's face. Tears slid down Zalman's cheeks.

"And you, Jacob, what's your story?" It was his boldest question yet. As Jacob pondered how he was going to answer the question, or if he was going to answer it at all, a sharp light invaded the barn, illuminating the skinny chickens in a cage, a tired pig that was opening one lazy eye.

Zalman jumped up against the wall as if stricken by a bayonet. The barn door squeaked shut, merging with the sound of Jacob's laughter.

"Don't be afraid, Zalman. That's just Frau Blanc, the widow who owns this barn, this farm, what is left of it, that is." He addressed the squat woman, who bore a heavy bag in both her arms and, expressionless, settled it down on the floor.

"Frau, this is my friend Zalman, who has also escaped from the town and found his way here." Then, turning to the boy: "Zalman, meet Frau Blanc, my savior, and soon to be yours too."

Zalman looked at the woman, then followed Jacob down the ladder. The Frau stood silently as the boys ripped open the cloth sack, laying bare its contents. Soft-boiled eggs, a loaf of black bread, five knockwurst sausages, a container of fresh milk still cold from the freezer. A trove of riches!

Zalman watched as Jacob cracked open one of the eggs and sucked the juices out. Zalman took the loaf of bread in hand, tore off a piece, and let the starchy taste fill his mouth before swallowing. As they ate, Frau Blanc stood in heavy black boots and a gray coat, watching them. Then she walked over to the cage of chickens that, filled with anticipation, were running frantically from corner to corner. She took a handful of seeds and scattered them in the cage as the chickens fought for their share. Then she walked over to the pig, which didn't bother to raise its head, patted its side where the bones protruded, and lay down a carrot, leaves and all. She approached the boys and watched as they ate.

"Smakuje dobrze?" she asked, her voice flat, heavy. The two nodded that all was good, not stopping to answer, as they relished the victuals.

Zalman now had a good view of her round face, or rather the wrinkles, for there were so many folds in the cheeks that one could barely make out a face, just watery green eyes, an upturned nose, thin lips whose inscrutability evoked the *Mona Lisa*. The woman stood for a while, staring at the two. Then, without a word, she left the barn, pulling the door shut behind her.

The boys, their bellies full, followed the shaft of sunlight as it sparkled, then disappeared, as the door creaked shut. All that was left now was the single beam that flashed from the hole in the roof, and, in a matter of hours, that, too, would be extinguished.

Later, Jacob explained that his father's cousins had been neighbors once to Frau Blanc and her husband. They were fine people, quietly sympathetic to the plight of the Jews. Jacob himself had never met the couple, didn't even remember the cousins, and yet his father had instructed him, repeating the admonition as the times grew more perilous: *If anything should happen, make your way to the farmhouse at the edge of the woods. If anything should happen . . .*

Jacob wasn't sure how long it had been since he arrived, sweating and out of breath, at the Frau's door, just a few yards from the decrepit barn. Without question, she had taken him in, shown him where to hide, how he could stay silent. There had been others before him, she revealed, but never told him who they were, how they had found her, or, more important, what had become of them. And Jacob didn't ask. In the same way she had accepted their presence then, it was no surprise that she acquiesced at the sight of Zalman. Frau Blanc was a woman of few words, but her actions, at least the way Jacob saw it, were thunderous.

Jacob figured that he had been hidden in the hayloft for weeks, perhaps even months now. And although he never admitted it, he was glad for Zalman's presence.

It was perhaps many more days, weeks, each sunrise and sunset folding into the other, that the two spent up in the hayloft. They sometimes talked as they bit into a wedge of cheese brought by Frau Blanc on one of her now-more-than-weekly appearances. They fashioned games of hide-and-go-seek, one hiding behind the chicken coop, or burying himself within the straw. They told each other fanciful stories of knights in battle and Martians with giant brains, all from other worlds, coming to save them.

Sometimes, when the silence became too oppressive and neither could sleep, Jacob had no choice but to listen to Zalman's endless questions. He would ask Jacob about his life at home before all the madness. What was his father's occupation? What sorts of dishes did his mother like to cook? Did he, like Zalman, have a brother or a sister who would play soldiers or read books with him? But then Jacob would clench his mouth shut, knowing that when, as the moonlight streamed through the hole in the roof, Zalman saw the angry look in his eyes, Zalman would finally stop asking questions. Instead, he spoke more about himself, how he loved the tangy taste of his mother's goulash on cold nights or the way his father hummed Yiddish melodies to himself when he thought no one was listening.

But there was one thing Jacob did share with the boy. On particularly cold nights, Jacob told him about his dream of building a house in a land he had never been to—of the colors, the texture of the rugs, the flowers in the garden. Zalman listened intently, imagining as if he himself were setting foot into the brightly lit foyer for a visit with friends. The boys tried to form a schedule so that their days had order, a semblance of normalcy, and so when blackness pervaded the barn and they could hear only the sounds of the night, a cricket, the pig snoring on the dirt floor, Jacob and Zalman slept. But always with one eye open.

And then one morning they heard the bar lift, the barn door open perhaps a little too quickly. In the loft they waited to hear the heavy thud of Frau Blanc's cloth bag as she set it on the floor. But before the realization came to them, that the old woman had been there only two days earlier, that their bellies were still full, they saw the glint of metal, heard the command that shook the ground like an earthquake, felt the chickens hit the wire cage as they flew about hysterically. And before their brains could register bold steps on the ladder and that *Yes, this was it, they have finally come,* they felt the sharp nudge of a pistol against their ribs, amid the shouts of *"Aus! Aus!" Get out!*

Jacob and his friend emerged from the hayloft, their bodies stooped like old men, their faces flushed with fear. The soldiers ordered them to sit, backs against the barn wall, as one of the men, a blond, blue-eyed Aryan, no older than Jacob himself, riffled through the cloth bag up in the hayloft, devouring the sausage and half slice of black bread that was left. Another, only slightly older, with dark eyes that resembled small bullets and a scar running down the right side of his face, walked over to the farthest corner of the barn, where a pile of dead mice snuggled in a corner, opened his coat and the zipper of his pants, and took a long piss. The other, perhaps the most innocent looking of all, with a white face and arched eyebrows that looked painted on and gave him the aspect of a fairy, and with platinum hair cropped in soldier's fashion, close to his head, walked over to the chicken coop, where all now except for one running in circles were pecking at the ground. Observing the birds with the mild curiosity of an academic, he hushed the animals, said something softly under his breath that neither boy could hear, then opened the latch and reached in. With one hand, he grabbed the bird and twisted its neck as Jacob and Zalman looked on, horrified. Just as calmly, he dropped the limp creature outside the cage, where the other chickens eyed it curiously. He stared down at the animal, a barely perceptible smile on his face, removed a clean handkerchief from his pocket, and wiped his hands. His companions didn't seem to notice. In fact, not one of them appeared interested in their captives; it was as if they had become another rock, or the skinny pig, still snoring in the corner. But when Zalman, finally taking his eyes off the terrifying scene before him, leaned over to whisper "We are next" to Jacob, the air split between them as a silver bullet whizzed by, lodging itself beneath a rotting shelf on which a bucket teetered.

"*Shaah!*" barked the older, who eyed them from his place against the wall, gray uniform still unbuttoned, fly open. He returned the pistol to its holster, closed his eyes once more, as if nothing at all had ever happened.

How long can a man hold his breath? Jacob wondered, forcing his eyes to look straight ahead at the motionless pig, which looked more dead than alive by then. The two boys stood against the wall as the ray of roof light flickered with each passing of a cloud. They stood, breathing, Zalman imagining again that he was watching a movie, waiting for the next scene, as Jacob dared not think of his family or his dreams for

14

fear that the tears would put an end to his inconspicuousness—so he didn't think at all, hoping to melt somehow into the wall behind him.

Someone barked, shattering the silence again, and soon Jacob and Zalman were outside under a sun that was more radiant, more alive, than either had seen in their lifetimes. And then their feet were moving on a day when the air was light despite the still-leafless trees, light and warm and full of promise. After about a half hour of walking, always looking straight ahead, never behind or to the side, they joined the others; some were women, and there were a couple of adolescent males like themselves. Most were ageless, different, perhaps, but essentially all the same in the eyes of their captors, who laughed and pushed them forward, ever forward. They walked. The group joined others, and more joined them until they were a mass, a great wave. Were there twenty, a hundred? No one took the time or had the inclination to count. Just forward, one step in front of the other, all silent, with brains that had long ago stopped thinking and hearts that, despite their desires, would not cease.

Ultimately, they reached a clearing, and with a stiff command and a prod, they stopped, nearly falling upon one another. Some of the older men, and a few women, sank to their knees; others fell in a heap, so sudden was the shift. And when they looked ahead, finally, at a sight that only a year ago would have made them cringe with terror, these men and women had only resignation in their eyes. They soon met others, this group all men who looked to be in their midthirties, with bruises lining their thin arms, giant holes in their shirts, their pants brown from dirt. Jacob guessed they were the ones who had escaped to the forest only weeks before he himself had left home. The men's fingers were tightly clenching the handles of iron shovels and were striking the ground, bringing up piles of earth and setting them in mounds at the perimeter of a growing, massive hole.

More shovels appeared, and after one earsplitting bark, they all had shovels in their hands and had begun to dig. Methodically, standing next to Zalman at the edge of the crowd, Jacob worked the soil, lifted the blade. *Hit, fill, lift, pour, hit again.* Out of the corner of his eye, he counted them, saw the black heavy pistols lying dormant at their sides. *Hit, fill, lift, pour.* Only a couple of the soldiers were standing now, poised, looking up into the sky as the grayness of an early dusk seeped into the atmosphere. *Hit. Fill. Lift. Pour.*

Three of their captors had removed their caps and were seated against an emaciated tree. Other soldiers were engaged in spirited conversation, maybe over their last encounter with a young fräulein at a brothel, all punctuated by raucous laughter. Closer to where he and Zalman worked, Jacob made out the blond hair of one of the soldiers who had captured them earlier. Next to him sat the older one, his protruding belly straining against the buttons of his still-clean gray shirt. Both men, caps covering their eyes, were dozing next to a naked shrub, their chins pressed against their chests. Jacob startled as his vision came to rest a few feet away on the face that had already carved itself into his memory forever. The white complexion, the arched eyebrows, the platinum blond hair, the almost angelic face. He was raising a flask to his lips, guzzling, wiping his mouth with the back of his sleeve. Yet his eyes gazed straight ahead, and for less than a moment, Jacob felt them meet his own. *Hit. Fill. Lift. Pour.*

"Psst, psst!"

His skin jumped, and he almost prematurely dropped the heavy shovel. Jacob turned his head slightly toward the boy, who was mouthing his name.

"Jacob, what do you think has happened to the Frau?"

Jacob shook his head, glanced back at the arched eyebrows. He could see as the soldier placed the empty flask on the ground that his thirst was not yet quenched.

"Jacob!" he was whispering, more urgently now. "What do you think will happen to *us*?" Arched eyebrows was looking away, toward his sleeping companions, the naked shrub. He casually flicked a speck of dirt from his collar. There were only perhaps eight of the soldiers in all.

"Zalman," he said, trying to keep his voice even, "soon I will put this shovel down, very gently. And you must do the same."

The boy was gazing at him directly now, eyes wide, and Jacob could make out beads of sweat beneath the dirty-blond hair covering his forehead.

Hit. Fill. Lift. Pour. Arched eyebrows moving now, toward his companions, calling out.

"Zalman, what was it your father told you to do because you were so good at it?"

The boy bit down on the bottom of his lip before answering.

"Run. He told me to run."

They placed their shovels on the ground and, beneath the first rays of moonlight, made for the forest.

PART II

BRICKS AND MORTAR

TWO

Jacob, 1952

Jacob sat at the counter of the coffee shop, sipping a cup of black coffee as he perused the sports section. He followed the Yankees in print and on the radio and had developed a keen desire to see Mickey Mantle hit one out of the park. But he had to remain content for now with voice and paper. He had neither the money nor the time to attend a real live, in-person game. He lifted the cuff of his sleeve and looked at his watch. It was a gift given to him by his uncle, American citizen Uncle Abe, when Jacob got off the ship less than a year earlier. Jacob had no more than an hour to go before he would walk the six blocks to Thirty-Third and Fifth for his class.

He hadn't been much of a student as a young boy, never having the patience for formal studies or rigid numbers, but after the first week, he'd actually started looking forward to English language classes every Tuesday and Thursday night. The exhaustion that seeped into his bones after eight hours of work bottling seltzer was absent on those days as he anticipated sitting in the classroom, taking notes from a blackboard into his own composition notebook. It helped that Jacob was an eager student. His hand was always among the first raised. When he was called upon to read first his rudimentary sentences, then paragraphs, and ultimately composition, he recited with a robust voice that reflected the confidence he felt after his hours of study and practice. The other twenty students, some from Poland like himself, a few from Austria, France, Holland, and even a couple from Japan, all listened, smiles on their faces, eyes shining with admiration. A few of the slow ones surely harbored a secret envy. But how could he help himself? Languages had always come easily to him. Besides, although he never cared for the assigned propaganda he had to read back home, he was eager to try books by American authors he had long heard about, like Mark Twain or John Steinbeck.

Jacob took one sip of coffee, which had now begun to grow cold, folded up the paper in case he needed it for coverage later, and placed it under his arm. He walked into the brisk air, joining the wave of workers seeking an evening refuge. After walking for a block and a half, Jacob began to feel a couple of drops. He unfolded the paper, placed it over his head, and quickened his pace. By the time he reached the school, the light rain had subsided, and he threw the paper, photo of the Mick and all, into the nearest garbage can.

The classroom was on the third floor of a building that housed a high school by day. Still feeling the rush of air as the front door shut behind him, Jacob turned right for the marble staircase and took the steps two at a time. When he reached the classroom at the end of the hall, he was disappointed to see he was not the first one there. Rick Tanaka, one of the Japanese students, who struggled with a new language and an alphabet that was even more foreign to him, was already seated. Ron Kransky, the skinny Pole no older than Jacob, was arranging his books, pencils, and pen neatly on his desk, sitting a respectable distance away from Rick. Again, the door flew open as Sophie Jenick, arms filled with books, an umbrella, and a bag of apples, rushed into the room, settling herself into a corner seat in the back. Sophie, a woman in her early twenties, short and round, her face framed by red ringlets, always looked as if she were late for an appointment, perpetually out of breath. Besides the fact that she knew just the basics of English, Jacob had learned from her essays that she was newly married and came from a town not too far from where Jacob had been born, and as a result of what they shared, she would sometimes smile shyly at Jacob whenever she saw him looking her way.

Jacob wondered about his fellow students. What were their true names before they were Americanized? He was glad that his own name wasn't too changed from the one he was known by back home.

Jacob flipped on the light, casting a bluish tone to the faces of his fellow students, who nodded at him in greeting. He removed a black-and-silver Parker fountain pen from his coat pocket along with a jar of jet-black ink that he fit snugly into a hole at the corner of his desk. He opened his notebook and began moving his lips quietly, for the third time, to read the page filled with meticulous lettering. By the time he looked up, the class was almost filled with students, and the teacher, a gentleman in his fifties wearing a chestnut-color tweed jacket and sporting a full beard of tight gray curls, was at the desk opening his attendance book. Jacob folded his hands on the graffiti-filled wooden desk where he sat in the first row, directly in front of the teacher's desk. He waited patiently, as always, as the teacher pronounced the list of names, but halfway through he realized there was a new name: Esther. He couldn't quite make out the last name, but he was sure that from the sound of it, it was Polish. Not wanting to appear too conspicuous, he allowed his eyes to remain on the open notebook before him. And shortly after, his hand was the first to shoot up when the call for readers was made.

He cleared his throat and began. "My Job" had been the topic for last week's assignment, and even though filling and stacking seltzer bottles wasn't the most stimulating profession, if it even could be called that, Jacob had managed to fill a page and a half with the tasks of his day. Setting the bottles in place under the machines, stacking them side by side in boxes, getting ready for the next morning's delivery. He didn't trip over any of the words, and he didn't hesitate in the reading. When he finished, in the interim between his last word and the anticipated teacher's praise, his ear caught something unusual. Clapping. It stopped just as abruptly as it had begun. Nonetheless, someone had applauded his essay, something never done before in class. He turned to where the sound came from, one row behind him, diagonally to his left. She lowered her head and her cheeks flushed, but not before he could see the color of her eyes. They were blue. The new girl had blue eyes.

The teacher, Mr. Rutherford, commended Jacob's mastery of the language and, scratching his scraggly beard, even offered a few comments on how interesting the job must be. Jacob smiled. It was an occupation about as bland as the taste of seltzer. The rest of the class proceeded with a grammar lesson on verbs, the conditional perfect tense. "If I had enough money, then I would buy a steak dinner." "If you had enough money, then you would buy a steak dinner." "If he had enough . . ." He copied the list of phrases from the blackboard, then, joining his voice with the others, recited the conjugations. Afterward, they reinforced the lesson by writing their own lists of "ifs" and "thens." "If I had a car, then I would not have to take the subway to work," he wrote. When they were finished, a few of the others, a heavyset Frenchman with a thick accent, and a fast-speaking typist from Holland who wore a black wig in a pageboy style (Jacob guessed she was probably a pious Jew), read their drills.

Instead of taking the usual break after an hour of instruction, since the slaps of rain against the windowpanes were becoming stronger, Mr. Rutherford dismissed the class fifteen minutes early. The next assignment involved writing an essay on their personal goals in life, making sure to use "If I . . . then."

Usually Jacob couldn't wait to get back to his apartment in Borough Park to begin writing. But this evening he wasn't so sure. It was one thing to write about what a person did for a living, and another to confess one's private hopes and dreams. He had to ponder the subject further on his way home. For now, though, Jacob had one goal: to catch up with the new student, who was already standing next to the classroom door, buttoning her coat.

"I have to thank you," he said in Polish, hoping that his quick breathing wouldn't betray the fact that he'd rushed up to meet her.

She turned abruptly, setting those eyes, which were now sparkling with innocence, upon his own. When she looked up at him, he could see that her blue eyes matched the color of her coat.

It took Jacob a moment to speak—surprising, as he was never at a loss for words. But now his tongue had to catch up with his thoughts, which were going in several directions at once.

"I just wanted to thank you for praising my writing, but I hardly think it was that good."

She laughed then, hearty, uninhibited. Her lips, painted a shiny coral, were full, and when she opened them to speak, they revealed a set of perfect teeth, a brilliant white. Jacob wanted to suspend time, to hold it forever. It seemed that his life was on the verge of something, but he wasn't quite sure what it was. Too soon, though, he heard the voice, soft, throaty. Like him, she spoke in Polish.

"It was silly of me, I suppose. I clapped when no one else did, so I should be apologizing to *you*."

Composed now, it was Jacob's turn to laugh. There was something about this girl that made him want to keep smiling.

"Not at all," he responded. "I liked it. By the way, I'm Jacob Stein." He extended his hand, and when she reached toward him, he found her hand settled in his perfectly.

"Esther Itzkowitz. I'm pleased to meet you. Today was my first day attending this class. I've had influenza these past few weeks, so I think I'll have a lot of catching up to do."

"I'm sure you'll be fine. We only meet twice a week, so there's plenty of time to study. If you don't think me too forward," he continued, switching over to English, "I would be happy to help you."

"Well," she said, matching his English with her own as she ran her fingers through her short brown hair, "the problem is, I don't have plenty of time to study because I work all day and most nights for my father. Oh, and he is—what is the word?—he is *waiting* for me now in the car."

"Oh, of course," he said, holding the door open for her as they exited the now-empty classroom and made their way down the marble staircase. At the bottom, she turned toward him, her blue eyes holding his in her gaze. And, reverting to Polish, she said, "Thank you for the offer, Jacob. So nice meeting you." Then he watched as she slipped into step with the pedestrians rushing home between the raindrops and got into a black Oldsmobile Super Eighty-Eight across the street.

Jacob walked several blocks to his subway station before he even noticed he had become drenched by the now-heavy deluge.

"Nice to meet you too," he said quietly to himself.

～

Jacob did not reflect much on things. He accepted what was and didn't ponder much on the why or the how. But just the same, he found himself thinking, as each hour went by, about the next time he would see Esther. He found himself dissecting each phrase, each word spoken between them as if he were a scientist in a lab and not a bottle filler. She said she was glad to have met him, but was she being earnest or simply polite? The rapidity with which she had turned down his offer for help made him wonder if she was as consumed by work as she implied or if it was just an excuse not to see him again. Perhaps she wasn't attracted to him. She appeared to be in her twenties, but maybe she was too young to seriously consider taking up with a poor young man such as himself. Or worse yet, perhaps there was someone else. These thoughts rambled through Jacob's mind as he brushed his teeth in the morning or bit into his salami sandwich during lunch break, even when his head touched the pillow at night. He was so consumed by the young woman in the blue coat that he forgot all about the writing assignment until the night before class. He had to stay up well past midnight fixing ink to paper. His aunt Rose remarked on the late hour as she tiptoed in, seeing the light still burning over the kitchen table.

"*Nu*, Jacob, you are up so late still. How is it you have so much work for school?" the old woman asked in Yiddish, pulling her pink fleece robe tighter across her chest.

"It is nothing, Tante," he said, raising his head just long enough to answer in English, his now-preferred language. "Don't bother yourself about me. I've just forgotten about some homework. You should go back to bed."

"Very well, then," she said, as she moved closer to kiss him on the forehead, "but try not to stay up too late. You do need to get up early tomorrow morning, you know."

Jacob didn't mind that his aunt and uncle treated him as if he were six instead of twenty-six. After all, it was his father's brother who had sponsored his journey to America and even provided him with his own bedroom in the couple's small walk-up apartment in Borough Park, insisting that he could stay as long as he needed. His aunt and uncle, who had immigrated to the US in 1937, had been spared the horrors of living through the war and were more than happy to provide safety and a future for Abraham's brother's one surviving child. As for Jacob, who had long ago forgotten a mother's loving touch, he was eager to help out at Uncle Abraham's grocery and also earn a paycheck at the seltzer-bottling factory. Jacob assisted Aunt Rose with the laundry and household chores, sometimes even broiling a chicken or making a potato soup for dinner. She was grateful for his help, certainly, as arthritis through the years had gnarled her hands and made her gait unsteady. But even if Jacob had not done all this, the childless couple loved him as their own. For Jacob, the love he received in their household was like water gushing from a hose, filling what seemed like a bottomless hole inside. He had no plans to leave anytime soon.

~

The next day, when he walked into the classroom, she was already there, but now seated second row, center. Before taking the seat in front of her, he nodded politely. She smiled back. Could it be she was really glad to see him? The class filled up shortly afterward, and the lesson began. Jacob, though, found he couldn't concentrate, as he felt her eyes upon his back for the duration of the class.

"Mr. Stein?"

He startled, his mind failing to register the words.

"Mr. Stein, would you care to read your essay for us?"

Jacob swallowed. Without thinking, he shook his head.

"I'm sorry, sir. Not tonight." He mumbled something about his throat.

"Very well, then. How about you, Mr. Polansky?"

It wasn't that he hadn't done a good job on the assignment. But perhaps this time it was too much. Too much of Jacob on the paper. And he wasn't ready to share it with the class. Least of all Esther. He felt his back grow hot.

Throughout the first hour of class, Jacob sensed the drone of a voice, copied notes from the blackboard mechanically, all the while feeling that he was running a fever. Maybe he should go home. But before long, he heard soft murmuring around him, saw the shuffling of feet. It must be the ten-minute break. His heart jumped as he realized he could no longer move. Not even a finger. But then there was a tap on his shoulder, the sound of a voice.

"Jacob, are you well?"

He looked up to the glittering crystal-blue eyes, the bow-like lips. He tried to compose himself.

"Of course, Esther, of course. I am well. I was just thinking about the lesson."

"I see," she answered. Jacob saw a twinkle in her eye as he got to his feet.

"Let's go out into the hall."

He escorted her into the dimly lit corridor, offered her a cigarette, which she declined. They spoke only English now as they stood, he facing her, she in a striped tan-and-white dress held by a red patent leather belt, hand pushing back the curl in her soft brown hair.

You can learn much in the space of ten minutes, he decided, for he did learn quite a bit about Esther Itzkowitz, who was much more than the color of her eyes. Like himself, she was Polish, but she had been born in Łódź, the city that would become a Jewish ghetto and a Nazi holding cell, where the populace dwelled before marching into Auschwitz. But Esther and her family had been lucky, taking their chance to come to America when they still could, just before the doors were slammed shut. Though there were a couple of cousins who had perished in the ensuing years, freedom for Esther and her family had never been a dream, a prize to be won as it had been for Jacob, but the natural order of things.

Jacob envied her, but only a little. He was glad that she had never known the fear of opening one's eyes at daybreak, wondering what if any terrors could befall you at any hour. Unlike Jacob, she wasn't a shell, consumed each night by the nightmares of the past. Esther was whole, her spirit filled with the promise of a happy future, while Jacob, though hopeful, was a survivor who still had his doubts.

She didn't need this language class, she explained. She had lived in this country for eight years now, a proud citizen for the past three. Her English was fair, she admitted, but required more polish if she were to succeed in the family business, where she dealt with the public daily. Almost immediately upon coming to the United States, her father had taken a huge portion of the family's savings and invested it in the one

29

thing that had stability, certain he would reap a profit in real estate. His first purchase was a twenty-room boardinghouse for the steady influx of immigrants from Europe who were looking to establish a foothold in Manhattan. Her mother's primary job was as a homemaker, caring for Esther and her two younger brothers, and since the woman feared any discourse with these strange Yankees, it fell to Esther, the eldest, to run the office, rent rooms at the boardinghouse on the Lower East Side, then the two new high-rises on the West Side, where her father presided as landlord. She also dealt with the utility companies, prospective salesmen, painters, plumbers, and carpenters, rental fees, even the taxes. She was more than her father's daughter. She was the face of EMI (Esther, Menashe, Isadore) Realty. Her English could not just be passable; it had to be impeccable.

Jacob listened, his eyes never leaving Esther's face. He was mesmerized by her success story, a story he had little hope of accomplishing himself, not living in that small apartment with his elderly aunt and uncle, not bottling tasteless seltzer, but he also heard other things, things that were unsaid. Esther did not have a suitor. With the business and school, when would she have the time?

As the lesson resumed and he refilled his fountain pen from the inkwell and began an exercise on adjective comparisons and superlatives—*good, better, best*—Jacob felt relieved. The ten-minute break had run out before the beautiful twenty-two-year-old immigrant (he had soon learned her age) could ask his story. What would he say? How much could he tell without frightening her off? He had an extra day to think about it, though, for soon enough the class was dismissed and she was hurrying into the shiny black Oldsmobile.

After many more chats between Jacob and Esther during the class breaks and a few after class, Jacob slowly began to tell her about himself. How he had been born into a poor family in Raczki, how he had remained hidden for weeks and months in Frau Blanc's hayloft, how he had escaped from under the Nazis' watchful eyes moments before he heard the gunshots, smelled the dust in the air, as the rest were dumped into a mass grave. How when he had returned to the home where he grew up, there was nothing to keep him there. Perhaps one day he would tell her the whole story, even though the prospect scared him. Not even his aunt and uncle knew the full story, not even his dear friend Zalman, who always had known better than to ask. But this girl—well, if he could speak the words to anyone on this earth, it would be to Esther, whose face, whose body, he knew had already become home.

After a matter of only weeks, their classmates realized there was something special between the tall young man with the narrow face and the pretty girl with the coral lips and the flip in her brown hair. Jacob and Esther always occupied seats next to each other now, exchanging comments and giddy smiles each time Mr. Rutherford turned his back. And even as Mr. Polansky or Miss Jenick read their essays, Jacob would find his eye wandering toward Esther's soft white hands, which remained firmly clasped atop the wooden desk. Jacob soon realized that their blossoming romance was already gossip for the students as they conversed during breaks. Sometimes as the couple whispered, heads bent together, they caught Mr. Rutherford, at his desk grading their papers, chuckling to himself.

One evening, as the two walked side by side down the staircase, just before they said goodbye, he readying himself for the four-block walk to the subway, she heading for the car across the street, Esther took his arm and pulled him close.

"Would you like to come to my parents' apartment next Monday before the next assignment is due? I think, being that it's a bit confusing, I might now need your help." Jacob hoped she didn't notice the blush that he felt spreading across his cheeks and, restraining himself from sweeping her up in his arms, simply nodded.

"Of course. I am available next Monday. Yes, that would be fine."

She tore a page out of her notebook and quickly scribbled the address before running out the school doors. As he watched her open the passenger side of the car and settle in, Jacob wondered what it would be like to sit next to her in the front seat of a car, to walk down the street arm in arm, to come home to a house that was their own.

That evening, as Jacob rested his head on his pillow, he prepared himself for another restless night. Ever since he had left his boyhood home, sleep had eluded him. And when, after several hours, he finally did fall asleep, his sleep was troubled, filled with nightmares. Since he had first set foot in America, it had gotten worse. Sometimes he thought he heard the steel shovel hitting the earth; other times he saw the face of the fair-haired Nazi as he snapped a chicken's neck. Worst of all was the touch of his mother's hands as she secured an afghan blanket around his shoulders. And though he felt those hands around him now, his body soothed by the only item he had brought from home, it brought him no solace. On more than one occasion, he would wake up flushed, his face and neck drowned in sweat. But that night, his sleep was peaceful as he dreamed of his date with Esther. She consumed his thoughts, leaving no room for anyone else.

~

Jacob brought flowers, pink and white tulips, when he visited her on the fifth floor of a high-rise on East Seventieth Street. Although he also lived in an apartment, the residences were about as different as the moon and the sun. Uncle Abraham's apartment served as a container, with its one kitchen, living room, two bedrooms, a bathroom, and the scents of hot coffee and toast in the morning; in this, the home of Esther's parents, the door opened to a seemingly endless array of long corridors where intricate moldings hugged the ceilings, red-and-black-lacquered cabinets with tall vases filled with exotic flowers stood against the walls, and the scents of rose tea and baked goods emanated even before Jacob's finger touched the buzzer by the door. He was certain that the flowers in his hand had already begun to wilt.

But before Jacob had time to reconsider, there was Esther, petite, her chin tilted up as she stood at the door in a white flared dress with green polka dots and a Peter Pan collar, again that bright coral smile as she pulled him inside.

The family welcomed him, all except for the father, who stood with a hawklike eye at one of the broad windows. The mother, wearing a black-and-white-checkered dress with heavy white pearls at her neck, reached to embrace him. After quickly surveying her face, Jacob realized that her mother's appearance was indeed a foreshadowing of Esther twenty years into the future, and he decided that he was happy with the outcome. Meanwhile, Esther's brothers, both short and skinny with pomaded dark hair and wearing identical pale-blue button-down shirts, could have been twins, except that Menashe, the elder, had a short growth of a mustache that he kept stroking. The two, smiles on their faces, pumped Jacob's hand furiously, coaxing him to come into the living room and watch the *Red Skelton Show* on their new Magnavox.

Jacob stood in the foyer for a while, unable to move. He had not felt such an assault of love since his arrival in New York Harbor. He sensed Esther's gentle touch at his sleeve.

"There will be plenty of time for television watching," she said, admonishing her brothers, "and that is not the purpose of Jacob's visit anyway." She led Jacob past a large oil painting of a woman in a gilded frame toward a window where her father stood still, hands in his pockets.

"Papa, this is Jacob, the boy I told you about, the one from my English class." The man's face betrayed neither affection nor disdain as he grasped Jacob's hand in his.

"Happy to meet you, sir," Jacob said. The father mumbled something under his breath that Jacob didn't quite understand, but his hand, when Jacob shook it, had been warm.

Esther led Jacob into the kitchen, and the first thought that came to his mind was never in his life had he seen such a light-filled space.

Sparkling rays cascaded from a chandelier in the kitchen (of all places), crystals glimmering like little rainbows; the cotton curtains that hung primly over a window near the sink were a bright white, as was the linoleum, shiny and clean with flecks of gold. Even the glasses for tea arranged on a counter reflected the glimmer of a yellow moon that could be seen peeking through the white curtains.

"Some tea?" Mrs. Itzkowitz was asking him, but already her hand was pouring the steaming golden liquid into a glass.

Before long, Jacob was seated at the kitchen table, sharing tea and slices of homemade sponge cake with Esther, her mother, and her two brothers who, lured by the scent of the sweet cake, had forsaken *Red Skelton* to join them. Before sitting down, though, Mrs. Itzkowitz had found a glass vase, filled it with water, and arranged Jacob's flowers in the center of the table next to the cake platter.

"Thank you, Mrs. Itzkowitz," he said between bites, finding his voice again. "It's so kind of you. And the cake is one of the best I've tasted!"

"It's nothing, really. An old recipe from back home," she answered, smiling broadly. Her accent was thick, unlike Esther's or her brothers'. Esther's father, who had disappeared no doubt into the bedroom shortly after Jacob's arrival, had yet to make his voice known.

Esther's brothers, both talkative, dominated the conversation with talk about the Yankees and the shows that had mesmerized them on the new TV—*Dragnet*, the comedy debut of *I Love Lucy*, and, best of all, the hilarious Milton Berle. As he bit into yet another slice of the cake, Jacob learned that despite the fact that their initials formed part of the company name, neither son had an interest in pursuing the father's real estate business. Menashe was on his way toward a career as a lawyer, while Isadore had already shown talent as a painter; it was his artistry that adorned almost every room of the house. That left Esther, who was preparing herself to stand by her father's side.

She looked on now apologetically as her mother pushed yet another slice of the cake onto Jacob's plate. He patted his stomach, laughing, and stood up, thanking her once more. He wondered if he would see Esther's father again this evening.

"Come, Jacob, I want you to see our new Magnavox," said Esther, standing, and, for the first time, taking him by the hand as she led him toward the living room, where the brothers were already seated. The room, even more lavish than the others, was painted white with more of the intricate molding against the ceiling. The furniture was the French provincial style, a circular couch of baby-blue soft velvet covered in sturdy plastic with matching blue and marigold toss pillows, and ornately carved arms in bone white. Two matching chairs, the kind you were afraid to sit in, at one end of the room, a round glass table with a gold base topped by the tallest vase made of china and filled with multicolored flowers, too perfect to be anything but artificial. And yet, despite the objects that sparkled from end to end, there was one object that caught Jacob's attention. A magnificent baby grand piano polished to a shiny black. The bench tucked beneath was covered in a faded toile in shades of blue and salmon-color pink. It was at this bench that Esther's mother, who followed them briskly into the room, urged her daughter to sit.

"Play that sonata," she beckoned, "so lovely, ah . . ." She closed her eyes as if reliving the memory. Esther's brothers clicked on the TV, Isadore moving to turn the dial so that the volume was dimmed and the picture sparked to life.

Meanwhile, Esther was bent over the keys, her eyebrows creased as she lifted her fingers, then placed them gently down again. It was beautiful, soothing, the shadow of a memory of Jacob himself before he was old enough for his thoughts to take form, Jacob sitting on his mother's knee. His eye wandered to one of the high-backed chairs where Mrs. Itzkowitz sat nodding, eyes closed, a dreamlike smile on her face. It was all almost too much for Jacob, whose world had shifted perhaps too quickly. Although he had walked from bleakness, hopelessness, into a future that glittered now with the prospect of fortune—a business, a home, maybe even a family—he still felt ill at ease. Especially in this home, with this family who had embraced him as their own, a home that forecast the promise of what life could be in America—glittering chandeliers, pale-blue French provincial sofas, the miracle of TV, and Esther stroking the keys of a piano. Esther in a white dress with green polka dots, the little brown bob that dipped at her forehead, Esther the girl he now knew for a certainty would one day become his wife. All too much for the young man who still felt he was nothing more than just an outsider.

THREE

Esther

S he didn't like lying to him. She wasn't the kind of a girl who was dishonest, pretending to be someone she wasn't just for her own selfish motives. She hadn't planned to tell a fib; it was just when it came down to it, she really had no choice.

Esther had known Sophie Jenick for nearly a year, ever since she and her husband, Paul, had rented the one-bedroom on the second floor of her father's newly acquired apartment building on the West Side. Sophie, who was the same age as Esther and worked part-time in a bakery around the corner, would stop into the office downstairs each month to pay the rent, and soon afterward, as she struck up a friendship with the landlord's daughter, more often than that. The two talked about the latest fashions, the new "Sea Spray" stockings with navy heel and seam for the exorbitant sum of $1.85 a pair, the popular bell skirts worn over crinoline, the latest Judy Holliday movie, or the lovesick melody of Nat King Cole's "Unforgettable." And sometimes, when they were not discussing popular culture, or when Esther wasn't helping Sophie with her English so she could better assist the shoppers at the bakery, the two talked about boys. Sophie, though married herself, was naturally curious as to why someone as attractive and personable as Esther still had no ring on her finger.

Esther, sitting opposite her at the desk in the office, shrugged.

"I'm too busy to be looking for a man. And where would I find one, anyway, here in the office looking at statements and receipts all day?"

Sophie, who had short fiery-red hair and an impish smile, agreed but secretly started to consider possibilities for her young friend who, after all, deserved a husband and family, perhaps more than others. So it was only a couple of weeks after the discussion that Sophie happened to mention the tall young Pole who had caught her eye.

"We're taking the same English language class together Tuesday and Thursday nights, and I can tell you, he is not only one of the smartest ones in the class, but with those green eyes, and a full head of brown hair, I know he is just your type. Did I mention how tall he is too?"

When Esther began to protest, Sophie pouted.

"These days, we girls can't wait till someone comes knocking at our door. And, Esther, my friend, I am most sorry to say this, but if you wait too much longer, you could be an old maid! Like those sisters down the hall in apartment 2B."

At this, Esther exploded in laughter. The women, well into their sixties, were plump and sullen. One even walked with a cane. Nevertheless, she had to concede that Sophie's remark did strike a hidden fear in her.

"Well, even if I did want to meet such a man, how would I? I am busy here all day, and I'm sure he must have a job of some sort too."

"I've been thinking about that," Sophie said, speaking rapidly. "Why don't you join our class? We've only just had three meetings, so it would be nothing for you to catch up."

The notion was so ridiculous that Esther could not help but laugh at the suggestion.

"Sophie, you must be eating too much of that rum cake at the bakery. You know I don't need help with my English. I'm giving *you* instruction!"

Sophie didn't say a word but merely arched her eyebrows. Well, maybe there was a way . . .

If Esther felt bad about deceiving Jacob, she had even more misgivings about lying to her father. Boris Itzkowitz was by nature a man of few words, but he was one who paid attention, making sure that both bills and payments were executed in a timely fashion, his finger always on the pulse of the vicissitudes of the stock market, braced for the next big deal. Besides his business dealings, Boris had no hobbies; in fact, he had only two great interests—global world politics and his family. He had always instructed his children that understanding the world was a necessity, and that was why whenever he wasn't engaged in business negotiations or reviewing blueprints, Esther could find him in the small downstairs front office, ear glued to the large radio, listening to Eisenhower's speech or the latest troop maneuvers over in Korea. He was, as his gregarious wife used to joke, inscrutable, as implacable as the stoic buildings he purchased throughout Manhattan. And yet there was an aspect about the stodgy man who always wore a black hat on his head that only a select few were privy to.

Esther knew that, for Boris, family was the one thing that could fill the hole he'd felt inside his soul since venturing to the shores of America, just before Europe would be swept into the inferno of war. Sometimes she would hear him make his way down the hall after sleepless hours next to his wife in the comfortable bed framed by gold brocade silk drapes, and with the sounds of motorcars and fire engine sirens echoing from the streets below. Once, late at night when she'd gone into the kitchen for a glass of milk, she found Boris sitting in his nightclothes, wearing his slippers. She realized it was his habit to sit, just sit, in his armchair in the corner of the vast living room. When, one night, she asked him why, he told her that even though he was here in New York, his mind was far away at another home, where his mother stood at the black stove stirring chicken soup in a giant steel pot. His father would walk in the door, tired from a day of haggling with customers at the fruit store, a twin brother and a sister quietly doing their homework at the kitchen table. This was the family that occupied his thoughts in the utopian land of America. Only once did he confess the reason to her, since he was not the kind of man who could usually put voice to his thoughts, that the day he headed for his new home with pockets filled with gold and promise was when he left something far more precious behind, now buried forever in the ashes.

These thoughts kept Boris awake at night, and it was why as daylight crept into the room, he could center his mind only on family, his new family, and the promise of what still could be. And it was also why Esther, his princess among princes, knew that she could ask this one favor of her father, and that he would say yes.

She didn't tell him the real reason she wanted to attend English language school, though. He had never trusted boys, never known one who had good intentions, either for business or when it came to relationships. He was obstinate when her mother would stand at his desk, hands on hips as he tallied a list of numbers, and pleaded with him to allow the girl a few hours to have her hair fixed at the beauty shop or, even worse, attend a dance with friends; and without raising his eyes from the paper, he would speak, keeping his voice low and steady, "I am busy now, Sally. Do not bother me with such nonsense." And with that, the subject was closed.

So when Esther approached him just as he was opening the blinds in the office and called him by the familiar pet name she had used from babyhood, he turned toward her.

"Papou, I have been thinking about the business. You know that I am the one who is meeting with our salesmen or tenants, and of late, I have become ashamed."

He looked at his one daughter as she stood before him, wearing a red-and-white-checked gingham dress, her reddish-brown hair throwing off sparks of sunlight.

"You—ashamed? You have nothing to be ashamed for. Who said that to you?"

She came to him, placed her long white fingers on his shoulder.

"Oh, no, Papou. No one has said a thing to me. But it is only what I feel when I am speaking to people. My English, it is okay, I suppose, but sometimes the words are confusing. Sometimes I feel as if I am coming from a different planet when I speak, from Mars and not Poland. Only yesterday Mrs. Ekstein had to explain the word *exchange* to me, and when I meant to say *mortgage*, by mistake I said the *t*, which should be silent. I feel so stupid!"

"Don't be such a silly girl! Money talks better than words," Boris answered, turning back toward the window.

"I can't help it, Papou. It is how I feel. Besides, would it not be better for the business if I could speak the right way, not look like such a greenhorn?" At the word and all its implications, he turned toward her quickly. A scowl that all too rapidly, she knew, could morph into anger, dominated his face. She pressed on.

"And so, I have a question to ask you. My friend Sophie, you've heard me speak of her? She has told me about a class she is taking where I can go to learn English. They have only just begun the sessions, and it would not be too late. It is at the high school on Thirty-Third, and since the classes are given at night, I will not be taking time from the business at all. Oh, Papou, it would make me feel so much better if I could, so *happy!*"

Boris gazed at her, taking in her young face, her hopeful eyes, still feeling the delicate touch of her hand on his shirt. The sun was full on her face now, lighting up her cheeks, which still carried the red glow she'd had even as a toddler. Her floral perfume enveloped him, lulling Boris again with its hypnotic fragrance. How could he deny her anything?

He was a soda bottler. An anonymous job, just another cog in the complex workings of the city. But somehow when he read his essay, speaking of his meager occupation, it was with the authority of a mayor, the confidence of a lion tamer. She had not meant to applaud when he finished, but the momentary silence that followed seemed somehow too sad, too empty. She simply had filled it and was surprised to hear that hers were the only hands clapping.

Esther was even more surprised when he approached her after class. At first, when she heard his voice so close to her ear, she thought the floor had somehow fallen away, but she soon heard her own words, apologetic, released from her throat. And then she told him the lie as easily as if she had lived it. As she spoke, his eyes, his dark olive eyes, even the sweet little dimple in the middle of his chin, never left her. When she finally entered the passenger side of the large Oldsmobile, its lights sparkling in the rain, she answered her father's questions mechanically. But her mind, her heart, remained in Jacob's gaze. And when she stared out the window at the streets of Manhattan as they drove past familiar storefronts, shut now, the stray cats rubbing their bodies against the concrete walls of alleys, the moon hidden beneath a violet sky, Esther could see only a shaft of light, and in it, the face of a boy and the promise of a thousand days.

FOUR

Zalman, 1953

Zalman's hand shook as he tore open the telegram. Although he was the first to admit that he was still naive about this modern means of communication, he understood enough to know that telegrams meant bad news. The first thing that his eyes fixed upon was the name—*Jacob*—and his heart beat faster. He read the short document again just to make sure. Zalman wiped beads of sweat off his brow as relief washed over him.

Married! His good friend would be married in the fall to a girl he had met just five months earlier. And he wanted Zalman to stand beneath the chuppah with him as his best man. Well, of course! At the same time that a sense of elation lifted the young man's spirits, he could not help but feel a gnawing apprehension, because there was something more to the letter. *We will talk.* Zalman knew the portent of these words. *We will talk.* The two had had plenty of conversations, first in person, then by letter. Innumerable discussions. The subject was always the same. Jacob wanted his friend to join him in New York. He was lonely for a *landsman*, one of his own. Jacob needed his advice, his encouragement, but most of all, his listening ear. Since their first meeting in the hayloft of dear Frau Blanc's barn, he had learned little of

Jacob's former life, but Zalman realized that for Jacob, he had become a touchstone, a necessary connection to a past that would forever bind the two.

He left the telegram on the top of the small wooden dresser, resolving to handle the matter later. He stood by the window and stared out at the wide spaces buoyed by the tall blades of wheat-color grass, now fragile, as if their backs were on the verge of breaking. The sun, promising a bright winter day, remained high in the sky. Soon, he knew, shards of light would be flashing through the grayness, and the rooster, flapping its wings in readiness for the day, would begin its insistent call.

Zalman reached into his closet, retrieved his muddy rubber boots, and pulled them over his stockinged feet. He wiggled his toes wrapped in the heavy wool socks he had been given back in Europe, and relished the warmth, if only temporary, before he pushed his arms through the sleeves of his heavy coat, also made of sturdy wool, and ventured out into the frigid air. He buttoned carefully over the layers—thermal polo, blue plaid shirt—as he missed his old sweater knitted with tight loops, torn now, and braced himself for the smack of winter in early March. And even now, as he set out on a day when his mind would be occupied by milking, feeding the chicks, even now, he remembered. It was like a virus in his brain, some days lying dormant, others, flaring up, consuming him like a fire. And no matter how many times Zalman reminded himself that today his bones were warmed by a coat, his belly filled daily with thick oatmeal and hot coffee that embraced his insides like a lover, no matter how many times he repeated to himself how lucky he was to be here in Minnesota, alive, still Zalman could not forget. And the fear haunted his movements in the daylight hours, terrorizing him at night.

Zalman placed his trembling hand on the knob of the door and squinted up into the sun before stepping out onto the porch. He could not help but marvel at the row of neat corrals that housed sixteen Guernsey cows waiting for their troughs to be filled, the chickens, fat and eager, already scratching the ground that lay dormant, waiting for the rows of corn that would grow tall and ripe until ready for the farmer's hand.

A day of milking would usually bring about four gallons per cow, and if he were lucky, perhaps he would get to drive the wagon with its special produce of milk and eggs to town later that afternoon. But first he would have to check on the newly hatched chicks in the barn; yellow and soft, they would burrow into the palm of his hand, and Zalman wondered at these moments if this was what it felt like to enter heaven.

He gulped, pushing back a recollection, and belched the bromide he had taken last night for one of the headaches he'd sometimes had since leaving the old country. By the time Zalman had ten squirts of milk in the tin pail, others had joined him—the farmer's two sons, both frail looking, with unkempt black beards and wire-rimmed glasses, looking more like yeshiva students than farmhands. Within minutes, two more came, survivors like himself, hauling large bales of hay, raking it, readying the feast for the cows while the steady streams of milk against metal kept beat as the roar of a wind banged against the shutters of the farmhouse. Sometimes, only sometimes, Zalman thought about engaging the others, also from Polish towns near the woods, but when he looked at their faces, intent on the hauling, the feeding, the daily chores demanded by a farmer's life, their eyes downcast with another secret preoccupation, he thought better of it.

By 8:00 a.m., the cows had begun to grow drowsy, their heavy lids drooping. The milking and feed work done, the men walked out into the open, breathing the air in huge gulps as if it were water, and led the animals to pasture.

The men then trudged back, not toward the rectangular building that held their small lodgings but to the farmer's house, where a breakfast of bubbling-hot oatmeal and fried eggs already plated by the farmer's wife was waiting on the dining table. Looking at the building with his father's eye, Zalman guessed it had taken no more than three months to construct the gray ranch house with its flat roof and simple porch. Before stepping up onto the porch, Zalman and a couple of the men dug into their deep pockets for unfiltered cigarettes and watched as the smoke drifted up against the blue sky. If Zalman ever gave it much thought, he would acknowledge that this was his favorite part of the day.

He knew that there were billions of people crowded into this world, which was becoming smaller by the minute. He knew that somewhere people were packed into rattling subway cars on the way to their jobs in the great metropolis, others standing chest to chest in foul-smelling cars meant for cattle. He knew in this world there were lines of elaborately coiffed ladies wearing ermine-lined coats, waiting to be served at fancy department stores; others, bare skinned, faces striped with fear, waiting for the executioner's ax. He knew these things, but as Zalman stood under a smiling sky, taking the smoke deep into his lungs, he tried to forget all that. In those few moments there was no one else in the world but him and the now-pink sky and the gentle touch of a breeze as miles of grass swayed as far as the eye could see. Zalman was at peace.

He stamped the dirt from his feet before entering the house and took his place at the table to the right of the farmer and his two sons just as the older man was reaching for a second helping of the oatmeal, which sat in two big bowls at the center of the table. He gave Zalman a nod as the young man took up his fork.

Rabbi Isaac Rozenstein, the dairy and chicken farmer who'd purchased the land with loans obtained from the Jewish Agricultural Society in 1940, had a round face framed by a dark beard that disguised an amiable smile. The rabbi, his wife, Golda, and their four children had arrived from Poland prior to the Warsaw Ghetto Uprising, thanks to the sponsorship of an American-born cousin living in Illinois. With only the clothes on his back and a few meager pennies in his pocket, Isaac had listened attentively in the tiny apartment of the Chicago tenement where his cousin and their family of five lived, as he learned of a man, a German-Jewish philanthropist, Baron Maurice de Hirsch, who was helping the Jews from Eastern Europe escape their oppressive history of antisemitism and worse, and settle them on farms throughout New Jersey, Delaware, Florida, and other states. Although the cousin himself asserted that he was too tired and disinterested for such a venture, perhaps Isaac could find his fortune through the generosity of Hirsch's society? Even though he had no experience running a farm, having never so much as seen a cow in his lifetime, Isaac jumped at the chance. And when he professed a desire to get as far away from the metropolis with its smog, crowded tenements, and general indifference, he soon found himself on more open fields, where not car horns or rattling dump trucks but the call of a rooster at daybreak and the melodic lowing of cows could be heard penetrating the air.

Since Jacob already had a sponsor living in Brooklyn, Zalman knew he would have to make his own way. So, at the suggestion of a fellow survivor he had met in a displacement camp, he became one of eighty thousand Jewish immigrants who entered the United States. Like Isaac, his benefactor, Zalman eschewed the cities and opted for the place closest to earth and sky. And although farming was as antithetical to Jewish mentality as viewing stars in the middle of the day, Zalman believed that this was a place where he would be needed. He discovered that there was a demand for farmwork in the States since large amounts of economic aid were being used to subsidize desperately needed exports to Europe. Yes, that was where he would begin his new life as an American.

During their months together in a displacement camp, and later as they shared an apartment in Berlin, Jacob had tried persuading, cajoling, and even begging his friend to join him in New York, but his pleas had had no effect. Even then, Jacob had helped Zalman get a job working next to him stacking boxes in one of several groceries that had been established after the war. Each knew that they would never make their fortune in a city filled only with the dust of memories. And it was Jacob, the more ambitious of the two, who would tell Zalman about the uncle he had living in New York, and the promise of America. Still,

Zalman was determined to forge his own path, and even though he owed Jacob his life, he knew that since the war's end, he had relied on him for too long. Instead, the cold vast lands of Minnesota would be where he would plow his own future.

"I hope this is to your liking, Zalman." The voice was soft, the words spoken in Yiddish.

He turned from his plate, his eyes meeting the blue knit sweater, the tear at the neck neatly patched, held up proudly by Miriam, the farmer's eldest daughter. He swallowed the last bit of toast and surveyed the garment, casting his eyes from neck to hem, lingering at the place where a barely distinguishable patch in just the exact shade of corn-flower blue to match the rest of the wool had been sewn. His eyes rested finally on her face, where two dots of red were slowly materializing on the pale cheeks.

"It's perfect!" he proclaimed in the old language, and watched as her lips took the form of a smile. "You know you really didn't need to do this. It would have served just as well with a little hole."

"You couldn't wear it like that. And besides, I enjoy sewing. It is my favorite pastime. I'll just leave it on this chair for when you are finished with your meal."

The girl bent down and placed the sweater neatly over the back of a side chair, her long dark hair, so long and thick, in fact, that, falling momentarily over the garment, it fairly covered it. She swept it back swiftly with one hand and disappeared into a bedroom off the hall.

A few minutes later, her sister, Anna, appeared carrying a plat-ter filled with freshly baked honey and poppy seed muffins, which reminded Zalman of the treats he used to relish back home as a boy. Unlike her sister, Anna closely resembled her mother. Tall and sturdy, she carried herself with a certain awkwardness, as if unsure how to navigate her bulk. Her hair, light brown with tight curls, topped a face that faintly looked like the work of an amateur sculptor, upturned nose slightly askew, a brow that protruded over owlish eyes. Naturally shy among the brutish strangers who sat silently devouring their meals as if they were racing against the dusk, she dropped the sweets on the table with a clatter and ran out of the room.

Zalman allowed himself only one of the poppy seed muffins. He couldn't risk another button off his coat. But then again, the possibility might offer him another encounter with the farmer's eldest daughter. He bit into the soft cake, his nostrils filling with the distinct aroma of the poppy seeds.

He turned to Rozenstein, who was already wiping the cake crumbs from his chin, a signal for the others that it was time to go back to work.

"Do you think we have met our quota for the eggs this week?" he asked, again in Yiddish. It was a silly question, of little substance or purpose, but Zalman felt compelled to fill the silence. Ever since he had found himself a free man, Zalman had developed a fear of the quiet, even solitude. Perhaps now, he guessed, the fear had turned into a phobia hatched in the pirates' room and the days when terror had replaced the sound of his own voice. And here, on this land in rural Minnesota, where he should feel closest to God Himself, there were times when sitting among his countrymen, each mulling over his own dark past, Zalman felt more terrified than ever.

"I'm sure we will meet that quota, and milk, too, thanks to the blessing of you fine men," he said in English, placing his hand on Zalman's shoulder and rising. As the men secured their coats, Zalman carefully removed the blue sweater from the chair and buttoned on the extra layers. As the screen door screeched plaintively behind him, he resolved to send Jacob his answer in the morning.

FIVE

Jacob

It was Uncle Abraham and Aunt Rose who walked Jacob down the aisle toward the chuppah. After each planted a kiss on his cheek, he stepped up on the bimah and turned. There were fewer than one hundred already seated, dressed in their finest; some remembered the day when they, too, had clasped hands and shared the cup of red wine, others dreaming of the moment when a holy bond, a sacred promise, would be shared. When Jacob turned to face the guests, he saw a multitude of beaming faces, each one like the other.

But he had little time to take heed of the guests, men who would soon lift the celebratory couple, women and girls who had removed their shoes as they joined in the joyous hora, because now she appeared before him. Jacob had heard others tell of that moment when you first saw her on the marriage day, the woman who would become your wife. And yet the words of his married friends had failed somehow to capture the feeling that overcame him.

Her parents, Boris and Sally, their arms linked with their child's, seemed to melt into the crowd of onlookers until Esther was the only one Jacob saw. She was clothed in streams of white lace, ruffles gathered at the cuffs and neck. Her face was hidden by a veil, and yet her eyes, forever an azure blue, glimmered like two stars beneath. The veil, which sprouted from a crown of rhinestones and tulle, fell back like a cloak so that when she walked, or rather glided toward him, it was with the regal air of a princess.

A tap on his shoulder and Jacob woke as if from a dream, remembering that he needed to move his legs toward her now, that indeed she was not an ethereal being, something of another world, but his Esther, the girl he was about to marry.

The words that united the two, the customary sweet red wine, the seven brachas, the prayers for a happy future, the ring placed on her forefinger, the breaking of the glass. And then the cheers that erupted, shattering the solemnity of the occasion, seemed mechanical, forgettable, even. Clasping her hand, he sensed the smallness of it, the delicacy of her skin. It was just as it had been that first time, and Jacob felt as if he had awakened from an exceptionally long sleep. As if now, after all the years that had come before, his life was only just beginning. And when he looked into her blue eyes, which were now shining with tears, he knew that she, too, felt the same.

Hours later, as he stood off by himself to take another breath before resuming the raucous dancing, a slap on the back startled him.

"So, my friend, how does it feel to be a married man?"

Zalman smiled up at him, his face rosy with drink and sweat.

"And I could ask the same of you? How does it feel to be a *best* man?"

"Not as good as you will feel tonight!" Zalman joked, pulling out a chair for Jacob who, dizzy with the frenetic pace of the klezmer band, had begun to rock on his heels.

Jacob was glad finally to be free of the kittel. He was starting to feel suffocated by the marriage coat, his jacket, and fancy black bow tie. He wiped his brow with a handkerchief. Jacob could not recall dancing this much in his life, ever. There was one dance of sorts with his new wife, though neither felt the touch of the other. Lifted aloft by a half dozen men, Esther and Jacob held on to the corner of a skimpy white cloth that separated them as they laughed, consumed with the absurdity of it all. In a few hours' time, he knew he would trace the curves of her long neck, sense the sweep of her brown hair loosened against his cheek, and his body shivered now with anticipation. Within the fuzz that his mind had become, he could hear Zalman speaking in their native Polish again.

"I swear, Yaacov, never have I seen such a thing. Goblets of ruby-red wine, roast beef dripping in its juices, and so many dancers! All this festivity—it is as if something has been waiting all this time, after so many troubles, so many tears, just waiting to explode to the surface. And we deserve it, finally. Yaacov, don't we deserve it after so long?"

Jacob remained silent and poured himself yet another glass of wine. He did not want to think about the past, pushing down his memories, that despair, the latent anger. Not today, he thought. Maybe not ever.

Zalman was talking again, an endless stream of words. Jacob needed to cleanse his mind. Perhaps another sip of wine.

"So different," he was saying. "The life of a farmer is so different than the way things are here. We move slower; even the animals are not so rushed. Not that I am not busy, oh, no—there is plenty to do, milking the cows, collecting the eggs, hoeing, and harvesting. I tell you, even the food tastes more ba-tampte, the sleep deeper. Next time, you and your pretty wife must come visit me in Minnesota. I am quite certain that Rozenstein will welcome you both."

Jacob wiped his brow again. Would Zalman ever stop talking? He'd have to have a serious conversation with his friend later. But not now. Where was Esther? The music had, finally, blessedly, stopped playing for more than half an hour, and the only sound was the click of utensils or guests biting into their steak or salmon, murmured voices confiding, expounding, occasionally the burst of raucous laughter. Jacob sat alone at the center of the long dais. Finally, Esther collapsed into the gold-painted chair next to him, her cheeks rosy from all the dancing.

He took her hand in his. It was okay; it was expected that the women would claim her for every hora. Tonight she would be his and his alone.

Sometime between the main course and the cutting of the cake, Boris came over to him. Jacob, who along with Esther was busy thanking guests, noticed his father-in-law only after several minutes. He turned in surprise and greeted the older man, who nodded and shifted his feet as if waiting for Jacob to address him.

His bow tie, Jacob noticed, remained impeccably tied throughout the evening, no wrinkle in his rented tuxedo. The only sign, in fact, that Boris had partaken in a night of revelry was the traditional royal-blue kippah that usually hugged the exact center of his balding head and was now slightly askew. After what seemed like an eternity, Boris spoke, but he directed his question to Esther.

"Would you mind, my dear, if I steal your husband away for only a few minutes?"

"Please, Papou, go right ahead," she said, and laughed as she turned to say goodbye to a woman whose bracelets clanged noisily as she wrapped her arms around the bride.

Jacob wasn't sure if it was a kindly benefactor or the executioner he was following into the vestibule off the reception area. He'd had only one verbal exchange with the short, stocky landlord since meeting Esther, and that was some months ago when he'd asked for her hand in marriage. Even then Boris's only response had been a curt yes, and with a nod of the head and a quick handshake, the affair had been done. But now Jacob wondered as he accepted a cigarette from his father-in-law, What could he possibly want to speak to him about? Perhaps he realized the marriage to a man of no means and a background that remained for the most part a mystery had all been a mistake.

"There is a matter that I've thought about for some time," he began in faltering English, "and it is something we need to talk about today. I'm sorry to have pulled you out of your own wedding, but now I think is the best time." Boris stopped to inhale the smoke from his cigarette.

"It's a matter of business, really, that I wish to speak to you about," he continued, "and I have to tell you frankly that I'm not happy about your prospects and your ability to care for my daughter. You must know that Esther is a very special girl, not only beautiful, but a person of immense talents in business, math, and language. So how could I possibly let her make a home with a bottle stacker?"

Before Jacob could open his mouth to speak, though, Boris stopped him, clenching his shoulder with his beefy hand.

"And that is why I'm asking you today, no, insisting, really, that you come into the real estate business, where you'll learn from me and from Esther how to work hard and, most important, how to make money. Now you are family, and besides, my own two sons seem to have little interest in the business." He finished, the last words catching in his throat, the only sign of emotion Jacob had witnessed.

With Boris's hand still fastened to his shoulder, Jacob began to feel faint, a reaction somewhat akin to the moment Esther had accepted his proposal of marriage. It was some time before he could find the words.

"I accept your proposal."

With his customary nod, Boris released his hold on the young man's shoulder, leaving him standing in the smoky vestibule, cigarette dangling from his fingers. It was difficult to move as the clamor faded and terror filled his heart. It was the same way Jacob had felt that first night alone in the barn. Boris had just offered him a prize, yet it was a prize clothed in insults. Perhaps he was just a bottle stacker and incapable of anything more, unworthy of Esther. But did he have any choice? If he were to reach any of his dreams, he had to keep going. He had to take this chance.

Jacob waited for the icy paralysis to seep from his feet before walking back inside and pulling out the seat beside his bride. The final strains of music were dying down, the din of congratulatory voices had begun to quiet, and it was not until he walked out into the star-filled night that Jacob realized he had forgotten to say thank you.

SIX

Esther

They held hands for an exceptionally long time, and finally, just before daylight shimmied quietly into the room, he fell asleep. But Esther could not. Such a strange man, she thought, stroking his splayed fingers lightly. After exploring each other's bodies in the way of first-time lovers, sensitive, curious, then ravenous, almost as if they were crawling into each other's souls, they lay in bed and talked. And after what seemed like hours but had been only minutes, he began to cry. Pouring his heart into hers, Jacob revealed nothing, nothing about his life before his world fell apart, and she couldn't understand why he had this sudden burst of emotion.

He told her about her father's generous offer, and even though she had guessed the reason he had taken Jacob aside, she was touched by how appreciative, how overwhelmed Jacob appeared. Something told her there would be more to come, for her father, like a clever poker player, was not one to show his hand too soon. A small worry emerged that Jacob, being proud, as most young men are, would reject those gifts when they were offered, but she let her concern slide off her, just as Jacob earlier had slid the tips of his fingers down her arms, heightening her desire. Still, she could not quite figure out the crying, and she felt helpless in the throes of it. At first she thought it might have been about his parents and the void he was feeling on this day in particular. Yet Jacob had never spoken of them with a snippet of emotion, only telling her bluntly that they had died in the war. Maybe he was just nervous, but how was it that his insecurities could reach such hysteria?

She held him in her arms, wiped the tears from his hot cheeks, and kissed the top of his head. She watched him sleep for many minutes before finally laying her own head on the hotel's satin pillow. The sudden emotion hadn't frightened her; on the contrary, she found it endearing. Still, Esther wondered, what new pieces in the puzzle that was Jacob would emerge tomorrow?

~

The way Sally fussed over the wedding and the sumptuous breakfast that followed the next day, one would have thought that the mother and not the daughter were getting married. In truth, Esther admitted that her mother had not had much of a wedding: a speedy writing of the ketubah, or marriage certificate, a brief ceremony in the local shul with only immediate members of the family present, and then the resumption of life as usual, with Boris occupying the office next to his father while Sally helped out in a nursery nearby. Soon enough, the babies came for her, and the first, the only, clear memory Esther had of her mother was of her standing behind her, plaiting her long hair into a thick brown braid, and later, admonishing her younger brothers for not washing their hands before coming to the table. Of course, she delighted in helping her mother with the cooking and the tasting of the cholent, one of her favorites, always resplendent with tender beef, thick potatoes, and lima beans, each ingredient Esther could not help but sample during the process. The move to America had been hard on her mother, what with the difficulties of a new language and learning how to navigate New York's bustling sidewalks and fast-moving buses.

Yes, Sally deserved this celebration, Esther thought. Perhaps more than Esther herself.

Esther stood by the head of the table next to a three-tiered stand of sterling silver on which chocolate sandwich cookies and mini slices of sponge and honey and apple cakes sat glowing, waiting for an eager hand. On each of the six round tables reserved for the guests who had spent the night, there were already platters of salty herring, hard-boiled eggs, and waves of farmer's cheese and yellow American on slabs of thick black bread.

Sally, dressed in a hot-pink-and-yellow caftan, drifted over to her daughter and hugged her so tightly the girl feared she might faint. Sally then kissed her hard on the cheek, her Helena Rubinstein lipstick leaving a bright-pink imprint that Esther casually wiped away with the back of her hand.

"The kallah! The kallah is here!" she enthused, using the Yiddish word for "bride." And as she surveyed Esther with a keen eye, she said, "What a beautiful outfit you have on. You look like a princess!" Esther smoothed the folds of her ivory wool suit and patted the large rabbit's-fur button at her neck.

"Mama, how could I not look fine? You're the one who checked all the Spiegel's catalogs, insisting I wear only white!" She laughed, but Sally's smiling face suddenly shifted to a picture of concern.

"Oh, my dear child, I have forgotten. Your first night as a married woman, your first night with a man. How are you this morning? I mean, are you well?"

Esther laughed again.

"Yes, Mama, I'm well. In fact, I feel more than well!"

Sally sighed, relieved, and released the hold on her child.

"That's good. Now where is that husband of yours?"

Jacob and Zalman were standing by a large coffee urn, balancing white-and-gold china cups on matching saucers as they waited for the coffee to brew. The two, it appeared, were engaged in animated conversation, Zalman shaking his head and shuffling his feet. Jacob prodded Zalman's chest with his forefinger. Fortunately, Esther thought, he seemed to show no sign of last night's anxiety. Noticing her out of the corner of his eye, Jacob brightened and beckoned her to him.

Esther walked over to the two men, loving the way Jacob wound his arm around her waist.

"Have you met my beautiful wife?" he said, beaming, as he swept the palm of his hand over the length of her, from the top of her head to her feet, as if she were the rarest of diamonds. In truth, she was enjoying this.

"Yes, my good friend; in fact, I have met her a number of times," Zalman answered, seeming to forget the heated exchange the two had had just a moment earlier.

Esther lightly touched the fur button at her neck.

"Please, why don't you two take your coffee and have a seat?" she said, and, winking at Jacob, "I see there are even a couple of bottles of champagne on our table."

Zalman looked at Jacob quizzically, and spontaneously each placed the dainty cup and saucer on the table, substituting them for the flute-shaped crystal.

Two hours later, after the last cloth napkin had been folded and the tables scrupulously wiped clean by the white-jacketed busboys, Esther and her new husband said loving farewells to her parents and Uncle Abraham and Aunt Rose, who looked small and uncomfortable in their winter coats, each one holding a large paper shopping bag filled to the brim with bagels and fishes, not to mention the cold victuals from the night before. Esther's brother Menashe motioned for the two to follow him to the car outside, where he would be escorting them back to their apartment in Brooklyn.

Esther stood by and watched as her father opened his arms wide so that Jacob could fall into his warm embrace. How odd but how wonderful, she thought, as she realized that Jacob, in a matter of hours, had become one of their own—family. As the young couple held hands in the elevator on the way back up to their suite, a lump formed in Esther's throat. A significant part of her life had just come to an end.

Of course, rationally, she knew that she wasn't taking a final leave of her mama and papa. She'd be seeing them again in six short days when the couple returned home from their honeymoon in Niagara Falls. After that, Jacob would join her in the bedroom of her family's spacious apartment, at least for now.

Still, an emptiness occupied a space in her heart. She was about to embark on a new and mysterious chapter of her life when all else that she had known was falling away like leaves that had been clinging to a tree before the snow. But as she packed the white nylon lingerie set into her suitcase and caught a reflection of Jacob's profile in the mirror, she reasoned that endings also mean beginnings, the business of building a future, a new life. After that, the emptiness in her heart slipped slowly away like a final leaf, and she tried not to think of it again.

SEVEN

Jacob

In the end, he couldn't persuade him to stay. No matter how much Jacob argued, cajoled, and even pleaded with him, Zalman remained obstinate, determined to go back to the farm in Minnesota. At first Jacob was frustrated. He even encouraged Esther to convince him, for he knew Zalman had developed a certain fondness for his wife, whom Zalman now looked upon as a sister. But no matter how much Esther smiled or batted her long auburn lashes as she spoke to him in soothing tones, Zalman would not budge. He simply grinned again, calling Jacob a "lucky man" to have such a wife.

Had the farmer's affection for Zalman, the promise of security, so changed him that he had found it difficult to turn away? Or perhaps it was the quiet country charm of the farmer's daughter that drew him back. Ultimately, Jacob concluded that it was none of these things, but that Zalman had found a home where he was as much a part of the land as the cows, the willow trees, the fields of growing corn.

As Jacob placed his arms around the man who had become more of a brother to him than his own had been, he tried not to let Zalman see the tears that were forming in his eyes. Adjusting the brim of his hat, he shook Zalman's hand one last time before getting into the new blue Ford sedan, a gift from his father-in-law, and driving north with his new bride.

"Best of luck to you and Esther. May you both have a life filled with mazel, many blessings. And don't forget to write! I look forward to your letters," Zalman said, this time in English, as he, too, averted his eyes.

"You too. You don't forget either. And all the best," replied Jacob as he settled into the driver's seat and locked the door just as an icy wind had picked up.

Neither man, however, was true to his word. It would be more than a year before Jacob would hear from Zalman. Perhaps it was because both had become too busy—Zalman with the daily tasks of keeping the farm sustainable, and Jacob with learning the business of real estate. Or maybe, as is usually the case with spans of distance and time, each had so much to say that neither was willing to expend the effort, and so said nothing.

Living with his in-laws and studying the numbers, the records, the contracts of real estate, while daunting at first, proved to be satisfying for Jacob. He enjoyed the stability of a home, his clothes laundered, his eggs prepared just the way he liked, and as he assumed more and more responsibilities at EMI Realty, he had come to realize that he was no longer standing at the door looking in, but rather a man, an important man, who was now part of the world he craved. Weekly, he would travel to see Aunt Rose and Uncle Abraham, noticing their hands becoming more gnarled, their backs more stooped with each visit. Yet, without exception, the smiles that flashed across their faces and momentarily shaved away the years appeared each time he would walk through the door. And since the day Jacob had left the seltzer-bottling company and his job of filling, sorting, and stacking, he hadn't missed it. Not one bit.

Although Jacob was content with his new life, paradoxically, the yearning, as if there was something more ahead, never left him. He liked his tasks, even if he had to dress up in a gray pinstriped suit and red tie for meetings with clients. He found himself waking, despite the alarm clock's shrill ring, ten minutes earlier each day, and as he placed his head on the pillow each evening, numbers and names and new ventures would float through his mind, directionless, like blackbirds. Jacob had a destination, though, and even if he couldn't quite formulate how he would arrive there or what it was, he knew that everything, even the terrors in his life, had conspired just so he could reach that moment. And something told him it was coming very soon.

After only a month of married life, Jacob also knew he had made a good choice in Esther, who was becoming more loving, more devoted to him with each day. And if it were possible, also more beautiful. Her chestnut hair, which had grown longer, sparkled as sun seeped through the windows in the early morning, and her eyes seemed more brilliant. But maybe, he concluded, that was just the way it was when women were in love.

Mornings Jacob would leave the city apartment with Esther and Boris, their bellies full of french toast slathered with strawberry jelly, hot coffee, and, for Esther, her rose tea. Each carried an attaché case with a dozen papers and pens along with lunch: an apple and bologna sandwiches for father and daughter, liverwurst with an occasional Hostess Twinkie for Jacob. Esther was a patient teacher, explaining the nature of the documents, tax forms, even stock market fluctuations. Jacob was a quick and avid learner. But over the course of a month, he noticed a peculiar thing. As he assimilated more knowledge, Esther grew quieter, less animated. The more papers she placed on his desk, the cleaner hers had become; the more tenants and associates he saw, the fewer work calls Esther assumed. As he grew fat with each new duty, with the knowledge, Esther had seemed to seep away, as if her brain had become a sieve. She no longer dressed for work, preferring to wear pedal pushers and to tie her hair with a bow just like one of the teenagers who huddled together on street corners. One morning, Esther decided not to get up for work.

Adjusting his tie in the mirror, Jacob approached her, concerned.

"Are you ill, my dear? Is that why you're still in bed?"

Esther opened one eye from beneath the covers.

"Not ill," she mumbled, her mind still saturated by sleep. Jacob walked over to the side of the bed.

"Then what's wrong?"

Rubbing her eyes now, she pushed off the yellow-and-gray blanket Jacob had brought from home and sat up. Jacob relaxed when he saw the familiar broad smile come to her face.

"Nothing is wrong, my love. Nothing at all. It's just that it's time for me to stop working, that's all. Your time to take on the business, to be my father's right-hand man. After all, my brothers will be leaving within a year's time, and Papou will need you."

"And what about you? I never meant to take your place." He knitted his eyebrows together, stared into her eyes.

Esther's face softened.

"Me? There is nothing I want more than to be your wife, to make you a home one day, to raise our children. Besides, I never much liked the business, anyway. Now come give me a kiss goodbye."

Jacob hesitated for only a second, searching her eyes before leaning in. He had a feeling that his wife wasn't being entirely truthful. She had never shown any sign that she was growing weary of the business; in fact, she was proud of the way she dealt with clients, enjoyed teaching him the ins and outs of real estate. But he had no time to deliberate the issue. He had a 9:00 a.m. meeting and he couldn't be late. He would have to accept her words for what they were. He preferred to think of himself as a lucky man to have such a wife. A lucky man, indeed.

Life, like the ticking of a clock, settled into an orderly beat. After the couple had lived together for nearly a year, the apartment down the hall became available, and the two happily began to set up a place they could finally call their own. Jacob's pride prevented him from accepting Boris's offer of living rent-free, and he used his now-substantial earnings to finance the two-bedroom habitat. Most days, Esther and her mother spent their time perusing the wholesale warehouses for furniture. Although Esther had never fancied herself much of a shopper, her mother's ardor for the task proved infectious, and the two set out on these missions with a glee and abandon Jacob had never before witnessed, nor could comprehend. One day, the two purchased a new round table with a Formica top for the kitchen; the following week, the small white refrigerator had been replaced by a larger-size appliance that defrosted automatically; and the week after that, Jacob came home to find Esther seated on a new turquoise silk couch that ran across the length of the wall, watching *The Adventures of Ozzie and Harriet* on a new thirty-six-inch Magnavox. Esther had also insisted that her beloved piano be handled by professional piano movers. At first, Jacob could not quite understand the need for such an extra expense. People whose job it was to move musical instruments?

One evening Jacob, looking slightly weathered from a long day's work, came home to find Esther pinning the last fabric panel over the small window in the kitchen, which overlooked the alley down below. She turned slightly, gazing over her shoulder as he walked in. Jacob was trying to balance his black leather attaché case, rolled newspaper, metal thermos, and, nestled in the crook of his arm, a stack of mail he had picked up from the locked mailbox in the lobby. He threw his burden onto the new kitchen table, then tried to make a one-handed catch of the thermos as it rolled to the edge. He was not in time, and before Esther could react, the vessel had fallen off the table, sending a mocha-color stream across Esther's shiny white linoleum.

"Whoops!" was all Jacob could manage as he stopped to grab the now-empty thermos while Esther rushed off the stool and began searching for a rag in the cabinet beneath the sink.

After removing his bowler and cotton jacket and hanging them up in the hall closet, Jacob returned to the kitchen and, as he encircled his wife's waist, he felt a sudden sense of déjà vu. Was this a memory or just a long-buried dream? The feeling passed, and he sprinkled her slender neck with tiny kisses.

"What would I do without you, my star?"

Esther stifled a laugh at his use of a new nickname he had adopted for her. She seemed to rather like this shortened, though mangled, version of her name, which he claimed was a metaphor for her blue eyes, "just like shining stars."

"You'd probably be an old and lonely bachelor, I bet," she said, pushing him away as she rinsed out the soggy remnant of a sheet that had been repurposed. Jacob went into the bedroom and changed into his tan short-sleeve shirt and a pair of beige khakis. When he returned, Esther was already ladling a large helping of steaming carrots to accompany the slices of meat loaf and boiled potatoes on his plate. He guessed there would be a refreshing dessert after the meal, a Jell-O and fruit mold left over from the night before, a recipe his wife had picked up from one of her housekeeping magazines. Jacob could not help but wonder what he would be eating if he had never met her. Maybe another salami sandwich, as he often had for dinner after a long day at the seltzer-bottling company. Along with a bag of potato chips. Esther was right. He would have been an old and lonely bachelor without her.

Both satiated and content after having had his dinner, Jacob began to feel his eyelids grow heavy, but he fought the pull toward sleep when he glanced at his watch and realized *Dragnet*, one of his favorites, was scheduled to come on the tube in five minutes. As he crossed into the living room, with his favorite chocolate-brown leather recliner in sight, Jacob's eye caught the stack of mail he had brought into the house before the fiasco with the thermos. Still standing, he picked it up, casually riffling through the bills and notices. A large official-looking envelope peeked out from the rest. It was addressed to Jacob only and had a government stamp on the back.

It was indeed a document, which at first he read quickly, and then more slowly a second time. As he did, a smile slowly seeped across his face until it seemed his cheeks could no longer contain it. He kept the words that would change his entire life to himself for a few minutes before calling Esther's name. Her yellow crinoline skirt lifted as she sprinted to his side.

"What is it? What's happened?" She leaned over, trying to make sense of the paper Jacob held in his trembling hand.

"It's from your father," he said, finally finding the words, "and it's a deed for a parcel of land in Brooklyn." The simple paper was beginning to feel like a fire in his hands.

She touched his arm lightly.

"I don't understand. What does it mean?" He looked at her face, her pale skin, her eyes a serene blue.

"It means a house, Esther. It means we can build our own house."

Jacob eased back into the brown leather recliner, but he didn't turn on the TV to watch his favorite show; instead, the couple sat talking, planning their future, for hours into the night. When they finally settled into their queen-size bed, their heads abuzz with their plans, their prospects, neither fell asleep until the soft edge of a sun could be seen rising over the city's gray skyscrapers. So it wasn't until late the next morning that Esther handed him the unopened letter she'd found next to the recliner on the plush green carpet. Jacob recognized the writing immediately. When he finished reading, he looked at Esther, tears forming in his eyes.

"Another big piece of news. Zalman is coming home."

EIGHT

Zalman

He remembered the story from all those years ago. It was something from the Bible. "King Solomon was not only the wisest king of all, but also one of the wealthiest. All that was the Euphrates River and then south in Egypt belonged to this great king. And even though he wasn't the eldest in his family, his father made sure that in spite of his closest advisers, and even Solomon's own mother, who conspired against him, Solomon would receive his due. And so it was that while still alive, David, the father, bequeathed the vast kingdom to his son. Having conquered his foes, Solomon went on to expand the borders of his kingdom west of the Euphrates, and it is said he owned twelve thousand horses with horsemen and fourteen hundred chariots, with colonies throughout Israel. Yet he did not remain content. He decided to take on the enormous task of rebuilding the Holy Temple with the help of Israelites and subordinate foreign nations. And what a structure it was! Stone and cedar, all overlaid with gold, housing elaborate decorations and tall vessels, a feast for the eyes! King Solomon went on to build his own palace, a citadel, a city wall. But there is nothing like the Holy Temple. And do you know how long it took Solomon to build that temple?"

Of course, Zalman already knew the answer. He had been asked the same question for so many years, and now, only a month after his return, he was listening to Jacob's story once again. But just to appease his friend, he shrugged and waited for the response.

"Seven years! Seven long years of building! Each stick of wood, each block of gold and metal, went into that temple! But I, no—*we*, we will build our castle in less than one!" And with that exclamation, Jacob would sit back in his armchair, put his two large hands together as if in prayer, and close his eyes. Zalman had no doubt that behind the eyelids Jacob was envisioning the home.

Once during the time of darkness, as they weaved tales in the hayloft, Zalman had asked him why he didn't tell more of his favored stories of King Solomon's life. The tale of how the ruler had settled an argument between two women who both claimed to be the mother of a baby. How Solomon proposed he slice the child in two to settle the discussion, and only when one woman gave up her claim to the baby to spare it from harm did he wisely determine who the real mother was. But with a wave of the hand, Jacob dismissed these and other tales of his hero as of little consequence compared to Solomon's other tangible achievement. Nor did he have any interest in talking about his namesake from the Bible, Jacob, who was not nearly as successful, or as commanding, as King Solomon.

"I wish my parents had given me another name," he declared that one time. "Jacob was the name of my mother's father, a thief and a swindler, an accountant of little merit who stole money from the glassmakers he worked for. He was not yet fifty when one evening on his way home from secretly filling his pockets at work, he encountered a couple of robbers who sliced him from neck to navel, leaving him bleeding in the street, his pockets turned inside out. I don't doubt that the crooks had some tip about this Jacob's underhanded dealings. Anyway, the point is that Solomon would have been a much better name."

Though Zalman was tempted to ask more about Jacob's family—he himself had let loose the details of his life, which flowed from him easily—something told him he should not push. So instead Zalman listened as Jacob finished his tale of Solomon still another time. He didn't mind it. Seeing the look of excitement sweep across his friend's face as he relaxed and placed his hands together gave Zalman a contented feeling as well.

Zalman hadn't planned for this: being here, in the stuffy Brooklyn apartment with the windows shut tightly and the drapes closed so that he couldn't see the face of the sun most mornings. The clattering of garbage cans, the blaring of horns in the street below instead of the nostalgic lowing of a cow, the rooster's insistent crow splitting the temperate air. He hadn't planned on it, but he hadn't planned on breaking his arm in two places, either, as he was making his way down from the hayloft where his shoe, still muddy from a rainfall the night before, seemed to have taken on a mind of its own, causing Zalman to go one way, his leg the other; and within a minute's time, he was six feet below on the straw- and dirt-covered ground, tasting the blood from a split lip instead of savoring the oatmeal and strawberries he had been craving only seconds earlier.

Broken in two places. The physical pain in his arm had seemed unendurable at times, the heavy immobile cast too constricting; all this, he knew, was to be expected. But Zalman had not planned for a different kind of pain—the pain of another loss. He thought he had become immune to it after the war and the iron door that had slammed down for good between himself and his family in death. At first it seemed like a hole in his heart, or a missing limb or a faded memory, and then there was a heaviness that took its place, and no matter how hard he tried to occupy his time with physical labor or engage in lighthearted conversation with the others at the farm, it was the heaviness, as if a quiet stone had settled deep inside his spirit, that never went away. And now there was the realization of yet another leave-taking, another loss.

He hadn't counted on it. He had endured fear, starvation, but how does anyone plan for an accident?

Finally, after an operation and two months when it became clear that he would no longer be useful on the farm, Zalman came to a sad realization. The farmer himself didn't want him to go, suggesting he conduct the business of the farm, the paperwork, driving the eggs and produce for sale to the market in town, but in the end his efforts proved useless. The farmer knew that Zalman's future prospects were no longer in Minnesota. As for Miriam, who did not plead or otherwise attempt to get him to change his mind, she stood quietly on the porch, shielding her eyes from the sun that last day in May, just before he set out for the train. He took her hand in his, the delicate fingers, their nails cut short, and held it for the first time, as if some romance had passed between the two, nothing but a promise, a hint of a future that could be, but now never would.

"I wish you great success," she said as he let go of her hand and, with his good arm, reached to touch the stitches on the collar of his blue sweater.

There was the long ride across the plains, the high grass and rambling hills and sky that opened to rain, oceans of rain in biblical proportions at dawn, and a silent darkness that painted the mountaintops in violet hues come evening. For Zalman, the days on board the train—the ride with its endless churning of wheels, and the tracks that seemed to move him forward toward eternity—began to converge into one long, dreary memory.

It was only when the doors to the car opened and he saw not the uniformed men waving truncheons, pulling back their barking dogs, but the faces of Jacob and Esther, who were waving now as they caught sight of him, that Zalman relaxed and thought maybe, just maybe, he could see a glimpse into his future.

~

As he sat in the back seat of the sedan, Zalman tried to focus on the scenes that unfolded before him as he stared out the window. People seemed to be rushing everywhere, mothers pulling their children along the street, an old man sweeping the sidewalk, throwing dust and litter up into the air, shopkeepers hurriedly closing their stores, the metal awnings slamming shut with a loud bang. And over all there was a muddy blackness that allowed only a sliver of moon to peek through the gathering clouds. This was the city life that he had chosen to escape, a life where daylight was something to be endured as men tied the laces of their fancy shoes and set off to work in stuffy offices, a place where the sun was just another star in a science book, the air and all of nature just another part of life, not the very reason for it.

But Zalman's thoughts were soon diverted as Esther's voice came floating to him from the front seat, where she sat next to Jacob. And with it, a unique floral scent he recalled: Shalimar.

"I simply cannot tell you how happy we are to see you, dear Zalman! Just wait till you hear our plans, the plans that you will very much be a part of. Jacob will tell you as soon as we get home. He has so much to tell you!"

As she turned toward him, he could see Esther's white cheeks flushed with excitement as she pushed a strand of her coppery-color hair from her eye. Her eyes, an unusual shade of blue, twinkled with such enthusiasm that he could hardly refrain from staring at her. A joy began to churn inside him, a feeling he had never experienced before, and he didn't quite know what to make of it. As she fixed those eyes on him now, he felt lucky to be the object of all her attention. Only once before had he seen such ethereal beauty. It was at Jacob's wedding, as he recalled those dazzling eyes set in the porcelain, nearly angelic, face. Only then her attention had not been on him, but another, as he stood off to the side, watching. Zalman turned back to the window, and as they sped by, he watched the lights from the stores and apartment buildings flicker in the distance. And with it was the image of the farmer's daughter.

Even if Zalman was not quite certain what lay ahead, Jacob's enthusiasm was enough to envelop them both. He listened as Jacob sympathized with his bad luck in falling and the consequences of his accident, and he felt Jacob's excitement at his return. He told him that on the very day he had received news of Zalman's accident, he had obtained the deed to land, a land that before this had existed only in his dreams, a prelude to his nightmares only fifteen years earlier. Surely it was God's hand playing a role in these circumstances. And now, here he was, not quite a rich man, but one who had started to lay the foundation for his future—and dare he say it—the house, the castle of his dreams.

Now, a month after his arrival, Zalman sat quietly listening to his friend as he once again narrated the story of Solomon, the wise king, the builder of temples. He realized that, for once, Jacob's heart was happy, and his soul unburdened. Like his hero, he'd be a builder. But he couldn't do it alone, he said, looking into Zalman's eyes. No, he needed the help of his good friend Zalman. Zalman, his brother. Zalman, his architect.

NINE

Jacob

One needs to plan well before building a house. Once you have the land allocated, then you must prepare and grade the site. That being accomplished, the foundation, a secure foundation, can be begun. Then comes the framing of the house, when you can stand back and gaze up at something for the first time, even if it looks like nothing more than a box with a few oddly shaped holes. Next is the installation of the windows and doors, and the roughing and siding, and even a two-year-old can tell that it's becoming a house. Then the professional electricians come in and do their work. Sometime after, there is another need, something important, especially if you are living on the East Coast, when each year the summers get only hotter, the winters more freezing. So heating and air-conditioning systems—fans—are essential to make sure the building is insulated and there's drywall, underlayment, and trim. Without a doubt, now it appears to be a home, but it isn't, not yet. No one would risk living in a space with walls yet to be painted, incomplete wiring, empty walls without counters or cabinets, unusable toilets, and sinks. No one would dare unless you were in hiding, unless you were running for your life and had no choice.

So you finish the heating and air-conditioning work, hook everything up to the water main. Now it's a house, but it does not feel like one. Well, then, you add sturdy wood floors so toddlers can run without tripping over gaps or nails, and plush carpet or maybe a shag in a bright green or blue, and pretty Dacron curtains that flutter when you open the windows in the springtime. And voilà, you finally have a house! But you still don't have a home. Not yet.

Jacob's mind began to race with these thoughts the moment he signed the deed to the property where he would erect his home, no longer a dream, a whim of the imagination, but a home framed with bricks and wood. Where he could stay warm and secure while drifts of snow piled in the streets or tempestuous winds shook the trees, and while the rain formed puddles on the road or danced on the rooftop of a home for all seasons.

It took little convincing for Zalman to agree to become the architect, once again Jacob's right-hand man. This time the new role was not in an escape, but a step toward a thing, moving toward hope. At first, Zalman balked, feeling unsure of his abilities in the trade, but Jacob had enough confidence for them both. After all, hadn't Zalman studied the meticulously planned drawings at his father's knee, visited the museums, office buildings, and the homes of bankers and art dealers that had sprung from the brain of one of the finest architects in all of Poland? Hadn't he salvaged the massive books on the art and techniques of this vocation, and Zalman's own rudimentary drawings that, though amateurish, possessed a spark that demonstrated that Zalman was indeed his father's son? All he needed was time to review it all again, to acquaint himself with the codes at the municipal offices in Brooklyn, and he could set to work.

After only three months, just as the street began to crackle with the mid-July heat, and the birds hid beneath the dry leaves, Jacob, holding the blueprint of his future home, felt that spring had begun. As he shook Zalman's hand, threw his arms around his stooped shoulders, kissed his cheek, he realized his dream was now Zalman's as well.

Jacob's responsibilities at work had kept him from visiting the site very often, over half an acre in Brooklyn's Mill Basin community, so Zalman, design in hand, supervised much of the construction. Often Esther accompanied him, the two carefully surveying a massive blueprint. As the house began to take form, she became emboldened, offering advice on trim and window size, then colors on the walls, the exact shade of marigold for the appliances. Sometimes she would ask Zalman to explain the measurements of a closet or why a bedroom radiator was placed so near to the entry. Zalman, who had lived among the Polish farmers, learned how to speak like an American, no longer such a greenhorn. The two discovered that they shared an interest in cooking, Esther explaining how to boil the bigos—a meat, potato, and sauerkraut stew he had loved as a child—while Zalman introduced her to sour cream with potatoes simmered in borscht. They also both loved music, especially the tunes each played on Esther's beloved baby grand, bringing echoes of home to the young immigrants. Almost immediately, the two friends came to realize they had something else in common as well: their love for Jacob, the man with the big dreams.

PART III

WINDOWS AND DOORS

TEN

Esther

The vacuum cleaner was so loud that she almost didn't hear the doorbell. Esther shut off the Hoover and pulled the machine to a corner of the living room before answering the front door, wondering if Jacob had again forgotten his keys. But when Esther opened the door, she was startled to see not her husband, but a woman perhaps ten years older than she was, with short wavy hair prematurely streaked with gray, holding a casserole dish covered with a red-and-white-checked gingham cloth.

"Welcome!" the woman exclaimed, breezing past Esther, then hesitating just before heading right for the kitchen. Esther, confused, quickly shut the door, and followed. The woman set the dish on the table.

"It's a noodle kugel straight out of the oven. I wasn't sure what to bring, but I thought, who doesn't like a sweet noodle pudding with raisins?"

Not waiting for a response, she pulled up the gingham cloth, and Esther watched as smoke rose into the air and, with it, a sweetly pungent though familiar scent. The intruder continued, "It's still hot, I'm afraid, so it's best to let it sit awhile to cool." Esther, makeup-free, her hair hidden atop her head by a yellow kerchief, stared at the whirlwind before her. "Thanks," she said.

"No thanks needed, honey," the whirlwind said, helping herself to a chair at the table. Esther followed suit, pulling out the metal chair and sitting opposite the woman. While she was trying to formulate her next words, the woman beat her to it.

"Oh, I almost forgot. My name's Flora, Flora Konigsberg. But most people call me Florrie, you know, like those Florodora Girls." She stopped briefly to laugh at her own joke. An awkward silence ensued as Esther, eyes still on the kugel, found her voice.

"I'm Esther. Mrs. Jacob Stein."

"Well, pleased to meet you, Mrs. Jacob Stein," said Flora Florrie. "I live in the house next door to you on the left. Well, I couldn't very well be in the house on the right because then I'd be living in a hole in the ground, being nothing's been built there yet." Flora spoke rapidly, stopping again to laugh at herself before continuing.

"I've been watching your house go up ever since it was a hole in the ground like the one next door. What has it been? About ten months or a year now?"

"A year. We began building just over a year ago," mumbled Esther, shifting her eyes finally from the kugel to the woman's face.

"So it has," said Florrie, leaning back and stretching her long legs in front of her as if she herself were the hostess and not Esther. "I don't want you to think that I'm a busybody neighbor or anything like that, but some afternoons when I wasn't listening to my show or sewing my dress patterns or waiting for the bread to rise, I couldn't help but peek out the front window and see you and your man talking to each other and directing the workers as the house went up, it seems, from brick to building in less than a day. A couple of times he'd come by himself, wearing a short green coat. A smiling, curly-haired fellow. And I knew just then that the two of you would make grand neighbors."

"No, that's not—" Esther began to protest, but the woman, not paying any attention, went on.

"It's a pretty house," she continued, gazing around the sunlit kitchen, appraisingly. "Much prettier than mine. Well, time does wear a house down. And I have been here going on eight years in June now."

"Really? Eight years you say?"

Florrie nodded as her eyes took in the white porcelain sink, the gold refrigerator with its own freezer attached.

"Mm-hmm . . . but our place isn't nearly as nice as yours. And we didn't build it from the ground up like your husband did. I could tell that you and your man designed the place yourself, because when I'd be coming home from the store with my groceries, you two would always be outside looking at some big poster spread out on the roof of your car. I figured it was some kind of blueprint, a plan for the house that you were huddled over. Not that I was spying or anything, because I'm not that kind of neighbor." She paused, coughed into her hand, and continued.

Esther wanted to object, wanted to let Florrie know that it wasn't her husband who pored over blueprints with her, but their dear friend, Zalman. But she thought it best to remain silent for now. The woman went on like a runaway train.

"Sid and I weren't so lucky, and besides, I wouldn't know the first thing about building a home. No, our house was built some ten years earlier by the Saccones, who lived there with their six kids—can you imagine? Six kids running around in that three-bedroom house with no basement! Mr. Saccone drove a hard bargain, but Sid, that's my husband, got him down to fourteen thousand." She swiveled in her seat, facing Esther.

"Hey, you got any kids?"

Esther, no longer shocked by the woman's presumptuousness, shook her head.

"No. We haven't—"

"That's okay, me neither," said Florrie, interrupting again. "But yours will come soon enough. Sid and I don't have any kids, and we won't either. I had a woman's problem when I was twenty. After a few years, they had to take everything out of me," she disclosed without any trace of emotion that Esther could detect.

"Oh well," she went on, shrugging, "I got three brothers who have a bunch of little ones, so I'm everybody's auntie. I take 'em to the zoo, or the park, do up Marni and Shari's hair with pretty ribbons. They're the littlest ones. And when any of 'em starts to squawk, well, I just give 'em back to their parents. That's the good thing about being an auntie. You only have to put up with 'em for so long. Don't get me wrong, I love each one of 'em, even Joey, the oldest boy. He's kind of quiet and serious, but I guess that's the way boys are at that age, almost twelve. But, like I say, I love all ten of 'em just the same. Matter of fact, I love all kids. That's why I work part-time at Murray's Toys on Ocean Avenue. I love to see the children walk in, their eyes all big, and smiling from ear to ear. When I bring down one of them little balls attached to a paddle, a bright-red Hula-Hoop, or one of those Tiny Tears or rubber dollies, you should see their faces! It's like I was Santa Claus or something. I swear I love them children."

Florrie sat back, looking satisfied, as if she had just finished a slice of Ebinger's blackout cake with a big glass of cold milk on the side.

"So? And you, you are young and healthy. I suppose you'll be having a few little ones running around within the year?" she asked.

"N-no, maybe not so soon. There is still much to be done in this house. Much work."

"Well, I wouldn't wait too long if I was you. I was already thirty when I found out that for me a family was a lost cause." She paused then, as if she had forgotten something.

"Hey, you got an accent! You from Europe? Poland, I bet that's where you're from!" When Esther nodded, the woman snapped her fingers gleefully.

"I can always tell! My husband's got family from there. Mine are from Austria, I think, but we've been here for a couple of generations already." Then Florrie got up abruptly and, again lifting the gingham cover off the lid of the Pyrex casserole dish, prodded the noodles with her finger.

"It's cooled off. Now I think you can put it in the fridge." Instead of waiting for Esther to make a move, though, she lifted the dish off the table, went over to the refrigerator, opened the door, and placed it delicately on the top shelf.

"Looks like you need some milk for your husband's coffee. I'll put you in touch with Mr. Ryland, the milkman. He delivers mine twice a week, so it'll be a snap."

Esther's eyes remained steady on the woman with the long legs and athletic build who had barged her way into Esther's home. Still, she couldn't help but feel a smile come to her face. She did not mind the neighbor's nosy questions, her presumptuous statements and bossy manner. And now, looking at the round curves of her cheeks, her soft hazel eyes, she realized something about Florrie reminded her of her old friend Sophie, who had moved to Baldwin, Long Island, just before Esther married, and since then Esther hadn't heard a peep from her. Not even a letter.

Florrie was standing by the kitchen counter examining a bowl of McIntosh apples.

"Where'd you buy these? In a supermarket? You should try Weiman's. I know the owner's son. They have the best produce. Get it straight from the orchard in New Jersey. I'll take you there sometime."

Without waiting for a response, Florrie glanced at the gold Bulova watch on her wrist, exclaiming, "Holy cow! It's nearly five o'clock! I've got to get my beef stew on the fire for Sid. He likes all the juices from the meat and carrots cooked in just so. I'll give you the recipe sometime!"

Then, without another word, she went to the front door, which Esther hadn't bothered to lock, put her finger to her lips, touched the new mezuzah, which Esther's parents had purchased for her in Israel, and left. Esther remained seated, staring at the closed door for some minutes. When she stood up to finish the vacuuming, she realized that the smile she had greeted her new neighbor with was still on her.

~

Sometimes when Jacob was asleep at night, Esther would slip out of bed, move carefully down the hall to the bathroom, and switch on the light. Then she would turn to the mirror, which reflected the pink and white tiles on the walls, and examine the image in front of her. Brown hair almost, but not quite, to her shoulders, longer than she had ever had it since she was a kid. Naturally wavy, there was that bob, the little wave suspended above her eyebrow. No sign of gray yet, but when there was, she knew she would color it first thing, not at all like Florrie, who didn't seem to be bothered by her streaks. Her lips, unpainted now, were fuller than she would have liked, her nose a little too pert. But it was her eyes, she knew, that were her outstanding feature. Blue like the sky on a sunny day, her father used to say when she was little. They were framed by eyebrows that were like her mother's, who was darker by nature, and needed plucking only occasionally, and lashes that waved upward. Her features were set in a cloud of ivory, unobstructed yet by worry lines or wrinkles.

Esther would lean forward like this, elbows on the bathroom counter, nose almost touching the reflection, and think. A "pretty girl," as her father would say; "my beauty" is how Jacob put it. She knew they were right, well, almost. She was pretty enough, and she didn't need more than that. Often, on these nights with the moon still high in the sky, its light peeking between the edges of the white horizontal blinds, she would imagine herself a very old lady. The idea didn't frighten her; on the contrary, the thought of growing old was a source of comfort. She and Jacob sitting on rockers on the front porch in the way of old people, waiting patiently for the grandchildren to arrive. And there would always be visitors at the home, sometimes one of their own children, six in all, followed by the grandkids, boys climbing up on Jacob's lap until, after some coaxing, he got up shakily to have a game of catch in the yard. Meanwhile, she would walk back into the house with a couple of the girls and teach them the notes of the piano or how to cook a vegetable-filled chicken soup the way her mother had taught her when she was a girl. Often Zalman would walk over, joined by his own wife and family, and then they would all reminisce about the days when he lived in the extra bedroom before owning his own house, with its peaked roof and a large picture window. Nevertheless, he would always be there, sitting on the porch or at the kitchen table where all the important gatherings would take place. All under the room that the three of them had constructed only a few months earlier.

And they would see the seasons right there at her own front door, something she was never able to do in her old apartment. In the fall, when the leaves dropped slowly off the grand oak at the curb in abundant carpets of golds and reds, she would often stand at the front door, where she would peek through the screen and drink in the brisk air. And then, when icy winds began to swirl around the house and shake the timbers in a threatening way, she would wrap Jacob's woolen blanket around her shoulders and sip the tomato soup she had cooked earlier that day and sit by the sliders and look out at the backyard as drifts of snow fell in crystal piles until the bare-limbed trees looked like winter angels waiting for the sun of an incipient spring. And then it would begin all over again: the tiny white buds timidly arising from the branches of the willows, the yellow green blades of grass she would pick, holding them close to her nose, like feathers against the skin as she inhaled the intoxicating scent of spring. From then on they would spend their days outdoors, waving to the passersby who were always on their way somewhere. Jacob and Esther would mark the time by the seasons and the years passed, but the memories stayed, solid and good. These images flew through Esther's mind as she stared for minutes into the mirror, looking at her reflection and the dreams she had for them both in Jacob's house.

ELEVEN

Zalman, 1958

He could hear the music even before he turned the key in the lock. The dulcet tones of Debussy's piano piece, "Clair de Lune," floated in the air, mesmerizing him, and, combined with the scent of beef roasting in garlic and onions, made him forget the day at work and placed him at ease.

Dropping his case filled with drawings against the sofa, he sat down and leaned against the blue-striped pillows. If she noticed him there, he was not sure, for she continued to play, her long fingers dancing across the keys. She was, he knew, as hypnotized as he.

His mother had preferred the old Yiddish melodies, but looking at Esther now, he was transported to the two-bedroom home in Raczki, his mother letting the dinner go cold as she was coaxed to play yet another tune, which would wash away the cares of a young boy who studied perhaps too many hours and worried perhaps too much about an increasingly hostile world that he was still too young to comprehend. Zalman had a vague memory of his father and older brother being there, too, all listening as she sang the familiar ditties, her voice light and jovial. But it was Mama he remembered most, and today he could see her in the slope of Esther's back, the rise and fall of her hands against the keys. The way her skirt, a bright crimson, fell draped over the bench. The song was different, "Clair de Lune," but it did not matter. He was with Mama again. He was home.

It was Esther's favorite and almost the only thing she played as the day turned into a fine evening mist. Zalman almost always arrived before Jacob, who kept late hours at work back in the city. Several months earlier, he had listened again to the dreamlike melody that, as her fingers moved along the keys, reached a sweet crescendo. It was aptly named, he had told her—"Clair de Lune"—the light of the moon. She seemed surprised that he knew so much about the song and the poem it was named for, which ended, *The melancholy moonlight, sweet and lone/ That makes to dream the birds upon the tree/And in their polished basins of white stone/The fountains tall to sob with ecstasy.*"

She stared at him then, amazed for some minutes once he had finished reciting the poem he had long ago learned by heart. Finally, she asked, "What else is it you know, dear Zalman?"

"Oh, not very much at all, but I do know a bit about very few subjects which are often of no interest whatsoever to most people."

She turned her body away from the keys and pedal to face him fully.

"I'm interested. I would say I'm *quite* interested."

"Well," he continued, lowering his head as he tried to remember the details, "I know that Debussy was something of a child prodigy and studied music at the Paris Conservatoire at age ten, where he remained for some time. He was a brilliant, an extraordinary pianist. But some consider his personal life, like many of the other masters of his time, much more interesting.

"He was close friends, shall we say, *awfully close* friends, with a young woman who was a singer, and of course a married woman. Well, as you can imagine, the two embarked on an affair. But nevertheless, Debussy remained good friends with the husband. I don't recall the man's name, nor even the woman's. But it was actually the husband who introduced him to French writers, one of whom was Paul Verlaine, the author of the poem which gave rise to the song you were just playing. Debussy had a few scandalous affairs after that. He married twice, had a child—a daughter, I believe, who died a year after he did. This is all the stuff of gossip, I suppose, and perhaps that is why I enjoy it so much. But the music, well, the music is the real pleasure here. Don't you agree, Esther?"

Esther listened intently to the history lesson as it had been delivered, partially in English, part in his native Polish, trying to let all that was said sink in. Finally, she could do nothing but utter, "I like the song, and I play it so often because, well, I just like it so much."

"Well then, that's really all that's important, right?" he exclaimed, slapping his knee before urging her to play the song yet again. And so she did, again, and often each week, as the year when the three of them lived together in this, Jacob's castle, drifted on. And before any of them realized it, they had lived in the house together for two years.

And now, as her fingers struck the high chords of "Clair de Lune," Zalman could not help but feel his heart soar again into that magical place, led by the enchanting song. Listening to Esther play never failed to transport him to a feeling of contentment and peace. He had tried moving out on more than one occasion. He was now an established architect with, thanks to Jacob's connections, numerous clients of his own. Yet he knew, and so did Jacob and Esther, that those attempts were halfhearted at best. He contributed, of course, to the upkeep of the home and had even, thanks to his farming experience, taken over the landscaping and gardening so that lilacs and gladiolus bloomed at every turn. He insisted, too, on paying rent to the couple who, though they objected at first, relented if it meant keeping their boarder and friend within the home.

Why did he do it? Why did he remain as a guest whom, despite his contributions of time and money, he knew he would forever be? Why did he stay? The question troubled him as he lay in his bed awake at night, the bed that should be occupied by a fair-skinned child, not a

Polish immigrant with rapidly thinning hair and all his worldly possessions in a brown attaché case. As the first hazy rays of sun appeared over the rooftops and the shadows deepened below his eyes, Zalman in bed would turn again toward the wall. He had always been a good child who had followed the rules when he was a student at the gymnasium, an obedient son who listened to the advice of his parents, and eventually a practical man who always tried to adhere to what was rational, what was right. And he knew for a certainty after six months, after twelve, and now, that he needed to leave this house that was not his.

He stood each evening leaning against the metal pole, looking down at the scuffed shoes of the passengers as the D train rumbled through the echoing tunnel, feeling the prickle of anticipation spread beneath his skin, the realization that something was holding him back. He did not mind the long ride, the hours spent poring over drawings, the petty annoyances and frustrations, the delays and contracts rescinded, deals gone bad. He did not mind any of it because he knew that at 5:00 p.m., he would be putting his arms into the sleeves of his green cotton jacket, placing a gray hat on his head, picking up the full attaché case, and going home.

In truth, Zalman felt that he was a brother to Jacob, a member of the family. His childhood had been tainted each day by fear, the time spent on the farm, though happy, marked by the knowledge that, though appreciated, he was nothing more than another worker. But here in his home, sleeping in the bedroom next to Jacob and Esther, he felt more secure than ever. After all, didn't they both ask him, *implore* him, not to leave?

Now as he listened once more to "Clair de Lune," he closed his eyes, forgetting about his day, his aching feet, wishing only to make the moment last.

The last note played, but Esther hesitated before getting up off the bench.

"I think it was beautiful, just beautiful," he said.

"Oh, you silly! You always say that." She laughed, walking over and giving his shoulder a playful slap. "You are no help at all!"

He looked up at her, seeing his image reflected in her pale-blue eyes.

"I mean it," he answered. "You play that song better than anyone I know."

She raised an eyebrow quizzically. "Or perhaps I'm the only one you know who plays this song?"

Zalman got to his feet reluctantly.

"Is it a beef stew that I smell? Ah, the aroma! May I help you plate it?"

"Oh, no, please," she said. "Best change your clothes first. I need to just give it another stir, and it will be ready in minutes by the time Jacob gets home."

After running a spoon through the pot and lowering the flame, something outside the window caught her eye. She opened the latch and took a deep breath.

"I think I just saw a cardinal! Spring must really be here. Do you think we should start planting the rosebushes soon, Zalman? What do you think?"

But Zalman didn't answer. He hadn't heard the question, because he had been staring at the gentle waves of her auburn hair and the view of her leaning toward the window.

Something stirred in him, and he ran upstairs before he could think what it was.

TWELVE

Jacob

His house was not a home. Not yet. A home required the patter of small bare feet against the floorboards, the excited shouts of play in the backyard, the soft tinkle of a lullaby spinning slowly above the crib. A home required children.

When Jacob was very young, he wanted superpowers, to fly high above the clouds in command of a world he did not yet fully understand. As he grew older, as he observed his uncertain parents and all that was around them begin to collapse, he had longed for stability, a place from which he was not forced to escape, a place he could call his own. And now that he had found that thing, a home he had helped build with his own hands, a wife who welcomed him at the end of each day with hot soup and sweet kisses, things were still not quite right.

Jacob woke up each morning with a gnawing in his belly, and the gnawing grew each month as Esther emerged from the bathroom, her sad eyes traced with resignation. After years of working and striving and loving the woman he never dreamed could be his, Jacob had to admit one thing to himself. The things he had dreamed of and now had were as intangible as air without someone to pass them down to.

Jacob had one last dream, the same dream his parents had, and their parents before them.

Although neither he nor Esther spoke openly of the problem, there were subtle signs of discontent. Unlike Zalman, who appeared soothed once he walked through the door and sank into the blue velvet sofa as if all his cares of the day had been washed away, Jacob felt a tense shadow over him. Worse yet, he noticed that Esther seemed preoccupied even as she greeted him with a kiss at the door at day's end. Their lovemaking was now different too. The two came to each other without the customary excitement. They went through the motions mechanically in an almost businesslike manner.

Despite the veil of dread that had settled over the couple, Jacob tried his best to buoy his wife's spirits. Hardly a weekend passed without an excursion to a nearby park or Rockaway Beach, bleacher seats at a Yankees game if the weather was good. Winters when the weather was harsh, their time was spent delighting in a plethora of activities: Radio City Music Hall, the Metropolitan Museum of Art, a Broadway musical. Occasionally, they would be accompanied by Zalman if he found the event to be of particular interest, like a concert or an art exhibit; and Florrie might come, too, for her husband, it seemed, preferred to spend his free time watching *I Love Lucy*, reading the papers while smoking Camels, one pack after another. Jacob was always glad for the company of the friends who, unlike himself, could spend hours talking about nothing in particular. It was good for Esther, a diversion.

Whenever they walked amid the tussle of crowds on Forty-Second Street and a child on a scooter would cut abruptly in front of them, or he caught sight of a father trying to maneuver a large baby carriage, Jacob would hold his wife's hand a little tighter. There was so much he wanted to say to her, but at these times the words eluded him. He was grateful to have Zalman nearby with a joke, or a comment about the potholes in the road. And, at least for a moment, he would forget.

Jacob wondered if he shared Esther's thoughts, her worries. Did she know, could she guess as she slept with an unlined forehead and measured breaths, that he lay awake thinking of the house he had built, the future, and why he had been spared only to have a life with no heirs?

~

One evening, Jacob came home early to find Esther seated on the sofa, crying. Zalman was next to her, a consoling arm around her shoulders. When she looked up, seeing him at the door, the surprise served only to heighten her sobs. Jacob felt as if his heart might break.

When she finally lifted her head, he could see she was red faced, her cheeks awash in tears.

"Oh, Jacob, I didn't want to bother you with this. It is just one woman's silliness."

Jacob moved closer, touching her shoulder as Zalman removed his arm from her and, with a knowing nod, went quietly upstairs.

"Please, my dear, what's wrong?" said Jacob softly as he kissed the salty tears away from her cheek.

"I was late, and I didn't tell you. Oh, Jacob, I had even baked a chocolate cake yesterday to celebrate! This time I thought—I was so sure that—"

Jacob waited then as a new wave of tears flooded her cheeks.

"But this morning, oh, I went to the bathroom, and—oh, Jacob!" And again, emotion burst forth.

Jacob encircled her with his arms, feeling her body spent and fragile next to his. They remained locked in the embrace until finally Esther's breath slowed, her last tear dried. He wanted to tell her that tomorrow the clouds would part and, just as surely as the sun would rise in the sky, they, too, would have a new beginning. He wanted to say that he had been through worse, far worse, in his lifetime, and even though it seemed that he had lost it all, then like a dream he had found her! And things were good, after all, weren't they? He wanted her to know that the building of the house made of sturdy brick and stone, its bright-red roof and towering oak tree in the backyard, could signal only a bright future for them both, that this setback was only that, he was sure. But that evening, as the filter of darkness swept over the moon, Jacob didn't say any of that. How could he? He wasn't even sure if he believed the words himself.

THIRTEEN

Esther

The year was 1960. The Organization of the Petroleum Exporting Countries, or OPEC, was created, the first weather satellite was launched by the United States, John F. Kennedy was elected president of the United States, and a child, a son, was born to Jacob and Esther Stein. They named the boy Gary, after Gershon, an uncle Jacob favored.

After the birth, fittingly on the night of the November presidential election, Jacob and Esther felt they were also reborn. The veil of fear for the future that had enveloped the couple, and which neither had spoken of since the day when Jacob had comforted his distraught wife, had finally been lifted after all these years. Esther attributed their good luck to her fervent prayers, but also, probably for the most part, to one of her conversations with Florrie. As someone who had battled infertility herself, Florrie assured her friend that she had become educated on the new medical advances. She had a friend who had participated in an experimental trial for a new drug at the advice of her doctor. She suggested that Esther look into it.

The advice had worked, for within a month, Esther had found herself happily pregnant. And with that discovery, of course, the friendship between the two women was forever sealed. The first few months of

Esther's diet consisted almost solely of crackers and weak tea, so violent was her morning (afternoon and night too) sickness. But her mood was such that she found herself smiling even through this, and when she grabbed Jacob's hand so that he could feel the first strong kicks against her expanding belly, she felt such an elation that she believed her life was perfect.

Jacob changed too. He began coming home early, sometimes even before Zalman, just so he might gaze upon the changes in his wife and stand in the empty bedroom that would soon be their child's. His mood shifted as well. Instead of his usual sullen demeanor over the past couple of years, he had begun to take part in the conversations between Esther and Zalman at the breakfast table; in the evenings he focused on his television shows, like *Bonanza*, with a new intensity, and laughed heartily at the antics of Jackie Gleason in *The Honeymooners*. At night, when the stars made patterns of light against the ceiling as Jacob took her hand in his, Esther would often glance at him, finding his eyes calm, steady, his mouth posed in a half smile. Unlike before, she was not preoccupied with Jacob's past. He was sometimes quiet, but no longer lost in thought; no longer were his eyes filled with anxiety. This new Jacob was tranquil; he was happy. That was the best part of all.

Once more, Zalman tried to leave, and on one Sunday in September, he even started packing a few of his belongings into a suitcase. But when Esther happened by the open door to the bedroom, she became so distraught that Jacob would not hear of it. Again, he admonished Zalman to remain in the home. Esther still relied on him for companionship, for his assistance lifting, carrying when Jacob himself was not around. And what if Jacob wasn't available when the baby was coming, as his hours were more erratic than Zalman's? Would he dare jeopardize Esther? The child? In truth, Zalman needed little convincing, so that same evening he neatly laid his sweater back inside the drawer, his cuff links on the night table. He decided not to bring up the subject for now. Secretly, he was happy—happy to be a part of a family again, even if it wasn't his own.

During the final months of the pregnancy, Esther's mother came as often as she could. But as Esther herself grew rounder, her face full, her cheeks rosy, Sally shrank somehow, losing nearly twenty pounds of her former pleasantly plump self, letting her hair fade to a drab gray. Just before Esther's pregnancy had become public, Boris had suffered a heart attack one morning at work, and even though it had been a mild one, the doctors advised against overexertion. In the best of times, Sally had been a worrier, but now with a husband ill and a daughter with child, the woman was in a constant state of stress, so much so that Esther began to worry about her mother.

While mother and daughter were close, Esther kept a secret from her, one she would never reveal. Shortly after Esther had begun helping her father with the business, she'd decided what she wanted to do with the rest of her life. She wanted a career, to make important decisions, to meet with different individuals, where she would be in charge. Her plan was to eventually take over the business. Once, she'd casually mentioned the idea to Boris, who'd responded with his customary "We'll see." She knew, though, that if she prodded enough, he would eventually make her a partner.

But Sally, now that was another thing. Even though when she was young, Esther's mother had a temporary job taking care of children, she most enjoyed her role as a housekeeper, wife, and cook. Many times, as Esther looked on while Sally was sweeping the floors or making the beds, she would remind her daughter that one day she, too, would have her own home.

A week after Esther's engagement, her mother had suggested that soon she would have to give up her work in real estate. She'd need to assume her proper role as a wife and, later, a mother. After that, Esther had spent many sleepless nights. To go along with her mother's plans meant giving up so much, and yet it seemed impossible to have both a happy home life and a career. How could she go against her mother's wishes? Worse yet, Sally might feel unappreciated. After a while, though, Sally's voice had become a constant drone in her head. Her mother was a smart woman, and perhaps she did know what was best, after all.

Esther had decided to give up her dreams of running the family business. She'd encouraged Jacob to take over, let him be the man. And in the end, everyone had believed that she wanted nothing more than to make a home for her new husband. Everyone but herself.

But now, as she listened to Sally's cries, saw the circles beneath her eyes deepen, Esther wished her mother had something else to occupy her time besides a sick husband. And she hoped that the same fate would not await her.

On occasions when she wasn't visited by Sally during the day, Esther was joined by Florrie, who would pop in most mornings after the men had left for work, with a tin of warm muffins straight from the oven or material for a pattern she was sewing for a new skirt or dress. Once she walked in with a yellow-and-white baby blanket knitted by her aunt Yetta.

"Put it right away or else it's bad luck," Esther warned, and spit on the floor.

Most days, if it was sunny, the two ventured out for a walk in the local park or shopped at a flea market. When the weather turned foul and rain pounded against the panes, they would stay indoors, playing cards or listening to Frank Sinatra or Anthony Dominick Benedetto, the crooner, or as he was best known, Tony Bennett, on the radio. Mostly, though, they just talked. There always seemed to be something to talk about.

It was just before dinner at 6:00 p.m. and two days before her due date, on the night of the general election when the country would decide if it would be the serious, contentious vice president or the young, determined senator who would be the next president. Esther was setting down a plate of lamb chops and white rice when she felt a trickle slide down her thigh and leg. She wasn't quite sure what it was, a loosening of the bladder or something else. She quickly wiped it down with a napkin, but when it happened again, this time with a stronger gush of water, she called for Jacob.

Jacob and Zalman were sitting in the living room, reading the papers, when Jacob heard her. Shortly after, the doctor was called, and they headed for the hospital. Esther was nervous, Jacob almost delirious with anticipation as he drove, while Zalman stayed back at home.

They stood at the nursery window just hours after the birth. Esther observed Jacob as they brought the child to him. As he stared ahead, it appeared that Jacob couldn't seem to find his breath, and immediately the color seeped from his cheeks. He tapped on the glass that separated him from the nurse, her mouth covered with a cloth, and the tiny pink creature asleep in her arms. As the couple set their eyes on their miracle, it hardly seemed real that this placid infant with closed eyes and five fingers on each hand was an actual human being. That this being, this person, with Esther's billowy rosy cheeks, and long gangly legs so like Jacob's, was actually their son.

Esther's recovery was faster than any of them had expected. Even after spending a week in the hospital following an emergency C-section, she took to the child's care naturally, just as if she had been doing it all her life. When Jacob came home after a long day of business dealings (days that were longer now since Boris was still somewhat incapacitated after the heart attack), Esther would have his meal waiting for him, still warm on the kitchen table as she greeted him, her auburn hair brushed and shiny, eyelids coated a sky blue, her lips pursed in a pink kiss. If it happened to be a night when the baby was fussy, Zalman would help out by rocking the cradle as he had one eye on *Gunsmoke* or another of his favorite shows on the TV. Florrie, who was known as Aunt Florrie by this time, would visit often, adding an extra homemade blanket to the baby's crib, sleeking down his fine yellow hair. She would still accompany them on weekends, when besides the park, they would visit Coney Island or the Bronx Zoo. And by the time he turned five, the boy had even been to a couple of Yankees games and had begun what would turn into a formidable collection of baseball cards, including his favorite, Mickey Mantle.

As the house with its kitchen wallpaper decorated with green and yellow teakettles, a second air conditioner for the couple's bedroom, even a color TV, flourished, so did the child. Gary was not a rambunctious boy like most his age, but rather introspective, preferring time alone reviewing his growing stamp collection or reading the Berenstain Bears series. What he loved most of all, though, was accompanying Jacob to work and listening as his father patiently explained all about the buying and maintaining of apartments and houses, as well as the importance of saving for the future, even if it started with a few pennies in a ceramic piggy bank. Esther marveled at how the child was becoming each day more of his father's son. From the set of his jaw to his high forehead to his height, which made him appear at least two years older than the others in his grade, he was indeed the mirror image of Jacob. All except for the blue eyes. Those were hers.

By the time their son had entered first grade, the couple knew that despite their good fortune, they had another problem. But neither spoke of it.

$\sim$

Esther touched her fingertips to the mezuzah by the door before entering and placed the heavy packages filled with the week's groceries onto the kitchen table. She smiled as she heard the first dull musical note float up into the air from where Gary and Zalman were seated at the piano in the living room. She was glad that Zalman offered to give the boy instructions, and after only some initial hesitance, because he really would much rather have been reading the comics or organizing his collection of baseball cards or even watching the latest installment of *The Three Stooges*—which all seemed to be much more fun when you are only eight years old—Gary relented. And now that his interest had been piqued, she was sure it wouldn't be long before she heard the familiar melody of "Clair de Lune" once again fill the house, now by a much younger set of fingers. Gary was just about the same age she was when she had learned to play.

"What's for dinner, Mommy?"

Esther was startled to find Gary at her side as she stood pouring the noodles into a colander over the sink.

"Your favorite. Meatballs and spaghetti," she said, tapping the metal to get the last of the water out before adding the spaghetti into a large Corelle bowl. She wiped her hands on the red-and-white-checkered apron at her waist and smiled down at her child.

"No hello or a kiss for your mommy today since I came in the door?" She tried and failed again to make the tone of her voice sound angry. But the boy shrugged and lifted his chin as he allowed himself to be kissed on the lips.

"Hello, Mommy," he piped, and turned toward the bowl of spaghetti, reached in, and let a naked piece slide down his throat. But not before his mother had taken note of the extra freckles that had formed across the bridge of his nose, and the lock of hair curling upward at his forehead, signaling the need for yet another haircut since the last one only three weeks earlier. How handsome he looks in his Cub Scout uniform, thought Esther as Gary took a seat at the kitchen table, how much like a little man!

Zalman entered the kitchen and, almost as if he could read her mind, exclaimed, "Our Gary is certainly growing up, is he not?" Esther nodded in agreement, and placing her hand on Zalman's shoulder, gave him a quick kiss on the cheek, adding, "Our piano teacher deserves a kiss as well. Gary is coming along, I think. He's even beginning to enjoy playing!" Zalman smiled and took a seat opposite the boy, who had begun tapping his fork against the dinner plate. After taking a sip from the glass of water already set on the table, Zalman cleared his parched throat.

"Yes, I believe Gary has a talent for it, just like his mother." Before Esther could respond, though, Gary blurted out, "Where's the SpaghettiOs—I mean spaghetti!" He laughed at his own mistake.

"Okay," she answered, "hold your horses!" Esther poured the spaghetti into three plates, topping each off with four fully rounded meatballs. Then she grabbed a large bottle of Heinz ketchup from the refrigerator and squirted half the contents into each bowl and mixed the spaghetti and meatballs together until they turned a bright red, just the way her mother had shown her. She placed a dish in front of Zalman, and one in front of Gary, who was now making strange noises while still tapping his fork against the edge of the table.

"What are you doing making noises at the table? You're not five years old anymore, Gary, and you know your father would not approve of this behavior."

"Mommy, you told me to hold my horses. It's the horses making all the noise, not me. Besides, Daddy isn't here now," he said, and made one more neighing sound before stabbing his fork into a large meatball at the top of his plate.

Esther and Zalman exchanged a glance as each tried to stifle a giggle.

"Your father will be home very soon," admonished Esther before taking another dish to the table for herself.

～

Jacob did not get home as soon as Esther had hoped. She knew that last week a superintendent of one of his buildings in New York had been called back to his home in Puerto Rico due to a family emergency, and tenants had begun to complain about burst water pipes and burned fuses. She had also heard that he had wasted an entire afternoon with lawyers, only to find out that the closing of a newly built home just two blocks away from where Jacob and Esther lived had been delayed. But he didn't trouble Esther with the details.

It was at times like these when Jacob's life was so involved with the endless phone calls, writing his signature on the stacks of paper on his desk, shaking the hand of a client to seal another profitable deal, that Esther wondered what her life would have been like if she had not persuaded her father to hand the reins of the business over to Jacob. During these moments of reflection, she admitted to herself that, despite being a woman, she had loved it all. She loved the meetings, speaking with authority, disputing a clause in an impending contract, or balancing a sum without one number going askew, and the best part of it all: having people listen to her, to respect her just as if she were a man. These thoughts drifted upon her most nights when Jacob would come home late, exhausted but exhilarated at the same time. Now it was her husband who was the big deal.

But what choice did she have? As a woman, a married woman, she had no business running a real estate office. She'd be the object of gossip among the tenants and other building owners, but Jacob, her husband, would have suffered the worst of it. What kind of a man allows his wife to handle business dealings, leaving the house at dawn, and returning home with an empty thermos and tired feet? No, Esther had made her decision long ago that she could never allow her Jacob to endure such humiliation. And so, with not a little convincing from her mother, she had gone to Boris one evening as he sat in his favorite armchair by the large window. She'd kneeled next to him, placing her head on his knee. As Esther lay awake late into the night, she would replay their conversation in her head.

Using her pet name for him, she had convinced her papou to make Jacob a part of the business. At first, he had been surprised by her request. Boris was not like most men, who believed that their daughters should forever remain cooking soups and darning old socks.

"But my dear, you of all my children have a talent for it! You even convinced me to send you to school to learn English so that you could better speak with the tenants and businessmen. Why would you want to give all that up?"

Esther opened her blue eyes wide and looked up at her father, the way she had often done as a child, portraying the picture of innocence.

"Oh, Papou, I'll soon be a married woman with household obligations to take up my time, and maybe a family one day. It's Jacob who needs a step up now. He'll catch on quick, I can assure you. Jacob is too smart to be a bottle stacker for the rest of his life. And besides, I'm getting somewhat tired of dealing with people's complaints night and day, tallying numbers when I'd much rather be home baking a challah for Friday nights."

She had lied, and it had taken all her strength that evening not to turn away, to hold back the tears that were straining at the corners of her eyes. As usual, Boris had relented to his daughter's wishes, making Jacob an offer as promised on their wedding day. But the deed to their home had been his idea and a surprise to the daughter who had deceived them all.

As Esther slowly loosened her control over the business, letting Jacob take over first one project, then another, as she immersed herself into shopping and decorating the apartment and then a home, the regret would subside. And then, after Gary was born, there were even days when she truly gave the missed opportunities little thought. But now, with Jacob away at work most of the time, and Gary attending public school, she had begun to feel the yearning once again, more than she had before. She wondered what it would be like to fill the void in her heart with a job, if not in real estate, then maybe as a music teacher. Or maybe something else. Maybe another baby.

When he walked through the door, Jacob had not even bothered to remove the jacket of his new three-piece Louis Cardin suit or place his attaché case in the closet. Instead, dragging his feet across the floor, he plopped down on the couch next to his wife, who was watching an *I Dream of Jeannie* rerun, and gave her a quick kiss on the cheek. In that moment, she assessed Jacob's face, which had assumed the dull gray color of the TV cabinet. And yet, with the bright-green eyes and the dimple in his chin, after nearly sixteen years, he was still the handsomest man she had ever known.

"You work too hard," she said, returning her gaze to the TV screen. It was a phrase she had uttered nearly each evening since the death of her father over two years earlier. Jacob ignored her, his eyes scanning the room.

"Where's Gary? Doing homework?"

She turned again to look at him and placed one hand on his knee.

"Gary's been asleep for nearly two hours, dear. It's almost ten o'clock."

He lifted his wrist as if to look at his watch, then let his arm fall.

"I hadn't realized. It's been a tough day."

"Yes, I know," she said, standing. "I've got meatballs and spaghetti I can warm up on the stove." He raised an arm to stop her.

"Don't bother. I'm not very hungry anyway. I'll just boil myself a hot dog. I'm sure we've got a package of Hebrew National in the fridge."

Esther settled back on the sofa pillow and listened as the refrigerator door creaked open, then shut, and the pans rattled as Jacob removed a pot from a shelf. She couldn't pay much attention to the show now. When she entered the kitchen, Jacob was taking his first bite of a frank, tasteless without mustard or sauerkraut, but he seemed fairly pleased with it anyway. She put on the apron, which was hanging over a chair, and began washing the dinner dishes that she had been too tired to tackle earlier.

"Jacob, I need to talk with you about something," she said, swirling a sponge through the soapy water as she stared out the open blinds into the night sky, as if she could actually see something there.

"What is it? Is something wrong with Gary? Did he come down with a cold or the flu? We need to dress him in warmer clothes. It might be spring, but that doesn't mean there's good weather every day."

Esther shook her head, still staring out into the blackness.

"No, dear, it's not that. Gary is perfectly fine. And he has a closet filled with woolens. It's not that," she repeated. "It's just that you need to know about something. I see things that you don't even notice since you are not home that much."

Jacob scowled.

"Wait! What are you saying?" he asked, raising his voice. "Are you blaming me for not spending enough time with you and Gary?" He stopped, choking on a piece of the meat. Esther turned to face her husband.

Before she could go to him or utter a word, he cleared his throat and resumed, his voice an octave lower.

"Look, Esther, I'm trying my best. It's not an easy job, and I only wish I could be with you both more than just on weekends. I'm not complaining. Not at all, you know I've always said I'm the luckiest man on earth, after what I've been through, God knows!"

Esther stood quietly, the soaked sponge still in her hands.

"Yes, Jacob, I know. And you say it all the time."

"The luckiest man on earth," he repeated as if she hadn't heard. "I have a castle, I have you, I have Gary. And Zalman, of course, my right-hand man."

Esther looked down at the linoleum, which showed a few streaks of dried ketchup.

"Jacob, it's Zalman I want to talk to you about."

He picked up a napkin and wiped his mouth slowly.

"What do you mean to say about Zalman? Is there a problem? Is he sick? I see him always, and I don't see any problems."

"That's just it. You can't see the problem. But I feel it—call it woman's intuition. Yes, I feel it more than see it. The matter is, he needs to leave this house."

"Narishkeit," said Jacob, using an old Yiddish expression for "nonsense," giving her a dismissive wave of the hand. "Zalman loves it here. He's a happy man with a fine job where he doesn't have to put in long hours at work, and has you to cook for him, even iron his pants. Besides, you know how much he adores our son, just like he was his own."

Jacob rose from the table, removed his navy-blue jacket and, placing it in the crook of his arm, began walking toward the living room. But before he could get there, Esther appeared before him, blocking his way.

"Jacob, I know you're tired, and I so appreciate how tirelessly you work for our family, but I must speak with you about this *matter.*"

Her voice rose stridently on the last word. Jacob faced his wife and, noticing the worry lines that zigzagged across her forehead, the set of her jaw, the determination that hid behind the pupils in her blue eyes, he lay the jacket neatly across the banister, took Esther's hand in his own, and the two walked back to the sofa.

"Okay, then, Esther," he said, as he placed his arm around her and she nuzzled against his chest, "tell me what your woman's intuition says is wrong with Zalman."

"You know how much I love Zalman," she began, eyes still downcast as she breathed in her husband's sweat, "and how he is a brother to me as he is to you. And for Gary, well, he has become an uncle, and closer to our child than my own two brothers, who never have the time to visit. As you know, he's teaching Gary how to play the piano, helps him with his homework. And when you are not around, if Gary insists, he will even play catch with him, though he's not nearly as good a player as you."

She began to feel Jacob's body shift impatiently. She continued, "And while he loves us, perhaps you most of all, I've become convinced he's not happy here. Zalman, the old Zalman, used to laugh when I told him stories of how the old biddies in the supermarket would argue over pennies for the price of a can of peas or a half pound of Muenster cheese. And for his part, he never could stop talking about Rabbi Rozenstein, the nice farmer, the stubborn chicken who refused to lay eggs, or the color of the sky just as the sun rose on a Monday morning. But lately Zalman has stopped laughing, and he seldom tells those stories. He'll help me with a heavy package or two, sometimes drying when I'm washing the dishes, but he quickly goes up to his bedroom as soon as he's done. He seems to listen patiently when I talk about the news or ask his opinion on the color of drapes for the living room, or even how it might be a lovely day for the three of us to take a walk around the block before dinner. He listens, but his mind is very far away."

Esther sighed as she felt Jacob's arm tighten around her shoulders.

"But if he is unhappy as you say, Esther, what can we do?"

Esther took a deep breath before answering.

"We can let him go, Jacob. We can let him go."

~

For nearly five minutes, Esther lay her head tight against Jacob's chest. She did this for the comfort, but also because she was afraid that if she raised her head, he would notice the tears that were pressing now beneath the brims of her eyes.

She had told Jacob how much she had grown to love Zalman nearly as much as Jacob did. But more than that, she now needed him as a friend for the times when Jacob was not around, and to share their joy in Gary even when Jacob was home. Finally, she brushed her cheek against his still-dry shirt and stood up. Despite all she had told him, Jacob protested the decision, saying that if Zalman genuinely wanted to leave, he would allow him to go, but until then, she should not broach the subject. But Esther had grown tired, and so, only half listening to her husband's admonitions, she walked upstairs and went to bed.

~

Esther had an unusual habit. After everyone in the household had gone to bed, as darkness blanketed the home, leaving only a peaceful sense of contentment, she would pull out her baking utensils, the measuring cups and bowls, the tin loaf pans, along with the flour, baking powder, and whatever other ingredients were needed, and begin the task of baking bread. She had begun this weekly ritual only months after Boris had passed away, for the heat from the oven, the scents of raisins and cloves wafting through the air, always brought back the feeling of her childhood home, sweetening her dreams at night.

Wishing to replicate the experience for her son and the others fast asleep upstairs, like her mother had done so many years earlier, at 10:00 p.m. on a Thursday evening, Esther fastened the apron and set to work. That night, she would be making raisin bread, her father's favorite, and she was already thinking about the cinnamon rolls she had planned for next week, which was one of the recipes Florrie had given her. She worked without distractions for half an hour, sifting, measuring, and kneading the ingredients, cleaning the spilled flour and salt off the counter as she washed out the used bowls, a time-saving method her mother had instructed her in, and she was content that the two loaves would satisfy the family for at least the following week. If there were any leftovers, they could be sealed in aluminum foil and frozen for a later date. Just as she had slid the loaf pans into the oven, Esther thought she heard a sound coming from upstairs. Checking the dial on the oven, she quickly removed her apron, ran the water over her flour-streaked hands, and went upstairs.

Hearing the rhythmic snores that came from her bedroom and Zalman's room next to theirs, she quietly walked down the hall and turned the knob to check on Gary. The boy was sitting up in his bed, his hands covering his eyes as he sobbed quietly. She rushed to his side.

"Gary, my baby, what's the matter? Tell Mommy why you are crying," Esther said as tenderly as she could, trying to hold back her own tears.

It took the child a few moments to acknowledge her, as his sobs grew louder, his small body quivering with hysteria. Finally, he allowed her to remove the hands covering his eyes, hands that were by now bathed in his own tears. He took a deep breath and gazed up at his mother.

"Mommy, am I going to die?"

Of all the questions her child could have posed, Esther thought, this was one that she was completely unprepared for.

"Gary, oh Gary, why would you even be thinking of such a thing?"

The boy only stared up at her, his lip quivering as if he were about to cry anew. She wrapped him in her arms.

"Of course, you are not going to die," she assured him, as she inhaled the scent of her son, a mixture of chocolate candy and sweat. She stroked his hair, which had just begun to lighten with the new season.

"Tell me, are you thinking such things because of what happened two years ago? Because of your *zayde* Boris?"

He pulled back from her and shrugged.

Children are such funny creatures, Esther thought. Gary had barely reacted to Boris's sudden death; he hadn't even shed a tear. He was only six years old then, and she had considered him too young to comprehend it all.

"Gary, look at me," she said, tipping his chin with her finger so that his eyes were directly in line with her own. "Your *zayde* Boris was very sick and very, very old. You are a young boy with many, many more years ahead before you can think about dying."

"But I don't want to die ever!"

"My baby, please listen to your mother," she began, trying to find the right words as she spoke. "You do not need to worry about this, I promise you. The only worries you should have are to get a good grade on tomorrow's spelling test and how to earn your next badge for Cub Scouts. That's all. Trust that Mommy and Daddy will always take care of you. And so will God."

She moved toward him again then and felt his body relax as she encircled him in her arms.

"I love you so much, my baby," she murmured in his ear, and then tucked the blanket tight around him as he rested his head on the pillow.

As she closed the door behind her, Esther didn't worry so much about what Gary had confided in her, but rather her own words. Would the trust he had in her and Jacob be enough to quell her child's fears? Would trust in God be enough? She realized then that her son's words had matched her own unspoken fears, the fears that, now that she was a mother, she would always keep to herself. And again, she thought only about how much she loved this boy. And how she could never allow herself to think of the void in her life again, the missed opportunities, the children yet unborn.

Esther followed the aroma of baking raisin bread down the stairs and went into the dark kitchen, where she waited for the ding that would signal the end of the cooking cycle.

But that night, her cheek pressed next to the soft cotton of Jacob's T-shirt, Esther found it difficult to fall asleep. While her body was steeped in exhaustion, her mind was working overtime. Gary had planted a seed in her mind, and now as she lay staring into the shards of moonlight against the ceiling, she recalled the last time she'd spoken with Boris, the last time she saw his hands one atop the other, forever in death.

It was an uneventful conversation after her mother had handed the receiver over to Boris, prodding him to say hello.

"How are you feeling, Papou?" she'd said, half listening as she washed out a dish of applesauce.

"Okay," was the curt reply.

"Would you like to say hello to your grandson?" She knew she could always get an animated response from Boris when it came to Gary. Before he could answer, she stretched the extension cord as much as she could, bringing it into the living room. She waved to her son, who was seated on the rug counting his baseball cards.

"Come quick, Gary. Zayde's on the phone."

Gary took the receiver from her hand and listened as his grandfather posed the usual questions. How are you? How's school? What's new? And although the answers were always the same (Fine. Fine. Nothing.), Esther knew that just speaking with the child could lift Boris's spirits. The conversation always ended the same way.

"Do you know that you are my best boy?"

"Thank you, Zayde."

Gary handed the receiver back to Esther before plopping back down on the rug.

"Papou?"

"What a special boy you have!"

Esther smiled as she dried the dish and placed it in the cabinet.

"Thanks, Papou, but are you sure you're okay? Mommy says that you're not eating well. You barely ate supper tonight. And she made mushroom-and-barley soup, your favorite!"

She heard him bristle over the phone, picturing the scowl on his face.

"So what? If I'm not hungry, do I have to stuff myself? Did she tell you what else she cooked? Chicken. Boiled chicken and a potato. Every night the same thing."

"Mommy's cooking the foods that are best for you. We don't want you to get sick."

"You don't want. Humph. Everyone thinks they know what is best for me. I'm old enough to know what's best for me. And if I tell you I am not hungry, then I'm not hungry!"

Esther knew better than to insist.

"Okay, Papou, just be well."

"You too. You and your son and your husband. That's all I care about."

After hanging up, Esther joined her son in the living room. She picked up a copy of *Life Magazine* and perused the glossy pages, thinking how very difficult all this must be for her mother. By the time she had tucked Gary into bed that night, she had forgotten all about the conversation with her father. She remembered it only the next day when she got the phone call.

It was her first funeral. Until then, she had avoided attending the sad events, figuring that it was bad luck. She made excuses when her elderly aunt passed away at age ninety-four, did the same when she heard of her second cousin's demise. But now bad luck had caught up with her, and she could no longer avoid it. Her papou was dead.

Esther had always wondered what it would be like, how it would feel to lose a parent. Would she cry hysterically until she had no more tears to shed? Would she lose her mind? But when she heard the news that shortly after their conversation Boris had gone to bed and couldn't be awakened in the morning, Esther didn't scream or cry out. Instead, she telephoned an ambulance, then Jacob, and got dressed. By day's end, she had arranged for the funeral for the next morning, secured his plot at the cemetery, spoken with the rabbi. They decided that Jacob, and Esther's brother Menashe, would deliver the eulogies. Meanwhile, Esther was to make sure that her mother remained calm during the funeral. She carried a bottle of Valium in her purse just in case. She also had to find a way to tell Gary. She decided to tell him the truth. His *zayde* had gone to sleep, and he never woke up. He was old and he was sick, and now he was not in pain anymore. They would all miss him very much. The response seemed to satisfy the boy, who nodded and went back to reading one of his comic books.

Everyone remarked how stoic Esther seemed. Just before they entered the chapel, as she looked down at Boris's face, his body wrapped in white cloth and the tallis he had worn to her wedding, she bit her lip and moved on. She surprised herself. She wasn't anxious or especially sad. She had too much to do, to help her mother prepare for a life without a husband, to help her child understand what even she could not.

As she listened to Jacob speak, Esther was glad they had decided to let Gary stay at home with Zalman. It would have all been too real, too overwhelming, for a child of six. He spoke of Boris's devotion first to family, then to work. How as a poor immigrant, Boris had built a thriving business. How he had been respected by rich and poor alike. Everyone whom Boris dealt with called him a fair, generous, and patient man. A real mensch. But, most of all, he loved his family. His greatest joy was little Gary. And there was nothing he wouldn't do for Sally, Esther, her brothers, and Jacob, the man who had given his daughter such happiness.

"Boris was like a father to me," added Jacob, wiping a tear from his eye.

As Esther listened to the words, dry eyed, she was glad that it was Jacob, not she, who delivered the eulogy. She held tightly to her mother's hand. She was proud of her husband, who summoned just the right words when she could not. She also realized how much he and Boris were alike, in their silences, their ambition, their quiet devotion to family. And again she wondered about the family Jacob never spoke of.

Two years later, surprised by Gary's thoughts of death and his beloved *zayde*, Esther felt inadequate. How could she comfort him? How could she tell him that you never stopped missing someone who was gone? And sometimes you missed someone even when he was here.

~

In the morning, Esther had nearly forgotten about Gary's questions, her worries again turning to Zalman. But she was never given the chance to talk to him. That afternoon, as Gary remained studying in his room, Zalman walked in the door and immediately approached Esther, who had been arranging the flowerpots on the windowsill in the kitchen.

"The zinnias are looking very pretty," he said as he lifted one of the brown clay pots from the counter and handed it to her.

"Thank you, Zalman," she said, smiling at him, but his face remained expressionless. Esther had no time to consider her next words, because Zalman's came in the next instant.

"I'm leaving at the end of the week."

Suddenly all the platitudes, the well-chosen phrases, flew out of her head, and she had a feeling of becoming unmoored. She had prepared herself to speak, but she was hardly prepared to hear the words from Zalman himself. What had once been a fleeting feeling, an intangible fear, now had substance, a reality. And yet there he was, still standing next to her, waiting for her response. But all she could manage was an astonished "Oh." Zalman didn't offer any explanation as the two stood in awkward silence until Esther regained her composure, until finally the words came, fully formed from her mouth.

"I understand, Zalman. And as much as it pains me to say this, you've made the right decision for yourself. You've wasted too many precious years in Jacob's house, a house you helped build, with a boy you are helping to raise, and as for me, what a comfort you have been in the years when I was most in need!"

Esther paused only to rinse her soiled hands in the kitchen sink, and briefly considered switching her words to her native Polish so she could truly express her sorrow at seeing him go. But maybe she had said too much already. Still, there had been no response from Zalman, who remained standing a polite few feet away, the same blank expression on his face as when he had entered the room.

"You deserve more, my good friend," she continued, trying again to fill the void between them, "This home, this wife, this child, is as good as yours, but they are not yours. And we, Jacob and I, can't keep you from that. We've taken too much already."

As she spoke, her words were gathering speed.

"But where will you go? I hope you will continue to work with Jacob. I can't see that changing. Don't feel as if you must rush, you know. You will always have a home in Jacob's house."

Zalman shuffled his feet uneasily and wet his lips with his tongue. His eyes remained downcast when he finally spoke.

"I have plans. I've been thinking of going into partnership with a friend of mine, and if not, maybe I'll go back to the farm if the rabbi still has a place for me. Until then, there is an apartment in Brooklyn I can rent. We'll see."

Esther's voice dropped an octave.

"Yes, we'll see, I suppose," she repeated. But then she remembered something he had told her a few months earlier.

"You have a girl back in Minnesota, the farmer's daughter, who you've been writing to. Now I see. Well then, Zalman, whatever you decide to do, I wish you luck." She took a step forward, only slightly, to express her sincerity by sealing her wishes with a kiss on the cheek but thought better of it.

Zalman's eyes moved upward to look at Esther, seeming to take in her eyes, her face, her whole being. And then, without a word, or even an embrace, he went upstairs, where he remained for the rest of the night.

FOURTEEN

Zalman

S he persuaded him to stay one more week. Only one week so they
could all get used to the idea of him leaving. What harm could it
do? Even as he continued to pack his bag, Zalman could hardly contain
his excitement. He had arranged a special evening for Esther, a going-
away present. Leopold Stokowski was conducting at the Philharmonic
that Thursday evening, and he had managed to get two tickets. Jacob
heartily approved of the idea and promised to arrive home early that
evening, in time to take Gary to Little League practice. Besides, he had
no interest in listening to old-fashioned music.

Zalman led the way down the aisle as Esther surveyed the hall,
wide eyed.

"Here we are," he said, pointing to two seats in the center of the
mezzanine section. "Row D. Not too bad, eh?"

"Not too bad? Why, Zalman, this is marvelous!" she responded,
sinking down in the plush seat.

Zalman couldn't suppress his laughter. She was just like a child
entering a toy store for the first time. He opened his program, instruct-
ing her to do the same, as he leaned toward her, pointing out the list of

the musicians in each instrumental section, the names of the symphonies they were about to play.

"I'm sorry, but there's no Debussy tonight."

"Oh, that's fine, Zalman. You know how I love all music. It's going to be wonderful, just wonderful!"

Yes, he thought, sitting back, it was going to be wonderful.

For the next two hours, the two sat quietly as they let the music envelop them, creep inside of them, transport them. The rapid drumbeats seemed to lift them out of their chairs, and when the violinist played her solo, Esther was so moved that she grasped his arm. Zalman closed his eyes. He had never felt so happy.

The last strains of the orchestra signaled the intermission, but the two remained in their seats, unable to move, sharing the silence that now seemed unusual. When they finally rose to their feet, it was as if coming out of a dream.

"Is it like this always?" she asked.

"Well, I've only been to Lincoln Center twice before. The music is always beautiful. But this time, I guess it does seem more special."

"Yes! I just can't believe I'm here. Thank you, Zalman!" Impulsively, Esther reached over and gave him a hug. He turned from her as he felt a flush rise to his cheeks.

During the second half, as they listened to one of the lighter, merrier concertos, Zalman pointed to the movement of the conductor's arms, explaining the meaning. She leaned closer and, in a whisper, asked about the different sections of the orchestra or asked the year when a symphony had been composed. Although Zalman couldn't answer all her questions, he found himself enjoying his new role as teacher. Before they realized it, the waves of music swelled to a great crescendo. When the final commanding note had been played, Esther was among the first to get up as the audience stood. The applause, which seemed interminable, subsided, and the musicians took up their instruments for an encore. The applause was repeated as they completed one last rousing number by Beethoven. When Zalman glanced at Esther, she had the look of someone who had just gotten off a roller coaster.

Once outside, as they made their way toward the subway station at the corner, the two couldn't stop talking.

"I really loved so many of the numbers. Which was your favorite?" she asked.

He responded quickly. "It was the violin solo."

"Yes, it was quite moving. I noticed her fingers moving so quickly, so adept. How long do you think it takes one to acquire such a skill?"

"A long time, I'd guess. What I most enjoyed about the solo was how it reminded me of home."

Esther considered his words for a moment, the two linking arms as they walked down the stairs into the station.

"Zalman, did you love your mama and papa very much?"

He glanced at her and nodded his head. "Well, yes, of course. Why would you ask such a question?"

She looked down at the platform, strewn with Hershey wrappers and cigarette butts. "Oh, it's just that every now and then you mention them. You must miss them a great deal."

"I do. I try not to think about them or my brother too much. But when I hear certain melodies like the kind we heard tonight, or I listen to you play the piano, I'm always reminded of my family. Our home was always filled with music. When Mama wasn't playing the Jewish songs on the piano, my father would put on the phonograph, and we listened to everything from Chopin to Sinatra. Often, we would find ourselves—even my brother, who spent most of his time with his head in a book—humming along. When I hear a song like that violin solo, I remember that. That and the sizzle of my mother's potato pancakes in the pan, the rustle of the newspaper as my father settled into his favorite chair. But I try not to think about any of it. They were taken so suddenly. It was a different life."

"Zalman?"

"Yes?"

"Why does Jacob never speak about his family?"

Hearing his friend's name, something stirred inside him. They hadn't spoken of Jacob the entire evening.

"I don't know. He never has, not even in the early days. You're his wife. I thought you would know the answer to that question."

Esther frowned and shook her head. "You'd think that would be the case, but no. He never mentions them, not a word. And when I try to introduce the subject, he pushes me away, telling me he doesn't want to talk. Perhaps the memory is too painful. Still, it might be best for him to release all that, not keep it locked inside. Don't you think?"

Before Zalman could answer, the train roared in front of them, stopping with a screech. The two got into a crowded car and had to squeeze themselves into a double seat next to the conductor.

"Wouldn't you know it? No air-conditioning. And on a day like today!" Esther ignored the comment.

"Maybe you can get him to speak, Zalman. After all, you are his best friend."

"I don't know how many times I have tried, but it just seems to get him angry. He never wants to talk about the old days, even the times when we were together. Perhaps his head is too much in business. It's a big responsibility, taking care of a wife and young son. It seems the more I talk, the quieter Jacob gets. It is not good to be too quiet. Everything gets in your head. So I just keep talking, and he keeps getting quieter."

Esther's shoulders slumped as she sighed. "That's true, I suppose. In that, he reminds me so much of my papou." The car rocked as the train moved forward. He could feel her breath against his cheek.

"Oh, Zalman, I will never forget this day!"

He turned away, pretending to look out the window. He would leave in five days.

FIFTEEN

Jacob

Next to his family and his work, the thing that Jacob loved most was baseball. So he made sure that any free weekend was spent going to baseball games at Yankee Stadium, or assisting at Gary's Little League games, or, whenever it rained, reviewing and helping his son arrange trades of baseball cards as if they were conducting a big business venture. And much to Esther's consternation, father and son had often taken the opportunity for a game of catch in the backyard, even as ice melted off the bare branches of trees.

But one particular Saturday morning wasn't that kind of a day. In fact, it was just the opposite, a morning in April when spring was newly born and only a hint of a breeze carried the scent of the lilacs that had begun to peek through the neighbor's hedges. That morning, though, they had received a telephone call from the Little League coach telling them he was canceling practice after being taken ill with food poisoning as a result of buying a hot dog from a less-than-reputable food vendor. Nevertheless, as Jacob used to remind them, the backyard was "plenty big for a real game." And so it was the *almost* perfect day.

Jacob sat at the table and watched Esther at the stove, flipping french toast, white bread dipped in beaten eggs, then sprinkled with cinnamon before dropping the slices into the hot oil. It was Zalman's favorite. In the past week, as the date for his departure grew near, Jacob noticed that she was cooking all of Zalman's favorites. Meat loaf on Wednesday, fried chicken with rice for lunch before the concert on Thursday, a roasted chicken with sliced potatoes and Florrie's noodle kugel on Friday night, and now french toast on the weekend. He noted that, in the past, Zalman had shown her his gratitude with a friendly embrace or even just by clapping his hands in glee as he complimented the meal with every bite. But in the past week, his only response to her efforts had been a halfhearted smile as he lifted his fork to take the first taste. So great was Esther's disappointment that she began to wonder aloud if Zalman had not actually hated his life in their household, and if perhaps his joy had been a pretense all along.

Gary already had his Yankees cap on as he bounded into the kitchen, sitting on one of the new plastic swivel chairs at the table and placing the softball next to Esther's good china plate with its border of tiny red rosebuds.

"Gary! What have I told you? No baseballs on the kitchen table!" she scolded as he complied by shoving the ball between his knees.

With his fork, he stabbed a couple of the pieces of french toast that Esther had already sliced into neat bites and filled his mouth so that, as he turned toward Zalman, his words came out garbled. Even Zalman couldn't suppress a laugh as he reached over the table for the jar of strawberry jelly, dipped a butter knife inside, and meticulously spread the jelly over the remaining pieces on Gary's plate. "Thank you!" said the boy, burping simultaneously as he spoke so that they all nearly doubled over with laughter.

"Gary, you are quite the jokester!" Jacob said, a smile materializing on his face. He bent toward his son to place a kiss on the top of the baseball cap.

"A jokester without manners," replied Esther, and turned back to the pan on the stove, glad that the dour mood of the household had been lifted, even if only for a short while. Jacob turned to Zalman, who, having finished only one of the two slices on his plate, was about to stand.

"So, my friend, are you ready for a game of baseball with me and Gary? You can be catcher again." Zalman shook his head as he shimmied past Esther and placed his plate in the sink.

"Not today, Jacob. I have too much packing to do," said Zalman, and then, almost as an afterthought to Esther, "Thank you for the delicious breakfast," as he walked toward the front of the house and headed up the stairs. Jacob ate slowly as Esther began washing the dishes, setting aside a plate for herself for later, as was her habit. Neither seemed to notice that Gary had begun to fill the silence left in Zalman's wake with a torrent of words. He was talking about the other kids on the team, telling them that even though he wasn't nearly the best player, but with more practice, a lot of practice, anything was possible. Wasn't that what Jacob always told him? That anything if you just tried hard enough was possible. But Jacob was only half listening as Gary's words continued to invade his thoughts. Since Zalman had told Esther of his plans to leave, Jacob had refused to discuss the issue—neither with Zalman nor even Esther. It was almost as if he felt his silence would prevent Zalman's departure from becoming a reality. But he realized as his son chattered on excitedly that he could no longer prevent what was soon to be a fact. He resolved that that evening, after dinner, he would sit down with Zalman to discuss his prospects, maybe even make him a generous gift as a down payment for a home. Now he turned to his son.

"We'll work on that pitching stance of yours. You've got a good eye, Gary, so practice makes perfect. We'll get going as soon as I'm finished with my coffee."

"Finished yet, Dad?" piped Gary, without a note of sarcasm, as his father quickly took a last sip from the mug of steaming Sanka. He was proud of his son who, he had to admit, preferred books and music but had slowly developed an interest in Jacob's favorite hobby. In the last year he had caught Jacob's enthusiasm, so that the two, sporting matching Yankee caps and jackets, were nearly always the first to arrive at practice and Little League games. Jacob reliably told Gary that he was destined to be the best shortstop, or even pitcher, on the team, maybe even in the whole league. And, after the past month, Jacob was more convinced of this possibility than ever.

"Finished yet, Dad?"

"Yes, sir!" announced Jacob, and rising, watched Gary pop a last piece of french toast into his mouth, then adjust his cap, leaving a red slash of jelly across his forehead. He decided not to remark on the matter—after all, like the saying "Boys will be boys . . ." Jacob grabbed his cap as the two walked out the side screen door, sending a ripple through the yellow cotton curtains as a whoosh of cool lilac-scented air sailed into the room where Esther stood silently, the dry kitchen towel still in her hand.

SIXTEEN

Esther

E sther heard the sound before she saw what happened. It was like the howling of a wolf, but at a lower pitch, more guttural. Only later did she learn that it had come from Jacob just at the moment of impact.

She flew out the screen door, not stopping to glance out the window a second time, leaving the curtains rippling in her wake. Once outside, she saw Jacob, cap still on his head, his tall frame bent over Gary. The wailing had ceased and was replaced by the repetition of her son's name. "Gary! Come on, Gary! Gary? *Gary!*" Esther stopped, frozen, afraid of what she might see, before taking a few steps toward the two, who were positioned at the base of the giant oak tree. It was not long before Esther's wails blended in with those of her husband, for lying cradled inside his father's arms was her child, her Gary, his lifeless eyes a sea-glass blue, wide open, waiting for the hit.

～

The doctors said it was something called commotio cordis, a direct blow to the heart between beats. It was instant, a fluke, and deadly.

Still, for several hours afterward, she continued to hear the noise, the wails, the cold robotic voice of the white coat telling her nothing could be done. It was only afterward that she noticed Zalman, his red face awash in tears, standing by her side, holding her hand tenderly. Was it tenderly? Was that the word she would have used to describe it? She could not describe anything, for in effect she was numb, unfeeling, immune. It was only later that she realized Jacob was nowhere to be found. When had she seen him last? Kneeling on the ground? In the ambulance with its siren drowning out their screams? Were they still screaming, or had a shocked silence replaced the sound? Or, as they stood, not really listening, as the white coat explained so serenely that their only child was gone? But what did it matter? She didn't care. Not about Jacob. Not about anything. The only thing she could see were snapshots of Gary that floated now like a dream into her mind. Gary as a curly-haired baby. Gary climbing onto her knee, sitting playing the keys of the oversize piano, flipping adeptly through his baseball cards. Gary, eyes wide open, a dried slash of jelly, prophetic, still marked across his forehead. Instinctively, she moved her hand as if to wipe it off. But it was gone now. Gary was gone. She clenched her fist tightly, digging her nails into the palm of her hand.

The days that followed were a blur seen only through the constant veil of tears that accompanied Esther during mornings when she mechanically assumed the role of grieving parent, and nights when sleep eluded her as images of her only child clouded her mind. In spite of the phone calls, the bountiful meals, the hard-boiled eggs, peeled, a reminder of the circle of life *(Does life go on, does it really?)*, bagels of every sort, an assortment of cheeses for breakfast, and roast chicken and kishka, a stuffed derma, and corned beef and kugels—mostly orchestrated by Florrie—much of the food remained untouched. Jacob had, for the most part, disappeared into their bedroom, and when he was present, the person before them had been replaced by a ghost, at least that was the way it appeared to Esther.

As for herself, her lamentations could not be quelled, her tears could not be stopped. Never had she known such sadness, never even dreamed it was possible, not even after the death of her father. The loss of a parent, though sad, was the natural order of things, but a child—their child—in a simple wooden coffin? The sight of it was so against the mandate of what it meant to be alive, something that she eventually had to concede was beyond comprehension. So she no longer tried to understand it but let the feelings wash over her as she went through the motions of her day. And yet, like a refrain that invaded her mind, she recalled the mere sight of the coffin, so small, as she stood before it that sunny Monday morning, draped in black between Jacob and Zalman, blocking the stream of words that flew from the rabbi's mouth, words intended to comfort, the platitudes from family, neighbors, and friends. Her mother, Sally, afflicted now with Parkinson's disease and whose steady flow of tears nearly matched her own, stayed home that day, and on most days afterward, unable to summon the words that could comfort her daughter. Although she would call Esther on the phone occasionally, she often said little. The skies were threatening rain, or she had a new recipe for a plum compote, or if Esther had stomach problems, advising a cup of strong tea. What could she say, really?

Even Zalman, who seemed always to be standing at Esther's side with a plate of rugelach and a slice of sponge cake or offering a sweater as the air began to chill—not even he could penetrate the sadness, not even he could stop the endless torrent of tears. Only at night when the moon was high and the silence deep did she hear sobs coming from his room.

While Esther in those days and weeks after the funeral could not stop crying, Jacob was unable to shed a single tear. He passed through the days, a grim expression set in his face, which seemed remarkably to have aged ten years. He spoke little, asked for nothing, his grief impenetrable. Even without his saying a word, Esther knew he blamed himself for the accident. If only he had not hit the ball so hard, if only he hadn't pushed his son to be the best, if only the two had stayed indoors that day. If only . . . Esther didn't blame her husband; the thought hadn't even crossed her mind. She was too preoccupied with the loss and the fear of a lifetime of days ahead that would be spent grieving, childless. And so she did not voice any objection when after the week's period of mourning, the shiva, was over, Jacob announced he would be going back to work.

~

Time passes. In six months, a human can go from an embryo to a baby to a child staring with wonder between the bars of a crib to a toddler running out the door, from a boy whose future lay before him like a brilliant new day to . . . to what? To grieving parents, to nothing. No movement, no future, no time.

It was also a time of learning for Esther. Since she was a girl, she had filled her days with things to do; now all the tasks that had occupied her time seemed irrelevant, worthless. So she relearned new things, a new way to be. Florrie knew someone who managed a card store downtown, and with a simple phone call, Esther became the new cashier and salesgirl Monday, Wednesday, and Friday afternoons. She learned to sew—skirts and drapes and doilies—took a class in ceramics from which she brought home vases for flowers, and purple-and-yellow-dotted teapots. Esther joined a women's club, where she knitted and helped collect money for the town library, and while she did not always chat about mundane things like some of the others, she listened. And when she had quiet time to think (knowing full well that thought worked as a parasite to sanity), there was always Florrie, arm stretched out to offer a muffin and a cup of steaming tea or sit with her, watching *All My Children* or another soap opera, an outlet for her fears. But as the days cooled and the sun shimmered low in the sky, the memories of what she could no longer have filled her mind, and often, as Esther sat alone on the couch waiting for Jacob to walk in the door, tears would spring to her eyes. But in those months, Jacob was no comfort. Not to Esther and not to himself.

Almost too soon after the customary period, Jacob had returned to work. It was there that he could remain invisible, hiding as he went through his daily rituals of paperwork and visits to tenants, lawyers, and associates. When he came home late in the evening, he spoke little except for a customary nod of the head when he walked in, not even bothering to assist with the dishes, or carry the garbage outdoors. The flowers on the hedges had begun to droop, and the grass turned yellow from lack of care, as more cigarette butts scattered on the front porch and lay cold, dormant in ashtrays on the end tables. Except for when he took his meals, Jacob haunted the bedroom silently, reading the paper or going over material from the office. He steadfastly refused all her appeals to come outside, take a walk in the park, or see a movie. Of course, going to a ball game was out of the question. While Jacob offered no solace for his wife, neither did he complain nor even give voice to the guilt Esther believe consumed him even now, just over a year later. He expressed no sorrow, at least not openly, no anger or resignation. Her husband had become invisible.

It was Zalman who remained in the house, there to help her fold the laundry or ask if she wanted another cup of tea. It wasn't until a month after the tragedy that she remembered. He had been ready to leave, had packed his things and had even secured a new job. And yet he was there, as always, comforting, supporting. Filling the spaces Jacob had left.

But even though Jacob had become invisible, unreachable, Esther felt that during those days she understood him more than ever. He had always been an enigma in his refusal to talk about his life as a boy, before his parents and brother lost their lives brutally, she guessed, in the war. Now that she, too, knew tragedy, perhaps the greatest tragedy anyone could realize, she understood the relief that sometimes silence could bring. Sometimes, she reasoned to herself, it was better to close oneself off, not revisit the sadness. Finally, Esther knew her husband, why he never so much as mentioned what his parents were like in better times, if his mother had tucked him into bed at night, if his father had shown him how to throw a ball, as he had with Gary.

The sun was at its full height that Sunday after Esther and Zalman returned from a trip to the local appetizing store, where they had picked up a whole whitefish and some egg bagels, a rare dairy treat for the evening's dinner. They were entering the kitchen when they heard the sound of rummaging and drawers slamming upstairs. They dropped their packages on the counter, and Esther rushed up the stairs where she found Jacob in not their bedroom, but Gary's, where he was tossing armloads of their son's shirts, sweaters, and pants into jumbo plastic garbage bags.

"Jacob! What are you doing?" she cried, covering her eyes with her hand. She hadn't entered her child's room since that sunny morning in spring, and since then the door had been kept tightly shut.

"Getting rid of things," was the curt reply. In a frenzy, he piled a drawer full of white T-shirts into the top of the bag. A framed photograph of kindergarten graduates was lying on the oak floor planks next to the round aqua-colored shag rug, its glass pane shattered. Some of Gary's rudimentary crayon drawings had been hastily torn off the walls and lay crumpled and abandoned on the bedspread decorated with varicolored baseballs. The bed remained as she had left it, bedsheets neatly tucked into the corners.

"Jacob!" she shouted, surprised to find her voice screeching now. "What are you doing? You are destroying *everything*!" But her husband didn't answer, and instead picked up the pace, hurling the pink ceramic piggy bank, a smile still planted beneath the animal's snout, against a wall, where it cracked instantly, giving up a shower of coins that scattered like beach pebbles throughout the floor.

Esther ignored the mess and ran to Jacob, grabbing him by the forearm as he flung Gary's Cub Scout cap as if it were a discus. But her husband was silent as a stone as Esther found herself falling backward just like the articles of clothing, so that in a matter of seconds she was sitting on the area rug, stunned, glaring at the man before her. His face was puffed up, flushed, as a storm surged beneath his eyes. Was this the affectionate, tender man she had grown to love? Esther decided not to fight it anymore. She quickly picked up the Cub Scout hat, a couple of the torn crayon drawings, the shattered kindergarten photo, and Spanky, the stuffed black-and-white cocker spaniel that sat on the pillow atop the bed.

At first, she had not even realized that at the bottom of the stairs stood Zalman, his face a mixture of fright and concern.

"It's no good. Nothing is good anymore, Zalman!" she cried, descending the stairs and dumping the items on the carpet. Still standing, she covered the free-flowing tears that ran down her cheeks. Zalman stood silently watching her as, his arms at his side, he clenched and unclenched his fists. For several minutes he gazed at her helplessly until her tears were spent. Then, just as their eyes locked, there was a whoosh of wind as an object came flying down the stairs toward the two, narrowly missing Esther's leg.

"What the—" exclaimed Zalman as he lifted the shiny metal off the floor. It was a Little League team trophy for second place, the first and last Gary would ever receive.

Esther lifted it from his hands, caressing the torso of the figurine almost as if in doing so she could bring her son back to life.

Shortly afterward, Jacob came downstairs, huffing beneath the burden of two large garbage bags. This time, Esther did not so much as glance at her husband; he offered neither apology nor explanation as he pushed the bags through the door, lifted the car keys from a side table. The slam of doors, the growl of the key in the ignition, and then the emptiness of silence.

After moments of what seemed like an endless purgatory, Esther allowed herself to be led to the sofa, where Zalman tenderly lifted the trophy, still in her hands, and placed it on the coffee table in front of them. She felt that with Jacob's departure, the air, the life that had once filled their happy home, had vanished. She was finding it difficult to breathe.

Zalman was saying something. He was sitting next to her now, but it took her a long time before she could make out the words.

"You don't deserve this. I don't know what's wrong with him. I think he's going crazy."

Esther looked up at her friend, her eyelashes still dotted with tears as she nodded. "I'm worried that you're right. Crazy with grief. And there's nothing I can do to help him."

Zalman waited, unspeaking, listening to the clock in the hall chime the hour. She turned toward him, noticing for the first time that his eyes, small, overshadowed by heavy eyebrows, were perhaps more green than blue.

"Zalman, I don't know what I would do without you." After all, what more was there to say?

After some time had passed—she didn't quite know how long—the descending sun traced lines of light against the silver drapes, and the whirring blades of the ceiling fan in the upstairs bedroom hummed peacefully, lulling Esther into a blissful sleep. In her dreams, there was Jacob again as he was on the first night they had slept together as husband and wife. And even though barely sixteen years had passed since then, he appeared now as he was once: young, his cheekbones prominent, his face taking on a rosy hue, and his eyes intense, as if they could see right through her even though now they glistened with tears. Esther felt her heart lift then with the same hope. She leaned into her husband, catching the scent of the musk cologne on his neck, the rough stubble of his face scratching her cheeks. If only the world would stop, stop turning, stop everything. She desperately wanted the dream to stay, to hold on to it like a bright falling star. She felt herself pushing closer against his broad shoulders as his arm tightened protectively around hers, his nose nuzzling the locks of her hair, his lips sprinkling her neck with tender kisses like gentle drops of rain, his lips soft then urgent, pressed against hers. Only, she quickly realized, it wasn't a dream at all—it wasn't even Jacob now, but Zalman, kissing her with a passion she never thought him capable of. She pulled back instantly, opening her eyes.

Even days later, when Esther tried to make sense of it all, she found it difficult to recall exactly what had happened that late afternoon in June. All she knew was that her senses seemed to explode all at once. Zalman's face, once so familiar, was replaced by someone new, someone she could no longer recognize. A stranger. And yet, mirrored in those eyes, she saw the same confusion and surprise as her own.

Neither had heard the key turning in the lock, the step of Jacob's brown Florsheim on the ceramic tiles in the foyer. Only the howl, like the one Esther had heard just once before, but somehow now more desperate, as if someone had suffered a mortal wound. And soon she felt the scrape against her skin, even then knowing somehow that the scars would never heal, as fingers tore at them both with an animal vengeance, lifting Zalman whole, who offered no defense as he was slammed against the wall, as she heard the antique vase her mother had brought from the old country splinter into a thousand pieces, as someone emitted a cry, only once, as Jacob threw the man who was once his brother, his friend, down the porch stairs and onto the sidewalk below.

Esther sat on the couch where she had been dreaming only moments earlier, listening for the sound of a door, her husband's footsteps coming back down the stairs, but as the last streaks of light faded from the wall, and a few stars began to dot the horizon, only the silence remained. A silence that was deeper, more grievous, than even Esther had ever known.

SEVENTEEN

Zalman

As he stared out of the window of the moving train, Zalman tried to focus on the shifting scenery before him. Between an unsettled sleep and awakening, he watched as the sharp angles of gray blocks composed of brick and stone and metal gave way to the shimmering pastels of blue-green grass along the plains. Finally, washed by the sun, the mist opened up to bright sage-green stalks tinged a purple rose against a cerulean sky. So unusual were the colors, as if someone had switched on a bulb, that Zalman, every now and then, had to turn away.

In the months since he had left Jacob's house, he had tried, most times unsuccessfully, to avoid self-reflection. He found himself as he had when first coming to America, living at his cousin's house, which now, after knowing the comfort of family and home, seemed more foreign to him than ever. And despite intensifying his hours at work now with clients of his own and staying up nights for hours at a time watching old James Cagney or William Powell movies, he couldn't escape the surging memories of that day in early June. Why had he done it? He loved her; he knew that now, though it was not until Gary's death that he himself realized the feelings to be true. From the first day he had met Esther, he had admired her, even congratulated Jacob on his good fortune. And when, as he took up residence in the home, he came to expect the alluring scent of Shalimar as he walked through the door, the beauty of her slender forearm as she extended it toward him, martini in hand, the brush of her skin, the auburn forelock of hair soft against his cheek as she thanked him. *Thank you for helping me with the groceries. Thank you for reading Gary a story, taking him to the movies, teaching him how to spell "refrigerator," the names of all the US presidents, the musical scale. Thank you, Zalman.*

And yet, how had he repaid her for all her thanks, her limitless generosity? Betrayal. Betrayal of the one friend, the only brother he would ever again have on this earth. It was the fear of betrayal, he reasoned, as through the years he lay alone each night on the double bed next to the bedroom where Jacob lay entwined with Esther, his wife, that forced his decision to leave the house, still unsure of what the future might hold. Jacob considered him his friend, his very best friend, and had welcomed him as part of the family. He desired all that Jacob had—his wife, his child, his home. And yet, each time he remembered the magical strains of "Clair de Lune" that filled the house, the aroma of Shalimar, the lock of hair caressing his cheek, he knew that he could never go back.

Memories of that sunny morning when Jacob and Gary, caps on their heads, ball in hand, decided to play some baseball, flickered before him. The morning that changed everything. And once again, Zalman found himself helpless. Helpless to leave, helpless to stay away from her. Grief had changed them all irrevocably, but most of all, her. Bereft, lines of sadness etched into her face, she had become a broken woman, without a husband or parent to put her back together. So it was up to Zalman to slowly, patiently, reinstall in her a zest for life. Childlike, as she cast her blue eyes up at him during those dark days, he loved her more than ever. So it seemed only natural after Jacob stormed out with all the possessions that had defined their only son, and she leaned into Zalman for comfort, her lips quivering . . .

Jacob was right to throw him out, of course. Zalman, who had become Brutus to his Julius Caesar, deserved worse. Two days later, Esther telephoned him at his cousin's apartment in the city. She was not angry with him, not with him and not even with Jacob who, without a word, had gone back to work the next day and the day after that. Still, Zalman felt the sense of defeat and disappointment registered in her voice. She would leave the door open the following afternoon so he could come back and collect his things. He had done as she asked, gathering a few articles of clothing from the drawers, his briefcase filled with notes and architectural drawings, and finally, stopping at the piano bench where beneath was the "Clair de Lune" song sheet inside a slender book, *A Beginner's Guide to Piano*. He retrieved the booklet and stuffed it in the briefcase before shutting the door to Jacob's castle.

It wasn't the last he heard from her. A week after he had left their home for the last time, just as the first hints of light teased beyond the horizon, and still at his cousin's apartment, Zalman heard a strident ring slicing through the early-morning quiet. He jumped out of bed and ran for the phone in the living room.

Her voice, so dear and unexpected, sent shivers through his skin.

"Zalman? It's you, right? Sorry to call so early." And then, just in case, "It's Esther."

"Yes. I know."

"Look, Zalman, I'm sorry to bother you again. But I think we need to talk." He felt his throat clenching up on him and, fearing he might drop it, held on tightly to the receiver.

Hearing no response on the other end, she continued.

"Zalman? Did you hear me? I have something to tell you, but I can't say what I need to say over the telephone. It is—how do they put it?" For a moment she stumbled, trying to find the English word she needed. *"Discreet?"* She accentuated the *e*—"I have to be discreet. I will not take up too much of your time, I promise. Only we must be discreet, if not for us, then for Jacob. Zalman, are you still on the telephone?"

"Yes."

"Well. So, there is a place Florrie has told me about. It's near the school where she graduated college. Brooklyn College. Jacob would not be there. *Wolfie's*—that's it. Just like the animal. So I think maybe we meet there lunchtime. Twelve o'clock. Twelve o'clock to talk."

"There's nothing to say."

"Zalman, please." A high-pitched urgency.

"Twelve o'clock tomorrow."

"Thank you."

The phone clicked off.

~

Wolfie's on Bedford Avenue was only steps away from the towering arch leading into the imposing square of buildings and lush greenery of the Brooklyn College campus. Summer classes were in session now, and a handful of students, the young males in their short-sleeve button-down shirts and T-shirts, and the females in flowered sundresses, all with denim knapsacks on their backs, sauntered into the air-conditioned café as escape from the sidewalks, still thick with heat.

Entering the establishment, he noticed her immediately. She was seated in the back, facing him. Looking at her now, he felt as if the air had seeped from the room. Except for the hot-pink woven cape and hair prematurely streaked with gray (had he noticed before?), she could have been mistaken for any one of the handful of students chatting and smoking within the room. She was more beautiful than he remembered.

He approached the table with a barely perceptible nod and sat down. A thirtysomething waitress with stark buck teeth, her blonde hair pulled back in a messy bun, came over immediately. Introducing herself as Jean, she scribbled their order with the nub of a pencil—a

Lipton tea with lemon for Esther, and despite the tantalizing smell of juicy burgers and stacks of french fries being served at the surrounding tables, a plain black coffee for Zalman. Neither one had come to eat. Finally, her voice, familiar, light as ripples over a lake, broke the silence.

"How have you been, Zalman?"

He could feel her eyes looking at him intensely, though he was afraid to meet them with his own.

"Fine," he said, barely above a whisper as he unraveled the table napkin, freeing the utensils.

"You look tired."

He shrugged. He didn't want to be here. Still, he had a question.

"How is Jacob?"

"He's okay. What I mean to say is, he's holding up. We're still together if that's what you mean. He didn't leave me."

"No . . . I didn't think he would. And I didn't want him to."

"I know you didn't. You never meant for those few minutes to happen." Her voice was low, *discreet*.

"He was not himself, Zalman. He hasn't been himself since—you know. We were all changed. He couldn't be reached, he couldn't be helped, not in the way you helped me to—as the saying goes—take it one day at a time, one foot in front of the other." Her voice gained a newfound strength as she continued.

"I thought at first it was best to leave him alone, that he would come to understand that he was not responsible for what happened to Gary"—a catch in her throat—"he only wanted to throw the ball with his son."

The waitress came over with two mugs of the steaming liquid, set them down along with milk, still bubbling, filled to the brim in a metal tin.

"Anything else I can get ya?"

Both declined, and wiping her hands quickly on the black apron at her waist, Jean went back to the kitchen, leaving them to their beverages, which remained untouched.

Esther began again, quieter this time than even before. His chin still tilted close to his chest, Zalman couldn't help but glance up at her eyes, where droplets of water glistened, islands in a blue sea.

"After he came home that day, after all that happened, he went upstairs to our room. He didn't come down for the rest of the night, and if truth be known, I no longer had the energy for explanation, apologies—"

"But why would you?"

She placed her hand then on Zalman's, but it felt like a fire had lit in his tendons, and he quickly pulled the hand away.

"I don't know anything anymore, Zalman. I only know that you were—that you *are*—my very good friend. Maybe my actions, I don't know, sent the wrong message."

Before he could protest, her voice hurried on, more urgently than before as she stared down at the table.

"It had become like a contest with us, Jacob at work during the day, upstairs in our bedroom, while I stayed downstairs on the couch at night. I did not mind it, not really. The bed, the hall, all the rooms on that level, held too many memories for me, memories which had turned sour in only a couple of months. After five days of this war of silence between us, he finally came down one evening, made two cups of tea, and set them on the kitchen table. At first, he only wanted to know why. And I told him all that had happened between us was a friend comforting another, and truly, Zalman, you were a comfort to me. You brought me out of the deep water so I could breathe again. You showed me how to live. You were the best friend a grieving mother could ask for." She looked up at him then, noticed Zalman shaking his head, his lips tightly set.

"Anyway, I assured him of your loyalty and my love. He has forgiven me, it seems, but has yet to forgive himself. If he ever can at all."

"No," said Zalman, his voice low and groggy as if he had just awakened from sleep, "he hasn't forgiven me, this I know. And he would be a fool to do so."

"Oh, but that is the thing I came to you about," she said, moving her tea, now cooled, to the side so she could lean across the table.

"You know Jacob perhaps better than anyone. He would never like my saying this, but he is, as my mother would say about my father, '*a shtila marook*,' as silent as a stone, keeping all his worries locked inside. And because of this, I now know that he will one day understand and forgive you. You understand, I'm sure, how there's something, a secret something, that happened to Jacob many years ago back in the old country. It took this tragedy to finally pry open his lips, so that he finally told me all. He now knows the cost of holding on to bitterness until it is too late, and he can't afford to let that happen again. Oh, Zalman, I now know he will forgive you one day. Only please give him time. And then maybe you can even come back to us—our home. Not the same as things once were, never that. But maybe—"

The light shining off her auburn hair. A whiff of Shalimar.

The table shook suddenly. The unused utensils clattered as forks and spoons hit the ceramic tiled floor. Zalman was on his feet.

"No!" he exclaimed, not bothering to modulate his voice. "I don't want your forgiveness. All I want is for you to leave me alone!" Pausing only long enough to collect his straw hat, Zalman left the restaurant.

He did not turn around to look at her that afternoon, but if he had, he would have seen her mouth agape, still in midsentence, more astonished than sad. He hated the possibility that his abrupt departure might have hurt her, but he knew that he could not stay one minute longer in her presence. If he had, he might have weakened, confessed his true feelings for her. He could never allow that to happen. So he tried to convince himself that it didn't really matter how she felt. Nor did it matter that his curiosity about Jacob's past was quenched. None of it did.

Now Zalman needed to forget the past, to build a new life for himself. He vowed never to spend the rest of his days as a voyeur, as he had in the pirates' room during the war years, in the barn waiting for

Jacob's cue, watching Jacob's marital happiness unfold. From now on, he would be a participant in his own life. Zalman's life would be his own, and he would never look back.

As the train screeched to a slow halt and a blast of sunlight shot through the grimy window, Zalman scanned the platform for familiar faces. When his eye caught one in particular, he quickly stood up, gathered his things, and, just as the signal shattered the morning air, stepped off the train.

PART IV

CRACKS IN THE ROOF

EIGHTEEN

Jacob, 1934

J acob let his hand slide down the flank of the great horse. The black
hairs felt smooth and silky, falling away beneath his small palm, so
that after a few moments of stroking, he was no longer afraid. Almost
as if it sensed the child's trepidation, the animal stood as still as the gray
tombstones that lined the cemetery in the old town, its giant dark eye
open, staring only at the winding path ahead.

Somewhere farther afield, he could hear them talking. The man's
voice gravelly, punctuated by a smoker's cough, showed signs of a heavy
accent, hers warm and familiar, like water tripping over rocks. The
words themselves were incomprehensible. *Business.*

He decided not to pay them any attention, instead focusing on the
horse beneath his hand. "Good boy. Such a good boy."

It seemed like hours as Jacob and the horse remained together, but,
in fact, it was only minutes since the man had trotted the horse out of
its steel barn and coaxed the boy to come closer. Klaus, long past being
a pony, was a workhorse and no longer a frivolous colt, would never
harm a soul, the man assured. Only the flies that swarmed about Klaus's
coarse, bushy tail were subject to the occasional swat. But that was to
be expected. And, in fact, when she called to the child, finally, Jacob

startled, then ignored her, pretending not to hear. The horse was his friend now. Maybe his best friend in the world.

But she persisted in calling him, and when he heard a sharpness creep into her tone, he withdrew his hand as the horse, aware somehow of the unwelcome interruption, turned its head slowly and began sauntering up the hill.

He took his time trailing behind, and even when he had her in sight, crouching, her arms outstretched, expecting his ready embrace, he halted barely a foot away, his eyes fixing on the clouds of dust left in Klaus's wake. She crunched her brow, faking a grimace. Jacob became excited as he got closer, but then he came to a halt as out of the corner of his eye, a short distance behind, he saw another. Mama flashed the man a broad, red-lipped smile. The man was tall, even taller than Jacob's papa, and he stood now with hands clasped behind his back, the medals on his tan uniform sparkling in the early-afternoon sunshine. He was the owner of the big horse, and so, despite Jacob's love for the animal, he felt a sudden stab of guilt sear through his chest.

But soon his mama's arms were around him, and he fell against her bosom, inhaling the familiar scent of her soap.

"And have you made friends with big Klaus?" she asked him in Yiddish, pushing back the child's sandy-color locks with her fingers.

"Yes, Mama," he answered as the memory of his time with the horse sent a smile flooding across his face.

"And so, I suppose you should say a thank-you to Herr Reichert for letting you pet him, no?"

"Yes, Mama." He turned toward the tall man, but his eyes only fell in line with the glittering medals.

"Thank you, Herr Reichert."

The man reached down to pat the child's head but, thinking better of it, dug his fingers instead into his pockets as he bounced on his feet. Jacob took note that the smile on his face now matched his mother's. A few words in German flew from Herr Reichert's mouth—sharp, staccato. He tried to catch their meaning, but he had only just begun learning the language of the Fatherland in school. Before he could sort it out in his head, his mama spoke again.

"Herr Reichert says you are welcome to spend time with Klaus anytime you want. You may even ride him if you like."

Jacob nodded. He couldn't quite imagine how wonderful it would be to sit snugly in a leather saddle atop the great horse, his head nearly touching the tips of the clouds!

His mother was curving her mouth into the red-lipped smile again, a smile that, he could see now, was meant only for the tall man with the medals.

"Mama, can we go home now?" Jacob asked, willing her to glance back in his direction.

"Soon, very soon, Yankel," she answered, using his pet name. But much to his dismay, it wasn't so soon. As Jacob sat in the dirt next to a wooden fence, he picked up handfuls of the small, ubiquitous rocks and began to arrange them in neat rows. Meanwhile, his mother and the man had led the horse to the barn, where they remained until Jacob had finished three rows of twenty. Jacob felt lonely as he tried to preoccupy himself with the counting and arranging. Business, he thought. Mama and the man had so much business to talk about. But then he felt her slender fingers on his shoulder. It was time to go. The tall man with the shiny medals was nowhere to be seen.

As the two sat in the car, the ride was silent. Mama didn't talk; she didn't even smile. Her red lipstick sat on her lips, faded and pink. Jacob's papa was already in the kitchen, slicing potatoes when the two walked in the door. It was not that he particularly enjoyed domestic duties that were usually the domain of women. Nevertheless, as a mathematics teacher at a nearby yeshiva, his hours weren't quite as long as his wife's, who had worked for Herr Reichert as a secretary for the past two years. Jacob, being only eight, did not quite understand why his mother, a Jew, could work for the German government under the Nazis, who were openly dismissive, even contemptuous, of the large Jewish populace. Nor could he understand why his mama's work seemed more important than his papa's. All he knew was that he enjoyed these occasional outings to the country, where he could pet goats and now even a horse at the stables Herr Reichert owned. Even though—and he wasn't sure why—he didn't much care for Herr Reichert himself.

Seeing the two enter the small apartment, Shmuel, his father, put down the knife and wiped his hands, which were stained brown from the peelings, on a kitchen towel. He embraced Jacob's mama, his mouth pressing against hers, further lightening the lipstick, until only a pinkish smudge was left. Before he could acknowledge his young son, though, Jacob slipped into the room he shared with his brother.

The older brother barely noticed Jacob since Leon, as usual, had his nose buried in a slim book, this time *The Metamorphosis*, as he lay on his stomach on the bed wedged against the wall and small bureau.

"I'm back," announced Jacob as he sat on the bed across from his brother's and began to unbuckle his shoe.

"Did you have fun?" Leon asked, his attention still inside the Kafka tale.

"I suppose," answered Jacob as he placed the shoes carefully under the bed next to his album of stamps and the old book of fairy stories. He knew better than to divulge any of the details to Leon, who openly advocated against their mother working for Herr Reichert or anyone involved in the Reich, for that matter. At first, Jacob took his brother's reticence for jealousy, because only the younger child was asked to accompany Mama on these excursions to the country. The reason was simple, since with Papa at work, and Leon in school or at the library, Jacob was too young to be left alone in the apartment, as thieves in the town had been growing increasingly bold, and besides, who knew what the vandals might do to such an innocent mop-headed Jew?

So even though Jacob's mouth itched to tell Leon all about Klaus, the touch of the silky dark hair, his liquid-brown eyes, he resisted. He could not bear another argument between Leon and his mama, which the mention of Herr Reichert's name would surely arouse. Papa, meanwhile, would remain quiet at these times, at most gently admonishing his oldest child, "Please leave your mama alone. You can see how hard she works for us all. Besides, shouldn't you be returning to your bar mitzvah studies?"

Leon didn't particularly like learning haftorah, but since he didn't want to further anger his papa, he would reluctantly return to his room. Jacob, meanwhile, would pretend to busy himself on the floor with his wooden cars.

As Leon continued to stare into the book, an unusual feeling overcame Jacob, one of being overwhelmed by something that felt far greater than his eight-year-old self, or even Leon or Papa or Mama. It was like an enormous unstoppable wave, and lost in the center, young Jacob felt more alone than ever. It was not the first time he had experienced the feeling. The first time was when school had been dismissed early due to an electrical fire in the library, and he had found himself alone in the apartment, waiting for the rest of his family to come home. As Jacob had busied himself, removing the tin of biscuits from the pantry shelf, sharpening pencils for the subtraction exercises in his workbook, the mundane sounds so often taken for granted had become magnified. The wind had banged ferociously again at the flimsy windowpanes, the mice in the walls had scraped their feet menacingly near, and the sirens outdoors, omnipresent now, had shattered the still October air. Jacob had felt his heart beat so fast that he feared it might penetrate right through the wall of his chest. And now there was the feeling again. Something ominous was coming. Something awful.

No one would have guessed it, though, for the more anxious the child became, the more perfect was his pretense. Not even the great Lionel Barrymore could have done so well. For when he heard the soft knock against the door, and Mama's voice announcing that dinner was on the table, Jacob unclasped his hands from behind his head, brought his knees to his chest, and moved off the bed. He didn't bother to put the shoes, their soles still laden with dust, on his feet before rushing past his brother and seating himself at the kitchen table. "Roast chicken! My favorite!" he announced excitedly, picking up a metal fork. Yes, he thought, I am the greatest actor in the world.

Jacob's world fell into a dull routine of school, races down the winding cobblestone blocks with his two best friends, Victor and Aaron, home to do more work for school, and in a few more months, Ziegler's grocery, where he stocked the shelves with cans of lima beans and big sacks of flour. And before long it was the date of Leon's bar mitzvah. It was a small and tidy affair in the local synagogue, each line of verse overseen by the old rabbi whose ragged fingers shook as he held the yad against the sacred text, and Leon's voice, strong and confident, filled the air. The tiny synagogue remained empty save for the bare minimum, including his family and the men, none younger than fifty years of age, skullcaps on their heads, crying into their prayer books. And there was Mama, dressed in her fine royal-blue suit, a round matching blue hat set firmly over her fine curly hair, a net touched only by her long curving lashes. And there was Papa, his shoulder pressed against Leon, who wore his one brown tweed suit that Mama had washed already twenty times and ironed on the white kitchen table as the room streamed light through the window above the sink. And Jacob off to the side, watching Leon and the men's lips mouth the words in unison. He looked then at the fine seams, stitches sewn meticulously into his new tallit, which Papa had purchased for Leon a year earlier from Herschel's Judaic Goods Shoppe in another town. The writing a majestic gold and sky blue, the braided fringes a snowy white at the edge, hanging straight and pristine.

Jacob stood quietly dressed in a gray suit and striped shirt, a suit that had been his brother's only six months earlier, and one that, though his legs had grown as fast as stalks of corn, according to his mama, was yet too large for his eight-year-old body to fill. On his head was the skullcap knitted by his father's mother, a grandmother he never knew. His father wore the same, and so did Leon. All the same suits and skullcaps. All the same except for the tallit that Jacob was yet too young to wrap about his shoulders. For that, he would have to wait another five years. The music and Leon's voice swelled, sailing high into the air, escaping through the walls of the old temple constructed no less than eighty years ago.

Sometimes when he lay in his bed at night with only the amber glow of a nearby streetlamp spreading across his coverlet like a rippling wave, he swore he could hear that music—the melody of Leon's hafto-rah ascending into the air like the voices of angels. He pushed his head deeper into his soft white pillow then, wishing somehow that he could sail up into the air with that sound, up and away. Where would he go? Anyplace, he resolved, anyplace but here. But instead of escaping, Jacob only went as far as his dreams, for the next morning there he was again, rubbing the crust from his eyes to peek over at Leon's bed, still unmade, hearing the slam of the kitchen door as his brother and father left early for the brick school building five blocks away.

Each day, it seemed, as his mama adjusted the cap on his head and kissed him goodbye, there was another shop closed down, the Judaica Shoppe being among the first to go, glossy door shattered, the graphic yellow lines that Jacob came all too soon to comprehend, spray-painted on the windows, the shelves empty, shattered with the shells of ceramic menorahs and broken wine goblets. Soon after there was the kosher butcher owned by his father's second cousin, Mordy, the stationery shop, even the corner grocery that had been in the Goldman family for two generations, looted, stripped even of its counter and hanging green light fixture. By the time Jacob had turned fifteen, Papa was hearing rumors that it would not be long before the schools would find their doors shut. And then what would they do?

Jacob himself had changed too. As more shops, the library, and even the synagogue had turned into little but ghostlike structures, relics of the past, Jacob had grown so tall that he needed to bend his back each time he crossed the threshold to the bathroom, and his sturdy new shoes with the laces would become useless after only three months' time. No longer were even Leon's hand-me-downs useful for six feet two inches, as this stranger son, as Mama often lamented, had grown a full head taller than his older brother. She would often tell Jacob with a sigh that he took after her big brother, Gershon, who had grown to nearly six and a half feet. It was Gershon, she said, who besides being the eldest brother of five whom everyone looked up to in more ways than one, had such promise. He was on his way to becoming a surgeon, an orthopedic surgeon, or a bone doctor, as many liked to say, when one day while doing his rounds at a small hospital in Berlin, he contracted pneumonia, and in a week's time had succumbed to the disease.

In truth, Jacob remembered little of his tall bushy-haired uncle except that each time he would visit the family, he brought cinnamon-flavored cookies, which he would present to Jacob and Leon with a smile and a wink. Jacob liked to think that he was like his uncle Gershon in more ways than one. That he had promise. When he was younger, and he and Mama were alone in the hours after school was done, he would ask her to tell him stories about Gershon—the kinds of clothes he wore, the books he liked to read. And if she wasn't too tired, she would take him onto her lap, and as he angled in close, letting his long legs dangle to the side, she would tell him what little she remembered of Gershon. "What a mensch he was!" she said. Jacob absorbed the information as if it were manna from heaven, in the same ways he would look at the pictures in the book under his bed, as he let his head fall against her bosom and inhaled the air of her, the soap and talc as if she had just stepped out of a bath.

Jacob changed in other ways too. The child who was once talkative, curious, became more sullen. Meanwhile, Nazi soldiers began to appear like a swarm of bees positioned on every corner, occupying the few establishments that were left open: the post office, and the brau house where they would gather, lighting their cigarettes, tossing the still-lit butts into the trembling air. They ambled along with a proprietary swagger, as if they owned every inch of sidewalk. Which, of course, they already did.

And, as the years passed, Jacob's solemn, introspective nature turned to anxiety, and as he kept his feelings beneath the bone of his breast, it only made matters worse. It did not help that his mama was spending more and more time with Herr Reichert, as the business of the Reich, it seemed, was increasing as steadily as the clip of the horses that occupied his stables in the country.

Many years had passed since Jacob accompanied his mama on her work expeditions, for he was soon of an age when he could remain at home without the supervision of an adult. Like Leon, he felt the skin on his forearms ripple as his mama would return home, her red lips a little paler, her hat askew. The mere mention of the colonel's name would bring the taste of bile into the boy's throat, so that he even developed an acute aversion to horses. His papa, however, remained unchanged.

Whenever Jacob thought of his papa, it brought to his mind the elm tree down the block, grounded amid a quiet circle of greenery where birds pecked at the soil each summer, and where a gray frost clung against the slowly peeling bark every winter. But the elm remained stoic despite the shedding of its yellow leaves, the ravages of worms and ants. And so it was with Papa. Despite the sluggish demeanor of the few students whose minds were on other things as they slouched in their seats, the low click of the clock as the doors of shops and even apartments closed one last time, the intimidating growl of their German shepherds, the snickering grins of the soldiers, the growing quiet, the eerie silence in the streets, none of it seemed to bother Papa. And while his father's stoic nature, despite the threats that surely loomed larger than ever before, had once seemed admirable to Jacob, a strength to be envied, now he sensed the facade had begun to crumble so that even the elm, as he passed it each morning on the way to school, appeared silly and useless.

Jacob was smarter than they thought he was. And now that Leon was gone, enlisted in the Polish army, and now that Jacob himself had become a man (fully a bar mitzvah for nearly five years), it was time to speak up. But try as he might, he could not stop loving her. The work "appointments" with Herr Reichert had become more frequent, and now there were the nights, too, when she would slip in the door, birdcage hat no longer tipped stylishly to the corner of her brow, taking off her shoes so as not to waken the others, pretending that all was well, as it should be, in the morning.

It was easy to hate the German, as easy as slipping into his threadbare jacket and leaving while darkness still covered the sidewalks, as his parents slept in their beds. Jacob would wander the streets then, in the chill of dawn, circling the elm, striding purposefully past the school, its doors long chained and barred, past the old synagogue, its red brick still sturdy despite the shards of glass that lay scattered at the threshold. Jacob walked the street, picking up his pace, fueled by his anger, and yet unable to summon the hatred, which always seemed at bay, for his own parents. His mama, his mind told him, was nothing but a shameless whore, a traitor of the worst sort. His papa, once so revered, had become spineless, less than a man. Another leaf scattered in the wind.

His mama was making the coffee when he came home, refreshed somewhat by the brisk early-morning air. But Jacob's mind seemed just as consumed by his worries as when he left. Sometimes Jacob stayed out for an hour or so, or if the scent of an imminent spring greeted him on his way to work, he would remain outdoors and stay for as many as three hours, long past breakfast. When she saw him, as always, she would greet him with a bright smile, but it had been many months since she'd moved toward him with a mother's caress. He had rebuked her several times before that. There were lines of exhaustion beneath her eyes, more noticeable now that her face bore no signs of the makeup she so meticulously applied on the days she set out for work. His father, as unperturbed as ever, glanced up at his son, inquired as to the weather, and returned to polishing his sturdy brown work shoes, even though he had no need of them since the Nazis had issued an edict shutting down the few remaining schools in the town. How oblivious he is! thought Jacob as he poured some coffee into the chintz china cup. How ridiculous!

Jacob's mama settled into another kitchen chair and opened one of her old movie magazines. "Clark Gable is such a handsome man!" she exclaimed, half to them and half to herself. Jacob had a vague recollection of her using those very words to describe the movie icon yesterday and the day before that as well. She had only a couple of the magazines that she recycled for reading each day, and there was only one Clark Gable, after all.

His papa hummed an old Polish tune to himself as he sat intently carving the edge of a small object. This time it was a fruit bowl; there were many such objets d'art scattered about the apartment: a replica of a shoe, a large stirring spoon, a wide pot for the sad rubber plant in the corner of the living room. Now that he was out of work, his hands seemed eternally busy with new projects. Jacob decided that he'd had enough self-reflection for the day and was just reaching under the bed for his stamp collection when he heard a sharp knock at the door.

Unlike most of their neighbors, the family did not jump at such disruptions. Because of Mama's job, their refrigerator was always well stocked with meats, cheeses, and even the occasional bar of German chocolate. So they weren't frightened when Papa casually wiped the wooden splinters from his hands and opened the door—that is, until they saw the face that waited on the other side.

It took Papa a minute before he could find his voice.

"Herr Reichert! To what do we owe the pleasure of your visit on this fine morning?"

At the sound of the German words leaving his papa's mouth, Jacob came swiftly out of his room. There Reichert stood, somehow more stooped than he remembered, the face etched with jagged lines. Nevertheless, he was a commanding figure as he filled the doorway with his polished boots and shiny medals.

"Just a matter of business, dear sir," he said in German, a language that had become all too familiar, as he strode into the small apartment as if it were his own. Meanwhile, Mama's face took on such a deathly pallor as the colonel smiled (or perhaps sneered) down at them. Jacob, who long ago had learned to tamp down his feelings, sensed his heart quicken. Almost immediately, though, Mama's face resumed the mask of friendliness as she dropped the magazine onto the table and stood up. Never before had Herr Reichert visited the apartment in the little town whose walls now embraced a fearful silence. But soon, Jacob realized the colonel's eyes had set upon him, seeming to analyze each pore of his skin.

"My, my, Sarah! How your son has grown!"

Jacob realized he was expecting some response, but like his papa, he could muster only a glob of saliva, which stuck in the bottom of his throat. But soon his mama's voice captured the awkward silence.

"Yes, he is quite a tall one. He takes after my brother, God rest his soul. Certainly, my husband and I are no giants." Her response triggered the colonel's attention, and remembering the reason for his visit, he cleared his throat.

"Sarah, you are wanted back at the office. It seems a virulent flu, what with the change of seasons, has swept across the staff, and the girls, neither Vera nor Bertha, can lift a head from the pillow. And, as you well know, with the war effort surging, swift correspondence to the front is of the utmost importance. So since, dear Sarah, my typing skills are not nearly as proficient as yours, I'm afraid that you are urgently needed at this moment."

Jacob cringed inwardly at the endearment referenced toward his mama, but when he glanced at his papa, who still stood fixed next to the shut front door, and could detect no flicker of a response in his eyes, Jacob felt his own face redden with a burning resentment. At that moment, he did not know which one of his parents he despised more. He heard his mother's voice then, softly placating, rising into the still air.

"But, Fritz, tomorrow is the Sabbath. And even though there is no need of attending synagogue any longer, might I not have one day with my husband and son?"

The corners of Herr Reichert's lips dipped slowly downward, the pits in his cheek deepened, and his eyes emptied of color and darkened toward black. It was then and only then that Jacob felt his first premonition of the tragedy that would soon befall them all.

"Sarah, you are needed." Four words only. Low and swift. The imperative was set.

Mama's face looked on the verge of collapse.

"I'll just get my purse," she said, and disappeared into the bedroom. When she next appeared, she was wearing her cotton tan coat, a small black purse draped across one shoulder, her red lipstick impeccably applied.

"No! She is not leaving." His voice, his legs that had sprung up, had him glowering directly above the colonel, seeming to come alive as through a will of their own.

Jacob stood, fists clenched at his sides, looking down at the German, who in that instant seemed old, shrunken, smaller than he had when he'd first entered the room. For a split second, Jacob thought he saw the colonel shrink back, before a smile that could only be described as sinister enveloped his face.

"Well, well," he said, "who would think that the boy has grown *this* much?" The eyes, two rolling beads of black now, the cheeks curled like a well-traveled road. Jacob felt as if his face might burst into flames.

"It's all right, Jacob. It will not be for very long. Perhaps a day or two, isn't that right, Colonel?" Her voice was calm, steady.

But Jacob ignored her. Frozen to the spot, his eyes riveted on the German's still-grinning face. And before he knew what he was doing, his fists were punching that face, falling easily into the putty that was his skin. Jacob's fists pummeled the stalwart soldier, and continued to beat him, until amid the frantic shouts of his parents, his father's arms pulling him back, the veil of outrage finally slipped from the boy, until Colonel Reichert lay crumpled on the living room floor, a tired, quivering old man, senseless.

"Jacob! Jacob! What have you done? You have ruined us all!" his mama cried out, frustrated tears smeared across her cheeks. His papa, who had not uttered a word since he'd first opened the door to the chaos, stood silent still, then rushed to help the colonel slowly, arduously, to his feet. Once risen, his cap tenuously placed on the back of his head, he left the apartment, Mama quick at his heels, imploring, her cries racing down the hall.

Jacob stood for many minutes, fists raised, his breath coming fast. Somewhere far away he heard a door shut. Papa. He went back into his room and looked at the tidily made bed that was Leon's. What would his brother have done to the Nazi in their home? Probably worse.

Jacob thought there was nothing more despicable at that moment, and he blamed both of his parents for this breach in loyalty, for Leon's exit to join the Polish army, for the burned buildings, the isolation, the dead air that choked him by day so that he was forced to escape outdoors, and the terrors that plagued him at night. He blamed them for all of it.

Despite these thoughts that raced through his head like a herd of cattle running this way and that, he couldn't squelch the flood of hot tears that now seared his face. Unable to stop crying, he lay facedown on his bed. He thought his heart might break.

The next morning, after a long hot bath, Jacob walked into the kitchen and cut himself a slice of black bread. He found his papa sitting just as he was the day before, carving the finishing touches on the wooden bowl. He looked up at his son but said nothing.

After five minutes, when he had finished the piece and wiped the shards off the table, he turned to Jacob. His eyelashes were tinged with tears.

"You don't understand. I know that you couldn't help yourself, but Jacob, you should have held back your anger in the same way I have for these many long years."

Jacob lifted his head, but unlike the elder, his eyes had become daggers.

"In the same way *you* have held back? Don't make me laugh! What man allows his wife, the mother of his children, to sleep in another man's bed? And let us not pretend any longer that this is *business*." He spat out the word. "We both know what is going on here, how she sends him messages with her smiles, how she comes home spent after being away all night. And with a Nazi! Tell me, Papa, what could be more vile? Only you, the husband who stands by and watches this circus all in front of his nose! Leon saw it, and that's why he escaped from this home, willing freely to go into the army. Anything but this! Because you see, dear Papa, we, Leon and I, have come to own your jealousy. So that leaves me to be the man of the house, opening my eyes to this fiasco even if you cannot!"

Jacob turned from him, stared down at his coffee, feeling exhausted by this eruption of anger that he felt could go on forever. Yet, just as his anxiety had reached a climax, his father, Shmuel, became calmer, more reticent. Finally, he spoke.

"Jacob, my son whom I love more than my own life, again I tell you that you do not understand. You must accept the truth that I have come to accept many years ago, when you still wore a toddler's coat. There was a friend, a salesgirl at Mama's place of business when she was a typist for the linen shop which has long since closed. This salesgirl, Mildred, had a friend whose sister had married a German who rose in the ranks. They needed a typist and there was a job. At first, your mama said no, but then food was running low, and soon she discovered the job was more than just typing, that she would have access to certain papers which might be helpful to the Allies. Well, I cannot say more. All I can tell you is that the defeats the enemy has seen on the front, the foiled plans, well, she and a group of brave women are responsible for that. So, yes, I have had to stand aside these years when I would have liked nothing better than to crush his neck with my hands. But yet, I have held back. It's the price we have to pay for the greater good. And no one more than your mama. Jacob, she is a hero."

With that, his father rose, took the bowl in hand, and not stopping to gauge his son's reaction, went into his bedroom.

Jacob sat staring at the seat his papa had occupied only seconds earlier. So now he understood. But it was too late. His anger had already blinded him to any hint of a positive outcome. Late that night, soon after he heard the click of the key in the lock, and the tap of her heel on the kitchen linoleum, he had made up his mind. And so, as the first signs of light adorned the silent night sky, he wrapped what clothes he had in the gray-and-yellow afghan she had sewn for him. Jacob kneeled, pushed his treasures, the book of stamps and the large volume of fairy tales, securely underneath the bed and left. As he gently closed the apartment door, he remembered someone his parents had mentioned, a widow, an elderly Catholic woman who owned a farm on the outskirts of town. He would not see his mama that morning. He would not see his parents again. And it would be a year later, at war's end, when he learned of Leon's death in battle, his papa's demise in the gas chambers of Auschwitz, and his mother's hanging as a traitor and conspirator. Only then did Jacob realize that he was an orphan.

NINETEEN

Esther, 1968

She listened patiently, and after he was done, not quite knowing what to do with her hands, which remained clasped firmly on her lap the whole time, she lifted them and ran her fingers through the thick strands of her hair as if to massage the information into her brain. Jacob hadn't noticed, though, hadn't turned toward her as he continued the tale in a low, barely audible monotone. And now he was moving slowly, almost ponderously, away from the window where he had remained during the course of his monologue. She was at the window, she realized then, the window where she had once stood as a young bride, staring ahead, imagining her life as it changed with the seasons, each year bringing new mysteries, new pleasures. The same window she stared through one sunny day in April, her eyes unbelieving, on the afternoon that would put an end to all those dreams.

It took her a few minutes, her eyes simply staring ahead. If anyone were to ask her about the weather outside, she could not have responded, feeling it was all the same to her now. She ran Jacob's words through her mind but could only come to the same conclusion. He had hated his mother for associating with the Nazis, but more for turning on his father, a betrayal of them both. Whether she had her reasons—whether her actions were patriotic, even noble, didn't matter. For Jacob, the betrayal was a sin that was unforgivable. But Jacob was no longer that impetuous young man who condemned others perhaps too easily. There was something inside her that convinced her that Jacob, the man she knew and loved, could now find forgiveness. Even for Zalman.

A gentle breeze fluttered the first buds of the apple tree in the garden, and just as it did, Esther felt she understood it all. No matter that she had done nothing, that she had only looked upon Zalman as nothing more than a dear friend. Jacob had already banished the man who had been his best friend, more than a brother to him. She resolved then to meet with Zalman once, to offer an attempt at a reconciliation between the men. But if he rejected the idea, if he deemed it hopeless, then she would have to let it go. She would tear up the paper with his cousin's phone number and address, and for Jacob's sake, even though it pained her, she would have to erase Zalman from her thoughts. Whether he stayed in New York or went back to the farm in Minnesota, it would all be the same to her.

But as Esther stood quietly, choking down the tears, another fear edged its way inside her brain. What if Jacob's feelings for her had also changed from love to merely tolerance? If he could relinquish the mother who had raised him so lovingly, then how might he treat her?

A new decade, the seventies, was fast approaching, and the culture was shifting at a rapid pace, especially for women. They were protesting war, burning their bras, demanding the right to be equal. And, in fact, Esther never considered herself an inferior, having worked as hard as any man to maintain her father's business, and having even mentored Jacob in the tools of the trade when the times called for it. She could do it all again, become a female of the times, an emancipated woman. And yet, was that what she really wanted? A life without Jacob? But somehow with that notion in mind, she no longer cared if he mistrusted her, maybe loved her a little less. Esther resolved that she would put all her efforts into building a life with Jacob. And although it would be a shattered life, a childless life, she would try to regain his trust, and maybe he would love her a little bit more. She had heard his story, and at that moment, as she turned from the window, she made a promise to herself never to question him about his past, never to speak of it again, even if the ghosts of the past continued to haunt them both. Esther knew then that she would never have the life she had dreamed of, a good life. Being with Jacob would have to be enough.

~

Only once did she approach Jacob, days after her meeting with Zalman at Wolfie's. He had just closed on a large property in Midtown Manhattan, one that would bring in a good income in rentals for years to come, and Jacob was in a good mood. To celebrate, she cooked his favorite, a brisket with roast potatoes and green beans, its aroma filling the house as he walked in the door. Instead of a perfunctory peck on the cheek, he embraced her with a passionate kiss on the lips. Esther thought it might be the right time to have a conversation.

As Jacob sat scooping up the last forkfuls of brisket, which, he commented, fell apart just like butter, Esther felt her stomach surge. She knew she had to take this moment before she chickened out.

"Jacob, I am so proud of you! How far you have taken the business. And I know Papou would have been proud too."

Jacob smiled as he licked his lips. "I would like to think so."

"He would have been so very proud!" she repeated, afraid of the next words that waited on her tongue. He pushed his chair away from the table.

"Jacob, you're such a good man, a wonderful man! But I know you are still hurting. I know you must miss Zalman. Can you not reach out to him, see how he is? Just a few words only."

Jacob was standing now, as he turned toward her, a shadow over his face where only seconds earlier brightness had been. It was an expression she had not seen in a long time.

"Why are you bringing this up, Esther? Have you seen him, met with him?"

"N-no, of course not," she lied.

He looked at her then, into her wide blue eyes, and finding no falseness in them, said in a low voice, "Don't ever mention his name again." He turned from her and went into the living room.

As Esther cleared the last dish from the table, she knew that she had no choice but to abide by Jacob's words. She'd never speak his name again. And if one day Jacob decided to look for his old friend, it would be his decision. Not hers.

~

The days settled into a quiet monotony as Esther threw herself into a redecorating project with the help of Florrie, who more than ever before had become a fixture in the home, sitting at her elbow as Esther pored over reams of wallpaper peppered with orange-and-yellow sunflowers, holding the other end of the tape as Esther measured nearly the entire width of the living room for a new royal-blue velvet couch that would be free of its restrictive plastic coat. The flimsy tables were replaced by sturdy tan end tables that sat unmoved, like silent toads facing the new broad picture tube, this time a Sony, encased in its own highly polished black lacquer cabinet. Outdoors, the rumble of poured concrete could be heard for blocks as sweaty workers drinking cans of Coca-Cola replaced the front sidewalk. Even the backyard was excavated, the swing set unceremoniously now gone, the dwindling garden eradicated, replaced by lush hedges. All changed, except for the two trees: the golden apple tree that stood towering above the chaos, and the giant oak, a relic of the past and a reminder, at least for Esther, of what could have been.

And when she was done with the outside, Esther found new projects, glad that her mother had taught her the elements of home decorating, how planning and shopping could fill the time. She would carry stacks of glossy magazines on home decor, traveling into Lower Manhattan warehouses for a glossy metal-and-white Formica wall unit on which to stack Jacob's prodigious collection of Elvis records and her prized Beethoven symphonies. A furry shag rug in a dazzling blue that felt like pure cotton when she walked barefoot, an austere grandfather clock whose hourly sonorous melody echoed the passage of time, fresh Dacron curtains that matched the oat color of the grass wallpaper that now liberally dressed the walls in the living room. An orange papasan chair in the corner struck a comical note, and a lava lamp spewing yellow-and-blue bubbles, an optimistic element. And beneath it all, individual gleaming tiles set into the concrete floor, upon which each table was decorously adorned with plastic flowers. Shelves were erased, faucets updated, all transformed until Jacob no longer recognized any of it, if he had bothered to notice as he removed his wrinkled overcoat each evening, placed his hat on the small foyer table, and crawled upstairs. All transformed except for the black baby grand that sat in the corner of the living room, just where it was placed on that first moving day. Unplayed. Unchanged.

~

Nights Florrie returned to her husband, Sid, who seemed now more than ever a part of the big-armed chestnut recliner that had appeared in place of the tattered aqua corduroy one. As for Esther, she became marvelously inventive in the kitchen. Each night, dinners were transformed into a different exotic land. Mondays, instead of tired meat loaf, there was beef bourguignon, and on weekends, her special arroz con pollo, and a sugar-filled pineapple upside-down cake. And finally, when Esther was done moving and changing and transforming, she lay down in the new king-size bed with crisp white sheets and the gray-and-yellow afghan sewn by the mother-in-law she never knew—the one memory she had of her. She placed her hand on Jacob's arm and traced the dark hairs with her finger. Always he would take that hand in his and wind it around his neck. Wordlessly, he would set his lips upon hers, and they made love. In this way, she knew he was still her husband.

~

Esther waited on the gas line, which because of the oil crisis seemed to stretch longer with each passing day. License plates ending with odd numbers were restricted to odd-numbered days, those ending in even, the even-numbered ones. Esther was an odd, and so that day, February 3, was her day. An odd. She laughed to herself at the notion. So perfectly described, she thought, tapping her fingers on the leather-wrapped steering wheel of the new white Honda Civic. She had always considered herself somewhat different, although outwardly her life belied the fact. Her life had taken a tragic turn, yes, but now it was well ordered, she knew, and she was in control. Yet she had always expected something more. She still did. "Lady, does that car move?" She stepped on the gas. Late that afternoon, when she walked in the door, big brown bags from Macy's and Abraham & Straus dangling from her arms, she set the purchases on the sparkling white tile floor with the gold flecks and looked around. Chairs and sofa and ottoman and lamps—all of it, all the things she had used to fill the hole inside of her. But it was still there; she was off. She was odd. Her eyes fell on the silent piano. Again, she saw the image of Zalman sitting quietly on the couch, a smile on his face as she played. Before she picked up her bags, she had made a decision.

~

"Jacob, we need to talk."

Her husband glanced up from his *Daily News*, the round spectacles he wore for his failing vision perched on his nose.

Esther knew better than to wait for an answer and continued, "I have a favor to ask of you. I've been thinking lately, probably too much, but I want to do something with my life. Not that I want to go back to Papou's office, since so much has changed there with forms and new tax laws that I could hardly keep up, but something else, something different. And I know you probably think me a bit meshuga, somewhat crazy, but, oh, Jacob, I think I'd like to go back to school. Even though I'm in my early forties, there are many women nowadays working in professions outside the home, and besides—" She was about to add that she had no children to rear but thought better of it.

"Well, it's like that song I heard on the radio yesterday, 'I Am Woman.' I am woman! Hear me roar!" She feigned a laugh. She could feel his eyes still on her.

"I'd like to study to be a teacher. Maybe a music teacher," she added.

"Fine, Esther, do as you wish." He returned to the paper. "Since when do you need to ask my permission?" She remained in place, staring at her husband's expressionless face. Fine, he had said, fine.

~

Going back to school was both easier and more difficult than Esther had anticipated. It certainly took a lot more effort than deciding between the gold brocade or black-and-white herringbone drapes for the dining room. And while she had never considered herself on a par with the American, those who had the privilege of being born here, she excelled in her English studies that first year in 1973, and she soon came to realize that learning words and concepts ("variables," "hyperboles," and the like), along with concepts outside the business sector, proved much more challenging. Her matriculation from Kingsborough Community College to Brooklyn College proved less arduous, though, once she had mastered some of the more complicated intricacies of the English language. Finally, she could delight in the familiar territory of music, as she recalled her fingers dancing over the cream-colored keys, and the new tunes with their numbered notes designed for the instruction of the children. She would adeptly type out essays on the new Smith Corona typewriter, which took its place next to the vase of plastic tulips on the kitchen table, transferring her scribbles into comprehensive essays on music education and motivational skills for the primary grades. And a few months into her junior year, as her hand was always among the first to shoot up while others remained palm down on the desk, as her voice rose stronger in cadence, piercing the steady silence of the class-room, as the well-researched papers were returned with the bright-red slash of an A, Esther gained a newfound pride. At age forty-three, she was now considered a mentor, a role model for the younger ones. She, Esther Itzkowitz, the Jew from Brooklyn. Who would have thought? By the time she had taken her first step toward the podium to receive her diploma and shake the chancellor's hand, as she glanced at Jacob smiling ear to ear as he fanned himself with the commencement program, she knew she had made the right decision.

If there was one person who wasn't totally happy about Esther's decision, it was Florrie. As a friend who had stood by her side during the vicissitudes of the past few years, Florrie was encouraging at first about Esther's transition to a professional woman, while having no similar desires of her own. Esther had even made the tenuous suggestion that her friend seek employment at Clara's Bakery in town, which always had a sign for a clerk in the window, and whose prune danishes could definitely use Florrie's expert touch.

"Why in the world would I want to work there?" asked Florrie, crunching her eyebrows as the two women sat at Esther's dining room table, knitting heavy wool scarves to be donated to the poor in Appalachia. "Sid still has a job and makes enough for the two of us."

"Well, since the toy store has been closed for some time now, I thought the job would give you something to do," said Esther, looking down at the long needles, averting her friend's angry gaze. "And besides, everyone knows you're the best baker in the neighborhood."

Florrie sat up straighter in her chair, working the needles furiously.

"I don't need to be baking for those stuck-up women in town who don't even know how to turn on an oven! So they can take the compliments for my brownies and apple cake as they stuff their fat faces? No, thank you! . . . Damn, you made me miss a stitch!" she cried, attacking the wool again, almost as angrily as she had attacked her friend.

Esther went into the kitchen for a glass of water, as Florrie, who was never at a loss for words, continued to mutter to no one in particular.

"Such a ridiculous idea! I've got plenty to keep me occupied. Plenty!" And again, "Why would I ever need to go back to work?" And the unspoken question: Why did Esther need to?

As a stream of cold water from the tap filled the glass, Esther pondered Florrie's reaction to her suggestion. What could bring about such an extreme response, such anger? It reminded her of how Jacob would explode at the mere mention of his parents' names. She realized now that his response came from deep pain, the pain of abandonment. Maybe it was the same with her friend. As Esther became busier with her schoolwork, she had less time to spend with Florrie. Maybe Florrie thought she was being abandoned. And maybe she was just a little bit jealous too. So Esther never offered another suggestion, instead enlisting Florrie's help with checking her papers for typing errors, and later, reviewing some of Esther's innovative ideas for lesson plans. But while her heart tugged a bit each time she thought about how she and her best friend were growing more distant, she realized that another feeling was intruding upon her heart, something nearing happiness. It was something that Esther had not felt in many years, not since her life had been shattered, the day she tried to never think about, the memory continuing to twist the blood vessels in her heart like a rag wrung dry too many times. Esther feared that if she shed a tear, it would precipitate a million others. She chose instead to dwell on her work, which was more fulfilling and even more enjoyable than her decorating trysts. Many years before, Esther realized that true happiness, the complete bliss that was brought about only from the comfort of family and home, would always elude her. For now, though, she settled for contentment. So Esther found her slice of contentment in the change that had come about.

Mornings became a hurried affair, with Esther packing lunches for them both: a tuna sandwich with an apple for her, salami on a roll with a sour pickle for Jacob, and sometimes an added treat for them both, throwing in a Hostess Twinkie—but not too often. Jacob, who had always been on the thin side, was beginning to develop a paunch. She ran the day's lessons through her mind as she stirred Jacob's bubbling oatmeal, set down a small glass of orange juice for herself, and when the kettle sounded, steaming Sanka for Jacob and a rose tea for herself, poured into metal thermoses. The two exchanged a quick kiss behind the open pages of his *Daily News*, then Esther, car key in hand, rushed out the door, leaving her husband prepared for the day, her home spotless.

And in this way, the days, months, and years passed, filled with classroom activities, conferences, and the occasional lunch with colleagues, shoveling snow in the winters, watching baseball games in the summer, and nights that offered only a temporary respite until the preparation for it all began the next morning. Such a life offered scant time to think, to muse about the past, to project long term into the future. Esther thought, though, that was probably a positive thing. It was not good to think too much.

But there were those times when she looked out the kitchen window on a Saturday morning, noticed the light-green buds appearing on the trees outside when she would move to open the latch on the window just a little, breathing in the scent of a new spring, and remember. He would have been a man now, she allowed herself to think. Handsome and strong and tall, of course. Successful—maybe a doctor or a lawyer, or perhaps someone who would have joined Jacob in the real estate business, with little time for the trivialities of home, but always making the time to visit his mama. She could imagine him, shoulders back as he strode through the door, bending down to kiss her cheek, then seated at the kitchen table with his father, as he eagerly awaited the bowl of her special chicken soup, with just a tablespoon of sugar added for extra sweetness. Standing by the window, with the dish towel in hand just as she had on that fateful day, these thoughts, irrational as they were, brought a tear to her eye, but more and more now it was also with a smile as she thought of her only child lost so many years ago.

Although her life was now filled with an abundance of new experiences, new people, Esther hadn't forgotten her friend Florrie. When she had first embarked on her teaching career, the two had decided to get their hair permed into the popular new short shag hairstyle. Not that Esther exactly needed a perm, but she wanted to share a special day with her friend, whose kindness and companionship had lifted her upon many occasions. Besides, it was Lincoln's Birthday, and they had the entire day to themselves. After several hours in the New York City salon, and admiring their new looks in the mirror, Esther restrained herself from gasping when she looked at the bill. Nevertheless, she reasoned, a special day out with her friend was well worth it. The two then continued down Madison Avenue until they reached the French crêpe café they'd heard so much about, ordered crêpes suzette, chocolate-and-pistachio macaroons, and mugs of hot coffee and tea stirred with spiral canes of sugar. It was like the old days, although at times the conversation lagged, as her own interests had shifted from home and cooking to music and students and books.

The two continued to see each other on occasion, watching soap operas, working on recipes for the cookbook fundraiser at their synagogue, enjoying the new *Star Wars* movie, or even taking in a baseball game with Jacob. But, as sometimes such friendships go, these events began to grow farther apart, as had their interests, until except for the customary greeting as each brought in the mail, their meetings stretched to months. She would think of Florrie as she recovered from a cold one dreary day, hoping she would see her at the door, not bothering to knock, holding one of her tightly wrapped kugels straight out of the oven. But, like so many other memories, this, too, was not to be. Just as she knew the splashes of rain she heard outside would seep into the ground tomorrow, so it was with their friendship. Buried forever. She wrapped the woolen afghan tightly around her and tried to sleep.

Esther rose quickly in the ranks of the New York City educational system. It was now 1978, and Esther had reached forty-eight, considering herself solidly in middle age. After five years teaching in the elementary schools, she "graduated" to a junior high school in the same district. And while she missed five-year-old Mary Alexander's spontaneous hugs each time Esther entered the classroom, music books, and third grader Simon Goldsmith's voice, which always rose several octaves higher and louder than all the rest, she had to admit that the prepubescent young teens posed far more interesting challenges daily and regarded her class as a sort of playtime away from their studies. Others showed a serious passion for the melodies and, on the rare occasion, even talent. One of these was Andrew Becker. Normally reticent in the classroom, the tall young man with a mop of bushy brown hair that she was always tempted to take a brush to seemed more suited for the basketball court than math or even music, but when he walked into Mrs. Stein's room, he fairly bounced into his seat, where he would open the music book, ready before the rest of the class had even arrived, for the day's lesson. And although it was primarily a class in vocals, Andrew showed a refreshing curiosity in how the notes came together and transformed to a unique sound. Often, at the end of the day, she would find him lingering at her door, asking a question about something that had transpired in class, or requesting a special tune he had heard on the radio. So great was his interest, or maybe she saw something special in the boy even then, that when the next semester had begun, she invited him to join the after-school orchestral class she was forming. He quickly accepted, and when asked to name the instrument he would like to play, his response was immediate.

"The piano," he said. "I've always loved the piano. It's closest to the real meaning of music, don't you think, Mrs. Stein?" Esther was delighted, and even though Andrew had never played before, hadn't even laid a finger on a key, he took to the instrument. Although her class usually ended past dismissal time, Andrew found it hard to pry himself from the old spinet, working and reworking a tune until finally Esther had to dim the first ceiling light, and only then did he stand up, pick up his book bag, and, shoulders hunched, walk out of the room.

One chilly Wednesday afternoon at 3:00 p.m., Andrew appeared at the door of the music room, the first to arrive—nothing unusual about that—but this time he seemed somehow different.

"Andrew, is something wrong?" she asked, placing her books on the desk. The usual smile that greeted her and the light that frequently shone in his eyes looked somewhat dimmed. He didn't respond, but stretched out his arm to give her a sheet of paper. Was his hand shaking? She perused the paper, a music sheet with hastily scrawled notes, cross-outs, the workings of an animated brain. It took her a couple of minutes to realize that it was a sonata, and on the top were the words "For Isabel."

"Andrew, did you—did you write this yourself?" He looked down at the floor, nodded his assent.

Esther removed her coat and sat at the piano bench. After studying the sheet for a few more minutes, she slowly tapped out the tune.

Once she was done, she turned back to Andrew, his face now creased by anxiety.

"Andrew—Andrew, did you write this piece? Are you sure you wrote this, because, well, it seems more expert." The boy's eyes shifted to the checkered linoleum floor briefly, then up again.

"Mrs. Stein, I didn't steal it. I swear!"

"Oh no, Andrew, I didn't mean that. It's just that I'm not sure how to describe it."

Esther looked up at the ceiling, trying to grasp invisible words. It was one of the few times she wished that her English was better, more adequate. But she didn't have time for more consideration, for the other students had begun to saunter into class and were already setting up stands and opening their instrument cases.

"Andrew, if you don't mind, I'd like to hold on to this for a while until our next session." He nodded, and still averting her gaze, assumed a seat on the piano bench while she walked toward the podium at the front of the class.

Later, after the last student had left, she removed the melody from the back of her piano instruction book. She ran her fingers along the keyboard, stumbling across the notes, correcting a couple of errors where the tune sounded off, marking the points that were unclear. But then she played it once more, listening as the notes spilled happily out into the air like hummingbirds freed from the nest. Then, letting her hands fall from the keyboard, she listened again as the tune played itself through the silence. And she found she still hadn't the words to describe it. An ascension on the wind and, after, a low mournful plunge where the melody moved as if on a current of succeeding waves. And yet, not quite. Her eyes sought the title. She believed the dedication was a secret infatuation, although she knew of no one by that name in any of her classes.

Only when she heard the sweep of the custodian's broom against the hall floors and, looking up, realized that an edge of darkness had begun to dim the gray sky outdoors, did Esther get up, gather her attaché case and purse, and shut the door behind her. And when she did, she came to yet another decision.

"Jacob, I have a favor to ask of you." The two had been watching the latest episode of *Charlie's Angels*, a favorite. Esther had once even considered having her hair styled like Jacob's professed crush, Farrah Fawcett.

Jacob, ever in the leather recliner, leaned forward, slightly annoyed at the interruption.

"What is it, Esther? Is something wrong?"

"No, of course not. Nothing's wrong. I just had this idea, and I wanted to ask something of you."

She paused, traced the matching blue satin sofa pillow with the tip of her finger. "Well, Jacob, there is a student. Maybe you have heard me speak of him? His name is Andrew Becker, and he's in my special program after school. Well, he is—how shall I say this? The most extraordinary. Before this year, he'd never even put his finger on a piano key. He showed such an interest that I worked with him, some elementary tunes at first, but now, after only a year and a half, Jacob, he can play as well as I! But that's not all—he writes music. How he writes! He has written a sonata which has a tone like—I don't know—the voices of angels. 'For Isabel.'"

Jacob scratched the side of his nose and sighed, exasperated. "Esther, this is all very nice, but what does this have to do with us?"

"Not with us exactly. With me. The boy is quick, near genius, and I was wondering if maybe I could work with him, see what new masterpiece springs forth from his mind. It would be a couple of days after school, and I'd still make sure to have time for my schoolwork, have dinners ready by the time you would get home, never meet him on our weekends. And the best part is this could bring in a little extra money. So what do you say?"

Jacob shrugged in the same way he did whenever Esther approached him with a new idea.

"Esther, why should I stop you from tutoring? You are a modern woman, after all, the Betty Friedman of Brooklyn!" He returned his gaze to the TV just as the angels had begun to chase a criminal across a bridge.

Friedan, Esther thought as she sat back against the soft pillow, a contented smile appearing on her face. Her name is *Betty Friedan.*

Getting his father's permission for the weekly lesson proved easy, and within the month Andrew was seated, his knobby-kneed giraffe legs bent under him, on the piano bench of the glossy baby grand in Esther's living room.

Although she was reluctant at first to request a fee for her services, since she was not quite certain of the family's financial situation, and knowing that if pressed, she would gladly have provided the lessons without a dime in recompense, she worried about what Jacob, who was always concerned about the dollar, would have to say about her generosity. So she asked for fifteen dollars for the hour, and to her relief, Andrew appeared at the door, a ten and a five in hand, no questions asked.

At first, they had practiced the standards: *Sonatina in G Anhang 5* by Beethoven and Schumann's *Wild Rider Opus 68, no. 8.* And beneath fleet fingers, the old piano seemed to take on a new life under the boy's affections. Listening to him play, she knew now that her mother was wrong about Esther's skills as a child. At Sally's suggestion that one of her children take up piano, which she considered a sign of culture and breeding, Esther had begun lessons when she was only eight. She took to the instrument easily and had an affinity for it, soon playing the classics. Her mother, especially, had delighted in this, learned the meaning of the word *prodigy*, and often used it when speaking of her daughter. But as she listened to the notes ascend now, saw the boy's fingers fly adeptly over the keyboard, Esther knew that she had never been a prodigy. Andrew was. He was more than that. He was a genius.

After only the second lesson, though, she could tell that he was ready, having mastered most of what she had to teach, and so she asked him to show her the song. He glanced at her apprehensively, then brought out the paper from the pocket of his coat. Esther listened to the notes; then she played the tune, questioning him on some technical points, offering a few minor suggestions. As he removed his hands, finally, from the keyboard and placed them at his side, Esther, now sitting next to her protégé, took a deep breath. She did not know how to begin.

"Andrew, do you know how good this is? How good *you* are?"

She watched as a deep crimson blush crept up his cheeks. She could tell that he was thinking about how to respond to the compliment, averting his eyes, looking down into the blue shag carpet. She continued, "Look, I have been playing since I was a little girl, much younger than you, and I couldn't even think how, *where*, to begin writing a piece like this. The song takes one away, how shall I say it, to a place of perfect peace, but at the same time, there is a deep sorrow that flows through it all. And when I hear it, when you play it, it gives me such a calm, happy feeling inside, and yet I am brought to tears."

She waited until, finally, his eyes met hers. He was brilliant, yes, but he was just a boy.

"It wasn't hard to write. I mean I was just fooling around down in the basement. I was playing *Pong*, and I was bored is all. And I wrote it." He shrugged. "It's no big deal."

Andrew glanced at his watch, in a hurry to move on. She looked at his hands, reddened, trembling, and found his humility endearing. There were only a few minutes left before his father would drive up, honking the horn of his Pontiac Firebird.

"Andrew," she said, "do you think—could you—write some more songs like these?"

The boy looked up, a smile, for the first time that afternoon, spreading across his face.

"Mrs. Stein," he said, "I already have."

The following week and the week after that, he presented her with more melodies, some childish ditties, others the beginnings of overtures. And while none exceeded the excellence of the first song, each one was impressive in its own right. With each tutorial, the time seemed to go more quickly, and Esther looked forward to their meetings almost as much as she enjoyed spending coveted weekends walking in the park or shopping in the department stores with Jacob. Besides his precocious talent, there was something about this young boy, a familiarity, a need that made her think that time spent with him was never nearly enough. She would have even forgiven the fee if as soon as he entered the foyer, he didn't open his hand to reveal two crumpled bills as an offering.

As the meetings stretched into a month, Andrew grew more comfortable, nearly settled into his abilities, and so became more loquacious as a result. Like most boys his age, he confessed a love for video games and comic books, Batman being his favorite hero. He wasn't much into sports, though, never felt like he was agile enough catching a ball or jumping up for a basket. Above all, he loved music.

One afternoon, during another of their sessions, Esther remembered something, and now that the boy's natural reticence was slipping away and they had become something akin to friends, she felt that the time was right.

"That song you wrote, the one you first gave me, it's called 'Isabel.' Do you think you could tell me why?"

"Isabel." He repeated the name slowly, sounding out each syllable as a trace of the old shyness returned to his face.

"Isabel is my mother's name."

But before she could respond with a "How sweet," he continued quickly.

"But I never knew her. I don't really remember her, because she died when I was three. Dad talks about her a lot, though. I know she was a kind person, and I know she loved me a lot. Dad says I look like her, and maybe I do. It's kind of hard to tell from the pictures."

Esther felt her heart clench. She had always guessed that there was a secret sadness behind the boy's eyes, but to lose a mother . . . and at such a young age!

"Andrew, I'm so sorry."

"It's okay. I'm not sad about it, and like I said, I barely remember her, just a few things like how she used to play peekaboo with me behind the drapes, and how she would take my hands in hers and we'd play Ring Around the Rosie, oh, and she would sing to me at night before she put me into bed. But that's about it. That's all I know."

"Andrew, I am so sorry," she repeated, "but how did she die? She must have been very young." He shrugged.

"Don't know. I just know it had something to do with her heart. Dad said the doctors even warned her against having a baby, 'cause she'd had this condition almost all her life. But she had me anyway, and she lived—at least for a couple more years."

Esther closed her eyes, absorbing the information.

"So young," she murmured to herself.

"Mrs. Stein?"

"Yes, Andrew?"

"Can we go over that last piece? I don't think I really got it right."

"Yes, of course."

And though the two never spoke of Andrew's deceased mother again, the knowledge had begun to consume Esther's thoughts until she found herself musing over how it must be for a man and a boy living in that household, motherless. She thought of Isabel, imagined what she looked like, the style of her hair, the way she moved, slowly, with a delicate motion, her long tapered fingers so like her son's. She imagined how Andrew must have felt when she kissed the top of his head before placing him in his crib in the evening. She thought of her when Andrew appeared at Esther's front door at precisely 5:00 p.m. Wednesday evenings, but also whenever she walked into class and looked out at the group of girls and boys chatting and laughing, all with families who were whole.

But Esther did more than think. She busied herself buying bracelets with colorful beads and woolen gloves, and music books for the boy, claiming them "extras," things her nephews no longer cared for, or small unused items she had found around the house. *Extras.* Andrew accepted these things with gratitude, never complaining they were "too much," nor did he display overt affection toward her. They were, after all, teacher and student.

When she heard that the Brooklyn Philharmonic Orchestra was playing at the Brooklyn Academy of Music in two weeks on Presidents' Day, impulsively, she bought two tickets—one for her and one for Andrew. She tried not to think about her first excursion to hear an orchestra that evening years earlier. She tried not to think about the man she was with, either, as she kept her eyes on Andrew during the concert, almost as much as she looked ahead at the musicians. Esther reveled in the expression of delight on the boy's face as he leaned forward, palms together, listening intently. She loved her role as a teacher this time almost as much as she had enjoyed being a student. Late that afternoon, still recalling the heavenly strains of the music and the light in Andrew's eyes as he witnessed the talent of the players, Esther was just getting the house keys out of her bag when she was surprised at the front door. There was her husband, waiting.

"Jacob!"

He came down the two concrete steps, took her arm, and led her into the house.

"I didn't think you would be home before me," she said, somewhat breathless from the surprise, as she hung her gray tweed jacket in the closet.

"It was much too sunny outside to be stuck working in the office," he answered, taking a seat not in his recliner, but on the sofa.

"Besides, anything I have to do can be left for Monday," he continued. He patted the spot next to him, adding, "Esther, come sit by your husband."

She looked at him quizzically before sitting down and leaning back to settle into the crook of his arm. A faint smile appeared on her face. Until now, she had not realized how much she had missed, longed for, this moment. She closed her eyes, briefly inhaled the familiar scent of his cologne as the two listened to the silences of the household. Finally, after a few minutes, she felt him shift slightly, heard the sound of his voice before quite comprehending the words.

"The show you saw today—with the boy—it was good?"

Esther turned her head so she could see her husband's face, and brightening, she responded, "The concert with Andrew, you mean? Oh, Jacob, if you could only see the smile on his face, the intense concentration he had just being there, watching the conductor, the musicians! It was as if he had seen a thousand such concerts, and yet such joy at his very first! The happiness as he joined in with the applause! Just like— like when we took our own child to his first baseball game at Yankee Stadium!" She felt Jacob's fingers dig deeper into her shoulder, and she gulped the air. The words had come out without her realizing it, and a waft of sadness consumed her.

"Good," he said. "I am sure the boy appreciated it a great deal." Esther felt her muscles relax, her heartbeats slow. But before she had given herself a chance to fully review the delights of the day, at least in her mind, Jacob, still holding her, continued, "And that is why I think that now is the time to stop."

Esther shifted again to take in his face, his eyes calm, gentle, his tone matter-of-fact.

"Stop? Stop what?"

"I think you should stop seeing him. Stop meeting with—" He swallowed before saying the name for the first time, "Andrew."

The request, as simple and sedate as it was, seemed to slam into Esther, making her feel as if she had just been in a terrible car accident, broken and weak.

"I don't understand. Why should I stop? I'm tutoring the child, an exceptionally talented child who has great potential which I am helping to nurture. Besides, I am bringing in some extra money, if only a little, and enjoying seeing him grow as a musician, even as a man. He's having fun is all, and so am I."

She watched as Jacob's lips formed a stern line where a smile had been only moments earlier.

"That's just the problem; perhaps you are enjoying this tutoring a little too much. Don't you see what you're doing? You have become a mother to this motherless boy, and for you, he has become like a son. But you are not his mother, and he is not—" He choked back the words.

"Gary," she whispered. But as a surge of energy took hold of her body, she determined not to go to that place of sorrow. Instead, she allowed her eyes to remain on Jacob's and steeled herself.

"Ridiculous!" she found herself spewing out the word despite her efforts to remain calm, but she was already on her feet.

"The idea that I'm substituting this boy for our own dear child makes no sense. And, Jacob, I'm so surprised that you would even propose such a thing! That you would try to take away this one bit of pleasure in my empty life." And again, she regretted the words almost instantly as she watched a dark cloud sweep over her husband's face. He stood to meet her eyes, his motions slow, defeated.

"Very well, then, my star," he said, using the old pet name, "if this brings you happiness."

Esther watched as he took the stairs as if he himself were carrying a great burden and disappeared into the bedroom.

That evening, Esther couldn't sleep. She lay, eyes open, watching her husband of over thirty years, lips slightly parted as he took deep, measured breaths. Only in repose did Jacob resemble the young, spirited man she had met in class that day long ago. Tall and confident, with just the measure of shyness making him all the more attractive, he had seemed to her then a giant of a man who could lasso the moon if only she had asked.

And yet she knew that in a few hours his eyelids would open, revealing green eyes, but also a man with deep furrows down his cheeks, the dimple set in his chin, a brooding forehead topped with a still-full head of hair streaked each day more with gray. A man, slow, stoop shouldered; a man, just past fifty, defeated by life, looking much older than he was. Out of the corner of her eye she noticed the twitch. It was the pinkie on his right hand, activated by a dream, no doubt. She allowed her own fingers to wander, touch the skin, feel the hand that was the one thing even after all these years that remained the same.

With both her parents gone, her mother descending into Alzheimer's before her death, which came not as a shock, but as a relief, her one true friendship nearly dissipated, he was all she had. She wished for more; she yearned for it, recalled the dream that she did not dare bring to the surface, a relic of another time. It had appeared to her many times before, just on the edge of reality, when she was a bride, a new homeowner, a young mother. If only she could go back, return to that time when the world was, as the poet Matthew Arnold once said, "a land of dreams." She was, she finally reasoned, irretrievably foolish. Esther curled her body into the fetal position, tried to make her mind go blank. But before she did, she had come to still another decision.

The following Wednesday, Esther informed Andrew that she could no longer be his tutor. His reaction was more calm than she had imagined it would be. Raised eyebrows were the only signal indicating surprise. And so, after the last note in Chopin's sonata had been sounded, Andrew shook her hand, looking more man than boy, thanked her for her help, and left. Esther shut the front door before returning to tuck the sheet entitled "Isabel" into the piano bench.

A few months later, Andrew graduated from middle school, and less than a year after that, word came that he and his father had joined family living in Chicago. Esther choked back tears when she heard the news. She knew that it was impossible to return to that happy time when he was student and she teacher. Just as she could never go back to those other times in her life, it was another door closed.

~

Yet again, the days settled into a quiet monotony. Sometimes when Esther was sitting at the dining room table grading papers, or polishing the surface of its shiny mahogany, she would glance at the piano, which had resumed its mute aspect, and think of Andrew, whose young fingers had raced so expertly across the keys. But more and more she would recall Zalman and the look on his face when he would walk in the door and see her seated at the piano bench playing the familiar strains of a beloved song.

Once and only once did Esther dare to challenge the normal order of things. It was five years after she had dismissed Andrew from her tutelage, two years after she had begun a new, more demanding job teaching music at the local high school. One evening as she sat alone, Jacob already having gone upstairs to bed, she even opened the piano bench, allowed her hand to explore the sheets until, reaching the bottom, she pulled out a page, now tattered and yellow. "Clair de Lune." She glanced at the notes, hearing the music once again in her head, but didn't attempt to play the chords. She returned the sheet to its place inside the bench.

The couple had just returned from seeing a movie, and Jacob was in an unusually jovial mood. After exiting the car, Esther stopped on the porch, which had recently begun to sag, and gazed up at the roof, now gray with the last remnant of snow, and took a deep breath.

She walked into the house and removed her coat. Again, she glanced around the room, her eyes skipping from the couch, the glass table, polished, as always, till it glistened, the flower-adorned wallpaper on the kitchen walls. Making herself a cup of tea, she asked Jacob to join her at the kitchen table.

As he did, he removed a Stella D'oro biscuit from its package and dunked it into the cup filled with hot liquid.

"That was a good laugh we had at the movie," he said, chortling at the memory. They had seen *Flashdance*. She watched Jacob as he ate the last bite of the biscuit. A late-afternoon sun was filtering through the blinds.

"Jacob, I have been thinking about—something."

As he bent over his cup, Jacob's pupils shot up. He knew all too well what the consequences of his wife's "thinking" had been.

"The two of us in this house, this very big house which each day is eating up more of our dollars. This year the boiler broke down, and by next year we'll need a new roof. The windows will soon need better sealing, and the freezer now works only half the time. The furniture is okay, I suppose, but is becoming outdated. We could use some new bookshelves on the walls or a new wall unit. But I don't think I've got the energy for decorating the place anymore. What I'm trying to say is perhaps we should go looking for an apartment to rent—just to see what is there—not to buy anything just yet. This house, Jacob, this house is too big for—for only two people." On these last words, she let her voice drift off.

Esther watched her husband's face for an expression, some sign. She saw none. She watched as he got up with great effort, the easy smile that had been on his face minutes earlier erased.

"No."

And with that simple word, he left the room.

TWENTY

Jacob

Jacob finally relented and hired someone new. It was Esther who convinced him that he could no longer carry the business alone, that he needed someone younger, with more education, who could keep up with the rapidly changing technology.

Morris Leibovitz was ten years younger than Jacob and also from the old country. He was one of the hidden children who survived the war living with a Catholic family. "Christof" (what name could be less Jewish?) spent four years studying the Gospel and praying the rosary while filling his belly with warm oatmeal each morning and a slab of roast beef in the evening. At war's end, he reunited with his parents, who had survived arduous labor in the concentration camps, changed his name back to the original, and began life anew in the United States. Working as an architect on some projects with Jacob, Morris was always talking about his "adventures" during the war, while Jacob said little. How could this man even begin to understand the terrors that he had endured?

Like Zalman, Morris was a gifted architect, a meticulous one, proud of his handiwork. But that was where the similarities ended. While Zalman was mostly self-educated, Morris was trained in all the best schools, had received certificates, and was also a licensed Realtor. He had far more knowledge on the new technology, handled the floppy disk with ease, and was able to navigate Microsoft programs on the new Commodore 64 in the office. He also took every opportunity to remind Jacob of his skills.

While Jacob acknowledged that the man was something of a show-off, he could not deny that Morris could contribute to the business and even take some of the weight off his own shoulders. So, after observing him for a few months, he extended an offer to Morris to be his assistant, with the possibility of becoming a partner one day. Morris jumped at the chance. Four months later, Jacob could no longer deny that Morris had become an asset. The business was thriving, more homes at a lower cost were being constructed, paperwork was reduced through the new computer system, rentals were in demand, and even some of the clients were commenting on what a pleasure it was to work with the new man. Still, as he watched Morris's fingers tap quickly across the computer keyboard, the man incessantly making glib remarks about the AIDS crisis or the starving children in Africa as if he were commenting on the weather, Jacob couldn't help but feel there was something about the man he didn't like.

Each time Jacob would come home and relay the achievements of his new assistant, even if he was a bit talkative, Esther would get more excited. She anticipated the day when Morris would become a partner in EMI Realty and assume half of the worries and labor that went into the business. She also saw this as an opportunity for friendship. Jacob was spending so much of his time with Morris already, perhaps the two who shared a similar past could become friends outside of the office too. She suggested that he invite Morris and his wife over for dinner the following Saturday evening. Jacob adamantly rejected the idea at first, but after Esther noted that she and the wife could become friends now that she was not seeing so much of Florrie, he relented. When he proposed the idea to Morris, the man rushed from his desk and flung his arms around Jacob.

"We'd be so delighted to visit your home, my friend," he said, using the term for the first time, "and Leora will be so happy to meet your wife. Oh, I know we will have such fun!" His reaction was enough to almost make Jacob regret the invitation.

Saturday evening came all too quickly. Jacob opened the door to their guests, Morris wearing a light-gray herringbone jacket and blue tie, and Leora wearing a mink coat over a pale-pink knit dress that strained at the stomach. As he helped her off with the coat, Jacob caught Esther's eye, questioning why she would wear a mink coat in April, but neither said a word. Morris extended a big box of Barricini assorted chocolates wrapped in a bright-red bow.

"How kind! Thank you so much!" Esther said, leading them to the couch in the living room. The couple sat and surveyed the room, as Jacob and Esther took chairs across from them.

"Your home is so lovely! I hear Jacob built it especially for you!" said the wife, her head and the blonde beehive that sat atop it swiveling from side to side. Jacob sat back, a contented look on his face. He had not forgotten the time a year earlier when Esther suggested they sell the home, and he hoped Esther had paid attention to the remark.

"Would you like me to take you on a tour of the house?" Esther asked, standing up. Leora smiled broadly, revealing the stain of her red lipstick on her front teeth as she wobbled on high heels, following Esther out of the room.

Morris looked at the two women appraisingly.

"So glad that the girls could finally get together! It's important since we'll be working with each other for a long time, my friend." Jacob gritted his teeth at the mention of "friend" but sat quietly. Morris took no note of Jacob's silence as he continued his nonstop monologue about the plans for a new office building on Thirty-Fourth Street, the problem with a nonpaying tenant who faced eviction, and a new software program he was looking into. Jacob felt relieved when he saw Esther and her new friend descend the stairs.

"Your house is just magnificent!" Leora enthused, showing the stain on her teeth again.

"Ready for some dinner?" asked Jacob.

During the dinner, which received no fewer compliments than the home, Morris continued his nonstop talk. He had abandoned his talk about work and was relating the adventure of being a child in hiding.

"I fit in so well with the family's three children, you would have thought I was baptized! Some of the neighbors were told I was studying for the priesthood! Can you imagine? But I suppose I learned to be an actor, a good little liar!" He laughed, scratching his balding head.

Jacob wondered why anyone would be proud to be a liar, but he guessed it was essential during the war. Even so, Morris seemed a little too proud of himself.

"Esther, I must get your recipe for these noodles," interrupted his wife as she bit into her piece of the brisket dripping in brown sauce.

"So glad you like it. It's an old recipe from my mother," answered Esther as she poured some more rosé into Morris's glass.

"Honestly, I don't know how you find the time to cook such delicious dishes, make your own curtains, and carry a full-time job. I barely have time to shop for groceries, and I don't even work."

"Just takes a little planning. You can probably do the same things, even better, I am sure," said Esther, returning to her meal.

As Jacob listened to their conversation, he was glad for what he didn't hear. Nothing was said about the reason Leora was so pressed for time, the twin daughters who were readying for college in a few months. Morris must have informed his wife of the tragedy in Jacob's life, and although he liked to talk, Morris stayed away from this sensitive subject.

"Morris, why don't you build me a home like the one Jacob built for his wife?" asked Leora as, after the dining room table had been cleared, they ventured back into the living room with glasses of tea, Esther's sponge cake, and the box of chocolates.

"Here we go again!" exclaimed Morris, laughing, then sitting down and spreading his knees on the couch.

"Well, I have yet to get an answer from you. It wouldn't even have to be this big for the two of us; maybe there's a lot available in this neighborhood. What do you think, Esther?" she pressed, swiveling the beehive in her direction.

"Sure," said Esther as she chose a strawberry crème from the box of chocolates, and in a lower voice, "That would be nice."

"Well, Leora, I'm not saying no. But that doesn't depend on me. That decision is up to Jacob," Morris said as, with a smile on his face, he turned to his host.

"What do you say, my friend? When are you making me a partner?"

Jacob took another sip of his tea, feeling the burn on his tongue. He said nothing.

After the couple left the home, Jacob helped Esther clear the coffee table and wash the last of the dishes before going to bed. Neither spoke of the evening. But after the new software system was installed and two more contracts were closed, Morris continued to ask, daily, about when he would become partner, and Jacob finally silenced him. Perhaps running a business alone wasn't as bad as it seemed.

~

The rhythmic motion of the great train rocked Jacob to sleep. Once again, in the dream he was seated on his mother's lap, cuddled into her chest as she read the words of his favorite fairy tales. It did not matter that he wasn't listening too carefully to the story, as long as he could take in her clean scent, as long as the brightly colored drawings of castles and forests continued to fascinate him. Her voice was melodic, like a song, a lullaby that soothed him to a peaceful sleep that he fell into soon after she had begun reading. He wished he could stay there forever. He was awakened by a screech, and then a sudden jolt.

"These engineers can't drive. They are always putting on the brakes."

Jacob opened his eyes and rubbed out the clouds. At first he had forgotten where he was, but soon the image of the boy next to him began to take form. He looked at his watch and again checked the large, overstuffed bag at his feet.

"Nearly an hour left to go until we reach Hamburg, Zalman. If you are hungry, I have another cheese sandwich in my bag."

The boy shook his head and ran his fingers through his light wavy hair. I can't properly call him a boy, he is nearly a man, Jacob thought as he observed his friend's serious eyes, the stern set of his lips, his chin. He wondered if he, too, had aged as much in the intervening years since they'd first met in Frau Blanc's barn. He wondered, too, about what lay ahead when he stepped off the train only to board a ship from which he would step off once again, this time in America.

He didn't voice his concerns to Zalman, of course. To speak too much was to take the chance that a torrent of regrets, a storm of long-stifled emotion, would burst forth. And that was a risk Jacob was unwilling to take.

"Are you sure we are doing the right thing?"

It was the third time since they had left the apartment in Berlin early that morning that Zalman had asked the question. And Jacob always had the same answer for him.

"It's absolutely the right thing. It is the only thing. Neither of us has anything left to hold us in this place. Not a father, not a mother, not even a straggly cat! We cannot even visit a cemetery, lay a rock on a grave. There are only crumbled buildings and ashes here. Not for us, two Jewish boys with hardly a penny between us, and no one left in the world."

"Well . . ." Zalman paused. "At least we have each other."

Jacob set his eyes upon the boy again as a smile came to his lips. "Yes," he said, "we will always have that."

~

Jacob opened his eyes just as the announcement came over the loud-speaker. He gathered his things and got off the subway at the stop in Mill Basin. During the five-minute walk, he relived the dream he had just had. Like all the other times, it had seemed so real, as if it were yesterday. And yet it was over thirty years ago since he had taken that last ride with Zalman, who had accompanied him to the ship that would take him to his new life in America. It would be nearly a year later that Zalman would follow him to stay with cousins before he would leave him once again.

In the dream he had been content, had no animosity toward his companion. No, it had been a good dream. A dream about two friends traveling toward a new life filled with hope. Not like the dreams he had when he fell into a troubled sleep most nights as he dreamed of sitting in airplanes that fell out of the sky and climbing giant ladders whose rungs shattered with each step. Always in these dreams Jacob was running, running to escape an angry inferno, or running toward someone, a child whose face he dared not see, a child falling from a mountaintop whose hand he had clasped only to have it slip away, to lose him in the murky depths far below. These were the dreams that dominated his night as Jacob lay in his bed, so that upon awakening, he would reach for his Esther and bring her close to him, holding on to her for dear life, afraid that she, too, might fall from his grasp.

But now, as Jacob lingered on the five-minute walk to his home, he tried not to recall those nightmares and to focus only on the beautiful evening. And he tried to recall the dream he had just awakened from on the subway, in which Zalman had appeared not as a rival, a treacherous enemy, but as the friend and the brother he had always been.

Jacob weaved slowly among the commuters emerging from the station, not stopping to purchase the evening paper or pick up a pack of mint Life Savers from a nearby newsstand.

He didn't hate Zalman. He never had. If Jacob had taken the time to search deep within his heart, he would admit that it was Zalman, not he, who had saved their lives. If not for Zalman, Jacob would have been just another solitary defeated young man in hiding, or worse. But Zalman had given him purpose. The child for those first few weeks had brought an innocence back into his life, and along with it a sense of anticipation, that things would be better. Jacob knew, too, that as the older, more experienced one, he would have to be the boy's protector, so that when the crucial time came, he would not think of his own fears, but only of the boy. He could not save his father, his brother, not even his mother. But maybe he could save the boy. After all that had occurred, Jacob realized that if not for Zalman, he himself would have fallen, only to lie buried with the others for eternity. Zalman had been the strong one.

There were fewer stores and people now, as Jacob turned the corner of the residential block. He averted his eyes when he noticed the few workers out late, digging up water pipes in the middle of the street. Watching the mounds of dirt ascend as a giant pit became ever larger had always unnerved him, reminding him of his near miss with death. But here, in America, the image had taken on a different, more pleasant aspect, as each slash of the shovel into earth meant hope, the beginnings of a new house taking shape, a new dream realized. And then, years later, as a small casket was lowered into the ground, the sound of the spade, the smell of damp earth frightened him as it never had before. He crossed the street.

As he neared the home, Jacob tried to recapture his dream. Zalman seated next to him on the train, standing nearby as his best man, staying up late into the night, meticulously drawing the lines that would some-day be Jacob's house, watching patiently as his son's fingers paused over the keys of the piano. And Jacob realized then that without Zalman, like the house, his life would have had no foundation. Again, he recalled when Esther had approached him with an idea. She wanted a new house, this time smaller, a new home only for two. But Jacob had swiftly denied the request. How could he move on to a new home? Without Zalman, how could he start again?

He wondered, too, why he had hurt him. Although there had been no words between the two men that day when he had thrown Zalman out of the home, Jacob knew that the man had suffered a pain, one so deep that only Jacob himself could fix it.

Jacob knew that it was not jealousy but fear that had incited his actions. He could not chance losing her, just as he had lost his parents, his brother, everyone he had. He would not let Esther slip into the hole. His fear had morphed into anger, an anger aimed at his best friend.

Jacob placed the key in the lock. He had planned on taking some time off from work in two weeks. That was when he would call Zalman. Jacob was sure his old friend would be glad to hear from him.

TWENTY-ONE

Esther

It was one late afternoon on the first of April when Esther, her arms filled with books and packages, pushed open the front door with her knee and set the items on the kitchen counter. A sigh escaped her lips as she removed a glass from a bottom shelf and filled it with a stream of cold tap water. An aggressive sun was boring its way through the half-opened blinds she had recently purchased when she heard a car door slam shut just outside. Perhaps it was Florrie rushing home to make her husband dinner. Their friendship as the years flew past had grown more distant, reduced to sporadic waves or hurried greetings in passing. Esther noticed at the last such sighting that her neighbor's hair had gone from a lustrous black to nearly completely gray. While Esther, who was already past fifty herself, would never consider such a drastic change, she had to admit that the color, at least on Florrie, was rather attractive, giving her the air of a sophisticated, mature woman. Perhaps she would tell her that the next time she ran into her, maybe even invite her in for a cup of tea if they had the time.

Esther looked at the stairs and decided she was too tired to change her clothes just yet, or even grade the five classes' worth of exam papers, and the groceries—the milk, apples, rye bread, even the Breyers coffee ice cream, Jacob's favorite—could wait. Taking her glass into the living room, she kicked off her pumps and settled into the sofa. And as she took another long sip of the water and patted down the wrinkles in the royal-blue satin pillow, she decided that yes, this was her favorite time of day. Just as her eyelids began to flutter in sleep, though, she was startled by the click of the lock in the front door. She looked up to see him emerging, leather case in hand, shoulders slumped as he dropped the briefcase on the carpet and removed his jacket. When he turned toward her, she could see deep dark circles under his eyes and that his face had assumed an ashen-gray pallor.

"Jacob! Why are you home from work so early?"

He barely met her eyes but bent down to brush her cheek with a kiss.

"I don't know, Esther. I just didn't feel like working. Maybe it's my stomach again. I'm just not right."

"Jacob, you work too hard. Good thing you planned to take the next few days off from work. You need to relax. Maybe we'll go up to the country, no? It would be nice to get away. Go upstairs. I'll bring you some tea, or maybe you want some of the chicken soup I made last Friday?" But she didn't receive an answer, and Jacob was already up the stairs.

An hour later, Esther was shutting the blinds in the kitchen and clicked on the lamp on the end table in the living room. She had refrained from going upstairs to change her clothes or even turn on the TV so as not to disturb her husband, as the house assumed a peaceful silence. When she heard the whistle of the red kettle, she removed a Lipton tea bag from the pantry and, using the earthenware mug they had purchased on a recent trip to Miami, she poured a cup of tea. Delicately ascending the stairs, she walked into the bedroom.

The room was mute except for the regular ticking of the alarm clock on Jacob's side of the bed. His head was turned from her, sunken deep into the pillow.

"Jacob!" she called in her best singsong voice. "Time to get up. Otherwise you'll be awake and keep me up all night!"

But then something changed. It was a feeling, a deep silence that she had sensed only once before on a sunny day in April when she looked out the kitchen window. She hesitated before coming closer. Esther placed the mug on the dresser and walked toward him. But even before she touched his hand, still the hand of a boy of twenty, she knew. She knew that she had lost him. That he was gone.

TWENTY-TWO

Riku, 1994

The first thing that caught Riku's eye was the cylindrical object tacked onto the molding outside the door of the Brooklyn home. He had a vague memory of the object placed at all the entrances of a home owned by one of his earliest acquaintances when he had first arrived in San Francisco. The object was simple, wooden, and it had the image of a star painted a royal blue on its face. Not quite certain of its purpose, he was certain of one thing—the occupants inside were Jewish. If he found the house suitable, it could easily be removed.

Standing on the expansive though wobbly porch, he rang the bell, and after a few minutes was warmly greeted by two older women. Riku lowered his head.

"Are you Mr. Matsuda?" asked the shorter one, smiling and offering her hand as the other, some inches taller, with her gray hair tied severely in a bun, stood by. Without thinking, Riku kept his hands at his sides and took a quick bow.

"Yes, Matsuda. Riku Matsuda. I called you on Monday." The shorter and, he thought, the prettier one, smiled again. This time he saw that it lit up her whole face.

"I'm so pleased to meet you. I'm Esther Stein, and this is my friend, Mrs. Flora Konigsberg. Esther and Florrie, if you'd like." The taller one, Florrie, acknowledged him with a smile and, biting her lip as she took his cue, a quick bow.

"I'm here to look at your home, but I haven't much time, as my flight is later this afternoon, and my family is waiting."

"Oh, of course, of course," said the shorter woman with the unusually thick auburn-colored hair, the one who was the homeowner. She took quick strides, leading the way into the living room. When she spoke, Riku thought he heard a slight accent in her voice, but he couldn't quite tell from where. Her friend, fast on her tail, stood quietly behind as Esther swept her arm across the space. The first thing Riku noticed was the size of the room—large, expansive, with giant windows whose light was covered by dark damask drapes. The couch, a royal-blue velvet, and matching shag rug seemed out of date, and the radiator, white paint peeling at the top, equally anachronistic. It rattled intermittently, and the floors beneath the rug complained like an old man, squeaking with every step. A baby grand piano gleamed in the corner.

The kitchen was not much better. The appliances were olive green, though showed signs of careful scrubbing. Every couple of seconds, a sad drip coming from the kitchen faucet broke the silence. There were cheery yellow curtains on the one window over the sink, and a yellow-and-orange tablecloth decorated the small, round plastic table in an unfortunate attempt to brighten the room. The toilet and small sink in the downstairs powder room looked like they worked, although he wondered how many years it had been since the carnation-pink tiles had gone out of fashion.

Upstairs, another shag rug in the hallway, a chocolate brown, was severely matted, but it lacked any sign of pet hair or the noxious stench of tobacco and looked as if its only fault consisted of several frequent shampoos. The bedrooms, smaller than Riku would have liked, seemed equally immaculate. Only one, the main, contained a bed, two night tables, and a dresser. The other two, somewhat smaller, were empty. One was painted white, a color for either a girl or boy, the other blue.

"Oh, I almost forgot to show you the backyard," exclaimed Esther before unlocking and pulling open the screen door at the side of the kitchen.

As the group stepped out on the small deck, he hardly noticed how rickety its planks were or the raw wood splinters that peeked out at every step of the chestnut-painted deck. His eyes focused only on the massive tree just steps away.

"I see you like our apple tree," Esther gushed, the smile now filling her face from ear to ear. "My husband and I planted it in fifty-six, the year he built this house. Come fall, you will see apples on every branch."

"Enough for sauces and pies for the whole year," added Florrie.

"We like apples," replied Riku.

"Shall we go back inside?" offered Esther, breaking the sense of unease that followed.

The women's eyes pursued him as they sat on the worn sofa, while, staying away from the two odd yellow chairs at either side, he seated himself in the straight-back leather recliner. As he did, he thought he saw Esther emit a slight gasp.

"Well, Mr. Matsuda, what do you think?"

He paused before answering, knowing full well he had no choice in the matter.

"I think we can come to terms."

"My friend is not selling the home, you know. It's just a rental." The taller woman looked at Esther, who nodded.

"Well, then, I think I have a few questions before I sign," Riku said, placing both hands on his knees as if to get up.

"I think you should know something before you do," said Esther, who for the first time met his eyes directly. The other one quickly put up her hand.

"Esther, I don't think Mr. Matsuda—"

But Esther pushed the hand aside.

"Florrie, I want him to know—please!" She turned back to Riku.

"I want you to know why I have decided to rent the home, and not sell it. Excuse me—" She removed a tissue from the pocket of her navy polyester pants and dabbed at her nose before resuming, "It's just that this house, this *home*, meant—it means—quite a lot to me. You see, Jacob, my husband, built it. He and his best friend, Zalman, who was an architect, oversaw every detail—the walls, the plumbing, the number of steps in each flight. It was all a dream of Jacob's, something he'd had a vision of since he was a boy. A dream to build his own home, a permanent home for him and his family. After I met him, it became my dream too. And even though we never had the family we hoped—" She paused, twisted the tissue in her hands, and took a breath.

"And though we never had that family, we have always loved the home, or maybe just the dream of it. And we did have some good years here, only I wish we'd had more. My husband is gone now ten years." She turned to the woman beside her. "Florrie, is it ten years already?" Her friend nodded, began as if to say something, then stopped. Esther glanced around the room as if noticing all that was in it for the first time.

"There was a time when I wanted to leave. I wanted to give it all up. The home was just too much trouble, too big for just the two of us. But now, the longer I've lived here, the harder it has become to part with it. Anyway, that's why I've decided to rent and not just sell it. One of my brothers is insisting I take a small place near him in Boca Raton in one of those retirement communities. But I just can't. I'm not ready to give up the home. After all, it had been Jacob's dream when he came to the US from Poland, when he survived the war."

Riku flinched. "Your husband—he was a survivor?"

"Well, yes."

He could no longer help himself.

"I too. I, too, am a survivor."

He saw the two women exchange glances, but neither spoke.

"I, too, am a survivor," he repeated, then sensing their confusion, continued.

"No, not from Poland, of course, but a survivor from the camps right here in the US."

"But that's impossible, there weren't any camps—" began Florrie, but this time it was Esther who interrupted her.

"Florrie—he's Japanese," she whispered as if Riku were not present in the room. "We imprisoned the Japanese."

Riku shifted his body in the recliner.

"Yes, that's right. I was only five years old, but still to this day I remember it."

He lifted his eyes to look at them once again, taking in their pale, lined faces; their eyes, alert, waiting. He wondered if they were sisters.

"My parents were born in Nagasaki, Japan, the place that was bombed, the city of all that awful destruction. But they were on US soil by the thirties, well before the war, a newly married couple. I don't think they even visited the few family members they had left behind. Of course, once the war began, that was impossible."

Riku sighed, kept his eyes down, scanning the palms of his hands as if reading the words he spoke.

"But I, well, I was born in the US. An American citizen, one hundred percent. Still, one can't escape appearances. And in that I am Japanese. So, yes, they saw my parents, and including me, a child of only five years, as their enemy. So after Pearl Harbor, the dreadful attack, they locked us up, even me, barely out of diapers! Does that sound like America to you?"

The women shook their heads sympathetically. As Riku sat silently, the memories floated before his eyes as if they had happened yesterday.

The smells. That was what he remembered the most. Horse manure on wood under the sheets of linoleum, all topped with layers of dirt, the corpses of insects. Over three years sleeping on top of it all, on those army cots. He never could get used to it. He never did. It was all so different from the sweet scents of his parents' fruit store—the oranges, lemons, the cherries like the best wine, which all came to be one with the air. He remembered it all.

Riku could never get used to the stench, just as he could not get used to the barbed wire along the top of the fence, the machine guns pointed at them during the daylight hours as they counted the minutes till sleep during the blackness of night. The name of their new residence, not a home, never that, had been burned into his mind: the Tule Lake Segregation Center in California. But he was born here, here in *this* country. A true American citizen.

During that time, he recalled, his father's hands were idle. His father, who had never missed a day of work in his life, would sit brooding, for what else does one do when hope is lost? His mother, a gentle soul, at least had comfort in the few friends she had made, other young women who would stare at their children each day, wondering about the promise of America, wondering what their lives would be like when it was all over. All the adults thought the children were too young to notice how radically their lives had been transformed. But even they could sense the change, as they went to makeshift schools taught by educated Japanese women and their visiting white neighbors, when they played ball in the mud outdoors with the barbed wire surrounding them, breathing the air that seemed to grow more stale each day.

After those years, Riku and his parents were freed, freed from their prison, able to go back to their homes. But the problem was, they no longer had homes or a livelihood to go back to. Their fruit store, all that sweetness, was gone, and in its place: a bicycle shop. Their home, the place where Riku had been born, wasn't theirs anymore. A white family, one he didn't recognize, a true American family, now lived there. When they returned, they felt not just the shock of coming back for the next few days or a month, but years, as the years of their imprisonment had changed their lives and the lives of over ten thousand like them forever. They had become different people.

Their imprisonment had caused them to lose something that they had always taken for granted. He still wasn't the same. The stress of trying to rebuild had become too much for his father, something Riku never realized until many years later. Less than a year after the family was freed, he died of a heart attack, leaving Riku to be raised by his mother, who worked in a grocery store just like the family had once owned. But he could tell that she was changed too. The lightness she always had in her steps, her easy laughter, the merriment that shone in her eyes, her smile, was gone.

Lost in his memories, Riku sank into a deep silence. And still the two women, each seeming now to blend into the other, waited. Perhaps they could guess what was in his mind; perhaps they had suffered too. Maybe that was why he felt this sudden familiarity with these two strangers.

"I never wanted children of my own. Never had a desire for them because my early years had been so difficult. Eventually, that all changed when I met my wife, Jenny. So now I find myself with four little ones, all under ten, and I am already fifty-seven years old!" At those words, for the first time since he had entered the home, Riku felt a lightness wash over him as a smile came to his lips.

Esther was the first to rise from her seat on the couch.

"Mr. Matsuda, I believe you will make a great tenant for this house."

"Good!" Riku answered promptly as he rose to his feet. "I'll take it."

TWENTY-THREE

Zalman, 1983

By the time word reached Zalman, it was too late. All he could do after learning about his best friend's death was sit quiet as a stone for several days. No one, not even Miriam, could coax him out of the bottomless hole. His best friend dead. How was this possible? His last breaths taken without Zalman by his side. Zalman, who had been there during the darkest times, when both Jacob and Esther were sure they were facing their last glimpses of this dreary earth. But there were times of joy, too, when they had been together, tasting the first delicious drops of freedom, men in love with the life they had begun anew. Yet now—*Why wasn't he there?*

It was the cousin who told him, Moshe, who had arranged for his travels to Minnesota all those years ago, and who now revealed the news as calmly as if he were telling him to put on a sweater to shield himself from the cold. Jacob had gone to bed one night and then . . . and then. That was it. Zalman hadn't asked any questions then and couldn't see the point of it. When he put down the phone that had delivered the news that sent him spinning back in time, it was as if something in his mind boomeranged, and for several days he couldn't regain his balance. Immediately, at 8:00 p.m. that evening, when on any other day he would be taking off his slippers, readying himself for a hot shower, he decided to go for a walk.

"Just going out to clear my head," he announced, putting his hand on the metal knob, before a blast of cold air slapped against his cheeks. He walked for blocks, as he had done on numerous occasions since they had moved to the town of Highland Park in New Jersey, where his cousin's best friend had lived for the past twenty years—not a grand metropolis like New York, but not a farm either. Also, his friend knew of a piece of business for Zalman, something to call his own. He had resolved long ago never to work for anyone else again.

So Zalman walked in this place he had barely lived in for a year, ignoring the vibrant sounds of the neighborhood, still alive with shoppers, strollers, and men winding their way through the thinning crowds—the Hasidim, Hispanics, Irish, and Italians as they came home from work. Zalman saw none of it. Not the young couples strolling under leafless trees, the dogs straining on leashes, shop owners sitting on hastily stationed bridge chairs outside, nodding at potential customers as they passed by. Today, as his eyes fixed on the scattered cigarette butts, rumpled sales receipts, and empty paper cups that rolled underneath the parked cars, he saw none of it. Instead, he had one thought swirling through his mind. It would have been so easy to call her, express his sympathy, suggest they meet for a coffee. So easy. So devastating, for the minute he allowed his mind to fixate on the idea, he was swamped by a sea of guilt, drowning, unable to breathe.

After about twenty minutes, he was lost. He couldn't find his way back home; the street numbers blurred, and the sounds of the neighborhood rolled into each other, creating a wild cacophony from which he could not escape. Zalman stopped at a street corner, trying to find his way, before realizing, finally, that he didn't want to go home at all. Lost, at least for now, was better.

TWENTY-FOUR

Riku

As soon as his family moved in, Riku set to work. First, he had the rugs lifted and the wooden floors hidden beneath the tiles scraped so that the light pine was revealed when the sun bounced off its surface in the morning. He covered the middle of the newly naked planks with the deep-red silk rug, whose design was scattered with delicate green-and-white renderings of cherry blossoms. Riku took pride in knowing that it was the very same rug that had been in his grandmother's home in Japan and that had adorned his parents' parlor when he was a child in San Francisco. And, with Esther's approval, he had placed the massive velvet sofa, along with the coffee table and standing lamp, upstairs in the main bedroom, replacing it all with a flowered chintz sofa, two end tables with small lamps covered with simple white shades, and the chinoiserie, black lacquered, which held his father's collection of painted wineglasses. The piano, though at first an object of mild interest to the children, remained untouched in the corner of the room.

When he was done with the inside, having painted the bedroom his daughters shared a soft pink and having set up bunk beds for his sons in the blue room, Riku turned to the outside of the home. Enlisting the help of his twin sons, he ripped down the rickety deck, which he calculated could withstand only a couple of years' worth of stormy winters. It wasn't long before the entire deck had been replaced with a sturdy one made of redwood in time for its first Fourth of July barbecue. Jenny, of course, insisted on starting a vegetable garden, which by summer's end would already be flowering with full red tomatoes, hearty zucchini, and ripe green cucumbers. The hefty apple tree that had overseen its share of mellow springs and tumultuous winters found a slow renaissance as leaves emerged on every branch, and the smallest of embryos that would blossom into juicy apples in the fall, bringing shade to the parcel of grass. The backyard with the oak overshadowing it all had become a peaceful place, with gentle breezes that weaved through the newly formed leaves.

Then after reconnecting the broken links of an old swing he had bought secondhand, along with a slide that required constant sweeping from dirt and leaves, he turned his efforts to the facade of the home, which with systematic strokes of the brush was tempered from its sunny yellow, which had taken on a dismal and sad hue, to a more sedate shade of greenish blue. Last, the family carried new wicker chairs and a wicker love seat to the porch, along with a green-and-white-striped hammock that Riku tied in the shade between two trees in the back of the house. When all was done, everything about the place echoed home to the Japanese American family.

Esther herself had settled into her new residence in Boca weeks before the family had moved into the home. Riku could tell that Florrie, though, kept a keen eye on her neighbor's house through the open slats of her own window shade. On the first of each month, hair tied back and dressed in a pantsuit, she would appear in front of the home, its path lined with new rocks, and step onto the porch that no longer squeaked. That was when Jenny would greet her with the monthly rental check, which Florrie would later deposit into Esther's account. Jenny had never asked her inside since, because as she and Riku had agreed, she didn't like the idea of turning a business relationship into something more than that. Nevertheless, she would usually catch the woman trying to sneak a peek into the home's ever-changing interior. As Jenny closed the door, she could see the shadow of disappointment wash across Florrie's face. Jenny was pleased that she would have no gossip to report back to Esther, other than the fact that they were good tenants.

Once his efforts were expended and the house made into the very model of his and Jenny's vision, Riku had little time to enjoy it. He was kept busy with his new job as a chemical engineer at Dow, which had recently expanded with home food management projects like Ziploc and Saran Wrap. Riku worked long hours, leaving at 6:00 a.m. and not returning until eight in the evening, when the night had dimmed the hue of the home's exterior so that it blended in with the dark sky. Yet even from down the block, as he approached, walking past the stately oaks at each curb, the garbage cans positioned like soldiers before every home, Florrie's house with the wooden bench in front, he could discern the lights of the home sparkling brightly. Not his home, not yet. But he hoped that one day it might be.

Often when he looked at his wife of twelve years, Riku would consider himself a lucky man. Although Jenny herself was highly educated, possessing a master's degree in business administration before embarking on a career in management at one of the largest hospitals in San Francisco, she had abandoned it all once their twin boys, James and Joseph, were born. After that, Jenny never seemed to complain or to long for missed opportunities, instead devoting herself entirely to the two boys and the two daughters to come. And, of course, to Riku who, she had to acknowledge, was the most difficult of all.

When he struggled out of bed each morning, rubbing the crust from his eyes, Jenny was already downstairs making sure the special green tea he loved so much was steeped exactly right, and then opening each of the shades in the home like a quiet little bird. Riku marveled how at day's end she looked much the same, her dark eyes bright, her cheek still dewy as he bent to kiss her in greeting. He knew, too, that Jenny, the daughter of wealthy jewelers whose parents had escaped Japan before there had been a hint of turmoil, and whose children had been free from the shame of imprisonment, having been born in the Northeast years after the war had ended, was far more than he deserved. He had loved her from the first time she appeared in one of his classes at the university back in San Francisco. Even then he could not take his eyes off the girl with the heart-shaped face, the girl with splashes of rose-color rouge on her cheeks.

Upon hearing the news of his impending marriage to the young woman he had described as a girl with eyes of brilliant coal and hair sleeked back in a bun resembling a scoop of mocha ice cream, Riku's mother, Airi Shiori, was ecstatic. She had resigned herself to the idea that her only son would be a lifelong bachelor. Riku sighed now, remembering his father's adage, "No coin has two heads," that happiness always has another side, for it was shortly after the joyous wedding that he was confronted by two tragedies. First, the loss of his job as a lab technician, and then, worst of all, the death of his mother after a series of small strokes. Airi Shiori's death was something he would never quite recover from. After all, a boy has only one mother. It was then that Riku was overcome by an illness, an illness of the mind that the family never spoke of. Just like those first few days when he was a young boy, after his arrival at the camp, when he found himself immobile, locked inside his own body without the capacity to speak or focus on anything around him but his own terrors. With time, the panic had passed, but Riku always harbored a secret fear that the feeling would someday return with greater consequences.

But now, after securing a new, more lucrative position on the East Coast and after twelve years of marriage, Riku still could not believe his luck. First came the twin boys, James and Joseph, and two years later, a girl, Abigail. Then in five more years, Leticia—Letty—the baby with the unusual emerald-colored eyes and ringlets of dark hair, arrived. And even though he knew he could never be the typical American father, the kind that coaches their sons' Little League games or dances with their daughters around the living room, even though he still winced whenever his colleagues would call him "Ricky," he was proud of his accomplishments in the country that had both punished and rewarded him. He was proud, too, that his children all had American names.

~

The family had been in the house for just over a year, and that Saturday morning the sun rose high in the sky, alight with flame, looking just like one of the round apricots his father had displayed in baskets around the perimeter of the market. Riku awoke early, watching the first rays sprinkle dots of light over Jenny's sleeping head.

He would allow her to sleep later than usual so that he could lie awake listening to the soothing silences of the house. After about ten minutes, his bladder urged him out of bed, so he eased his feet into a pair of blue terry cloth slippers underneath the bed and shuffled into the bathroom. After relieving himself, he let the cool water run over his hands into the drain and stared at his reflection in the mirror. His cheeks protruded like apples; his face was broad. He knew that if he permitted himself to smile more often, toss back his head and abandon himself to laughter, it would be a face that most might consider warm, even friendly. Something Riku no longer knew how to be.

Still in pajamas and slippers, he padded down the stairs to the kitchen. He opened the small white Frigidaire, pulled out a bottle of orange juice, and poured himself a large glass. He remained standing as he drank it all and then quickly poured himself another glass, taking it outside, where, placing the glass on a leveled patch of grass, he eased himself into a hammock strung between two trees.

What to do? What to do? He hadn't even told Jenny yet, afraid of what her response might be. It had been only last Monday when one of the directors at the company had called him into his office, placed a hand on Riku's shoulder, and, grinning, told him that he was to be promoted to department head, so pleased were they all with his work, and in such a short span of time! At first, feeling the hand tighten on his skin, as the words made their way into his brain, Riku relaxed. But just as he was about to offer his thanks, the boss continued. The new position was an excellent one, with more responsibilities, and still another, higher pay scale. It would, however, be a transfer only a few miles from the family's former home, this time at their center in Pittsburg, California.

Mike Harrison watched the shadow cross momentarily past Riku's face and loosened his grip. He added that the new position was only an offer and that Riku wasn't obliged to accept it, but could stay on in the hopes that a position might open within the department where he now worked. Not likely, but maybe in a few years. Nevertheless, the director encouraged him to take his time, perhaps as long as a week before deciding. Riku nodded, closing the door behind him.

Riku looked up at the sun, whose rays had begun to peek between the branches of the full-leafed apple tree. A cardinal alighted on one of those branches, skittered along the wood, and took to the air. He drew in a deep breath. What to do? What to do?

If he took the job, it meant uprooting his family yet again. But, as their only source of income, didn't he have a responsibility to secure the best income, the best position, so that all their lives would have a chance to improve? And even though the family had placed much effort into the home—painting, scraping, polishing, and moving furniture—it was still only a rental. Even though he had a dream of ownership one day, it wasn't *his* home. Surely Esther would be happy to see them go, to obtain a still-higher rental fee now that they had fixed up the house. And he would not miss the old woman next door, her spying eyes each time he would walk to his car, put the key in the lock. Still, a decision had to be made.

And then there was the matter of the job itself. Despite his confident demeanor in the workplace, he realized that it only masked his own insecurities. He understood numbers and formulas well enough, but manage a whole department of people? Just the thought sent his heart beating wildly in his chest. A decision. No matter what, he knew that Jenny would support him. Yet it was only his decision to make.

Riku closed his eyes. But the sun that had seemed so calming, so peaceful, only minutes before, was like a disk of fire now, attacking him mercilessly with its rays even though his eyelids were closed, and from which there was no escape. His eyes snapped open, taking in the patch of dirt, a grassy area that had been left untouched for years and that he and his sons had weeded only days earlier, the apple tree that loomed now threatening above him. Riku grew afraid when he realized that the thing that he had feared the most was happening again.

He felt the orange juice coming back up his throat, its acid burning, the black hairs on his arms becoming insects, crawling without mercy so that he couldn't help but scratch his skin as he looked toward the sky, seeking a reprieve, a shower of rain. Worst of all, even though Riku was already on his feet, he found himself no longer able to move, rooted to the ground and trapped in the prison, lying faceup on a tiny cot big enough only for a small boy, encircled entirely by thick coils of barbed wire. He felt flushed, sick. He wanted to run but could not. He didn't even know how to begin. He had to get out if only to stay alive. Get out. Get away from the body that had become a noose, tightening around him, sucking out his essence. And soon he was down, in that spot of dirt, still waiting for it to flower. He opened his mouth and felt the taste of salty wet tears. He wanted to call for Jenny but wasn't sure if his mouth was even capable of making a sound. Miraculously, in minutes, she was by his side.

"Riku, what's wrong? Tell me."

But he could not formulate the words, could barely utter a squeak. His eyes, which he knew were wild now, like a madman, took in her lovely round face, so like a Kewpie doll, her liquid-brown eyes. She asked no more questions; only seconds later Riku found himself being escorted like an invalid back to the hammock, for somehow he had been lying on the ground some feet away. He plunged into it, surrounding himself in the comforting folds of the striped green-and-white canvas.

"Riku, please hear me. You're having another panic attack. Take a few deep breaths. That's right. You will be fine. You will be just fine."

Jenny's soothing voice washed over him, an ocean of calm. Riku closed his eyes and kept them shut for how long he couldn't say. When he finally opened them, the sun's colors had paled, and he watched the impression of clouds as they sailed through the air. Jenny was stroking his chest quietly. He nodded, took another breath.

"Will you tell me now?" she asked, her voice low, patient, as if speaking to a young child.

"I didn't want to say, Jenny. It was my decision to make."

Jenny nodded, her face settling from concern into a smile. It was almost as if she could read his mind.

"You know we'll follow you wherever you go, whatever you decide. That will be the right decision."

He could no longer feel her hand even though it was firm in his grasp. And then his head began to shake. He could not stop it. His eye wandered to the kitchen window, where he could see their reflections in the glass. Abigail, nose pressed to the surface, tears streaming down her face. James, his hand on her shoulders, his mouth set in a tight line, looking older, much older than his ten years.

Riku couldn't help it. He was a man. He was Japanese. Imprisoned as a child, imprisoned still. Who would help him now that his mother was gone, his father dead? Just Jenny. Maybe Jenny. Still, it was his decision, resting only with him. After all, wasn't he the man? He was not sure who or what he was anymore. He had to see. He had to see now.

"Jenny, I need a mirror!"

"No, Riku. No, you don't."

"Jenny, please! I need a mirror!"

"You are here, Riku. You are here and I'm with you. Lie back down."

"But, Jenny, I must—"

"Let me help you, Riku. You don't need to carry this alone. Please let me help you."

He lay back in the hammock, allowing her to place her hands on the sides of his face. They felt soft, cool.

"Okay, Jenny," he said, "okay."

TWENTY-FIVE

Zalman, 1985

For the first time in the two years since he had heard about Jacob's death, Zalman jumped out of bed, dressed, even coaxed his sleepy daughter awake, switched on the Mr. Coffee, and placed two slices of white bread in the toaster. He looked out the kitchen window, which faced the courtyard below. Another gray December day, but today he felt as if spring was just beginning, and he couldn't wait to head out the door and take a nice deep breath. Miriam, still in her robe, walked in and stood for a while, observing her husband. She sat down at the kitchen table and watched Zalman spread margarine on a slice of toast, and when he handed it to her, she smiled.

One of the things that Zalman most admired about his wife was her quiet strength. Superficially, she was that shy girl, living in a farm-house amid rolling pastures, who had perhaps too blindly succumbed to her father's will. And, indeed, it would appear that she also deferred to Zalman in all things. Yet Zalman knew that she not only listened to him intensely but responded. With only a few words she would confirm his decision to come back east and indeed convince him that it was the right one. He was happy now for this quality in his wife, and he knew that she would accept his most recent decision, even if she did not fully understand it, and maybe persuade him that it, too, was right. This was a good thing, he reassured himself, because he had no intention of revealing his real reason for making it.

"Daddy, you can't be serious! You're actually making breakfast?"

Zalman greeted his daughter with a huge smile, the same reaction he had whenever she came into his view.

"Why not, Debbie? Don't you think your father is capable?"

She laughed, fullheartedly, still with that childlike innocence that made him want to run to her, hold her in his arms, and keep hugging her, as he had when she was just a toddler. Instead, he asked her if she would like a slice of toast, maybe some milk? She shook her head.

"I've got to get to school early to set up my project, and I'm walking over to Elizabeth's first." She grabbed her book bag from the counter, opened it, checked its contents before kissing both her parents on the cheek, and left.

"Make sure to keep your coat buttoned. It's cold outside!" reminded Miriam just as the door slammed behind her daughter.

At twelve, Debbie, the couple's only child, was a dark-haired beauty. With her mother's oval-shaped eyes and long lashes, her pale white skin, the luxurious hair that when occasionally let loose would sinuously curve past her shoulders, she reflected Miriam. In two aspects only did she resemble her father. The first was the color of her eyes—lighter, bluer than Zalman's, which had flecks of green. But it was her true nature in which she most resembled him. Steadfast, determined, and loyal to a fault, that was the essence of his Debbie behind her demure, almost angelic, appearance.

These characteristics occasionally flared up from her more passive surface, as when the family had moved from the daily routines of farm life to the more challenging sidewalks of central New Jersey. The girl was only nine years old and at first had ignored the taunts of her peers, bullies who assailed her, calling her "farmer" and "country hick," the girls who snickered at her gingham shirts in the corners of the playground. And she tried to ignore the boy with the shaggy blond hair, which seemed to be always in his eyes, who sitting behind her in class one morning joined in the torment, giving the child's long silky hair such a firm tug that she squealed out in pain. One day, finally, Debbie confronted the children. She told them she had as much right to be here as they, suggesting that most of their own grand- or great-grandparents were once farmers too. As for the names, well, she was proud to be a farmer, a "country hick," names she accepted as a badge of honor. What's more, the girl boasted, her father had been a hero during the war, living on sour milk and knockwurst, hiding until he and his friend faced down the muzzle of the Nazis' guns before slipping away moments before bullets could rip their flesh and their carcasses were thrown into mass graves they themselves had dug. At first, the children were awed by the audacity of their classmate, but shortly after, their interest was piqued as, in the school playground, they listened to stories of her father's heroism and the daily tasks of how she would milk the cows, care for the chicks so they would become good egg layers, and even how she spent her leisure time playing hide-and-seek with her cousins in the hayloft. And so the nine-year-old had stood up to the bullies until finally she won their trust and, eventually, their friendship.

Of course, she revealed none of these episodes to her teacher, not even to her parents, who eventually heard the whole story from one of the mothers, a neighbor who had been assisting in the playground when the incident had occurred, revealing it all to Miriam one afternoon when the two ran into each other at the supermarket. Miriam related it to Zalman, and the two decided that neither would say a thing, either in advice or praise to Debbie. Naturally, they were proud of her. Mostly, Zalman was surprised over the intense loyalty his daughter had for her family. That night Zalman stopped at the drugstore on the corner and purchased a giant-size Hershey bar with almonds. It was Debbie's favorite.

~

That morning, the morning he awoke with a purpose and a sparkle in his eye, Zalman arrived earlier than usual at his office. He unlocked the storefront and glanced up at the sign that proclaimed in neon yellow, WALLS FOR ALL. He sat down at the lone desk and moved his index finger along the list of names in the ledger. Satisfied with the number of bookings scheduled for the months ahead, he then checked the stack of gallon cans against the wall, confirmed the day's purchase, and by the time Oscar and Manny arrived, had the load along with brushes, rags, and the tarps laid neatly in the back of the truck.

"Hey, boss!" called Oscar, wearing painter overalls as he strode into the shop, followed by his younger brother, who was carrying a bag filled with two large bologna-and-cheese heros and a couple of cans of Diet Coke.

"You could have let us help with that stuff," he added, walking out again and taking a peek into the back of the white Chevy. "What time did you get here, anyway?"

Zalman shut the doors at the back of the truck and wiped his hands on the legs of his dungarees.

"Just a half hour earlier than usual. And still an hour before you two dummies got here." He laughed at the men and winked to let them know he was kidding. The brothers exchanged glances. They weren't used to their boss being quite this jovial, and certainly not this early in the morning. In the two years they had been working for Zalman Mendelson, they had known him to be a man who was kindhearted, generous, but also serious, all business.

"Where to today, boss?" asked Manny, the smaller and skinnier of the two, as he moved aside to open the ledger and placed his package on the desk. He came back outside, removing a Camel from behind his ear and rolling it in the palm of his hand.

"The Goodmans' over on Dobson in Edison. Just closed on it last Tuesday. We've got the whole downstairs today, first coat. Easy, off-white, that's most of what's in the truck. The rooms upstairs are a rainbow, each one a different color."

"That's just what I like, a little variety on the job," said Oscar, still standing by the open door of the vehicle as he looked up at the sky. Legs akimbo, hands on his wide hips, he appeared troll-like, a character from one of the cartoons Zalman's daughter used to watch on TV.

"See that cloud over there? Could be rain coming soon," he added, pointing a pudgy finger up at the sky.

"Why so worried? We're not working outdoors today," injected Zalman, jiggling the car keys in his hand as a signal that it was time to leave, then added, "Besides, everyone knows rainbows come out after the rain, and since we're painting rainbows tomorrow, I'm sure the weather will hold till then!" He laughed. Out of the corner of his eye, he could see the brothers exchange quick glances again, confused. But today he didn't care. He was happy, and if he let his excitement slip from his usual serious demeanor, it was okay. Today, for the first time in a long time, he was excited about the future, looking forward to it. He didn't even care when Manny removed another cigarette from a partially crushed pack that he plucked out of the pocket of his overalls, along with a silver lighter, offering the cigarette to his brother, and then lighting his along with the one he had been holding. Zalman leaned against the side of the truck and watched the men as, conversing in Spanish, they lingered in the doorway just outside the shop.

Looking at their expressionless faces, open and guileless, Zalman decided that he liked the two men. But he had liked them from the start. The workers, still both in their thirties, were, as luck would have it, neighbors of Zalman's cousin, Moshe, the same one who had told him about the farm in Minnesota, and then again helped Zalman's family find a place to live once he had made the decision to abandon his life as a farmer. Moshe had even gotten Zalman a job helping out at a kosher delicatessen in town when the family first arrived.

Oscar and Manny, along with their families—Oscar had two young sons, Manny, a baby daughter—lived in apartments on separate floors in a building a few blocks down in Highland Park. Moshe was a tenant in the same building, having left the old apartment years earlier, seeking escape from the suffocating and newly gentrified streets of Brooklyn. And when Zalman made the trip back east, it was only natural that he follow his cousin, where he quickly rented an apartment only blocks away on North Third Street. It all made sense, since he no longer knew anyone in Brooklyn. Not really.

It was luck, too, that Moshe was the kind of neighbor who liked to talk, liked to know everyone's name, what made them tick. So, when Zalman just happened to mention only a couple of months after starting the business that he was overcome by the labor of being a painter and that the old shoulder injury had begun to bother him once more, Moshe immediately thought of the brothers, both adept with a hammer and nails, who would be only too glad to finally have some steady employment. Moshe was gone now, having moved—made aliyah—to Israel only a year after Zalman had resettled back in the Northeast. But thanks to his cousin, Zalman was finally home; even better, he had Oscar and Manny too.

Reluctant at first, but after losing one day's work nursing his aching shoulder, Zalman finally acquiesced. Almost instantly after meeting them, he knew they were the kind of men who would make good employees, both possessing a quiet, serious nature. He could tell by their manner, their eyes that never wavered from his face, that they were honest. Best of all, neither minded making the trip from climbing ladders and hauling paint, not if it was for a job that paid well. Plus, they would be open to learning the business that Zalman himself had gotten the hang of only a couple of years earlier. But there was another reason for his affection. They reminded him of himself. Although they had come from Cuba as young boys on a boat secured by their father, and were about twenty years younger than he, there was something about their spirit, a stubborn drive to do whatever was demanded of them. And, like Zalman, they were loyal—yes, there was that too. He had hired them on the spot.

As soon as they pulled up at the curb in front of the neat but aging facade of the Cape Cod home, the skies opened up and the rain began to fall—large droplets splattering against the windows, the kind that would soak them to the bone. A young, very pregnant woman greeted them at the door, opening it wide so that they could sidestep in, each with fingers curled around the handle of a can of paint. As Zalman settled up, reviewing directions with the woman, Oscar and Manny ran out again, their heads still uncovered, and retrieved the ladder, tarps, rollers, and brushes, and, in a few minutes' time, they were standing in the front hall, dripping onto the dull wooden floor. Good thing the carpets weren't installed yet, thought Zalman, looking around the small living room. It was a good thing, too, in fact, that the rooms were bare, not a stick of furniture to be seen. The owner thanked them, and advising the workers to let themselves out by 5:00 p.m., she wrapped a broad sheet over her head and around her expansive belly and left.

The men started the preparations immediately, reaching up from the ladder to set tape against the moldings that stretched across the ceiling, then resting on their haunches to fit the blue tape close to the edge of the floor, making sure radiators and ceiling fans were securely covered, and fastidiously spackling each yawning gap. With the rain ominously swirling against the house, the windows would have to remain shut, at least for now. Almost an hour later, they had opened the cans to reveal the paint, a silky off-white with the consistency of putty. After slowly stirring the paint to radiance, Oscar began painting the downstairs bathroom while Manny attacked the kitchen, which left Zalman with the living room, where the least strenuous effort was needed. He could no longer take the risk of reinjuring his shoulder, maneuvering the brush to avoid wall ovens and sinks, even though Miriam had begged him to stay behind and run the business from the office shortly after he had hired the brothers.

"You are a boss now, not a laborer. You have enough paperwork to keep you busy without having to get down on your hands and knees to paint and scrape," she pleaded one evening as Zalman eased himself slowly into the kitchen chair and picked up his fork. His wife meant well, he knew, and hadn't she already followed him all those miles to a new home in a state where they had never lived, where she had neither family nor friends, and all because he had woken up one morning and decided he could no longer work for her ailing father, who was begging him each day to take over the now-expansive farm? Isaac would ask not a penny of his son-in-law, his only compensation having the security of knowing that the farm remained in good hands, in the hands of family, now that neither of his sons had an inclination to continue on as farmers. Looking down now at the pale strands of meat on his plate, Zalman considered lessening the load for once, his thoughts churning in his head. Couldn't he at least do Miriam this one favor? Spare her yet another day of worry?

So when she asked him again to sit back, to let others take over while he did the paperwork at home, Zalman didn't answer at first. He chewed the chicken slowly and dabbed at his mouth with a napkin. He took a long sip from his water glass, then turned to look at his wife, standing, holding the dish towel against her chest as if it were a Bible. She was waiting, as always, patiently. He opened his mouth, but no sound came out. How could he find the words? How could he tell her even now after fifteen years of marriage? Even now when she knew every wrinkle that wound along his face like a long highway, every word that came from his mouth even before he could utter it? Even now when she thought she knew him better than he knew himself? How could he tell her that he needed this job, this business that was his and nobody else's? Something that was his and his alone. How could she understand when he already had a family, a home? When he had her.

And so, as Miriam remained standing, her deep-brown eyes laced with concern, Zalman looked up from his meal and finally said the one word that would slow the frantic beats of her heart. "Please." Miriam blinked once, sat down, and began to eat.

Now as Zalman glided the roller along the expanse of wall, transforming the dim olive to a clean white, he felt happy. A sense of accomplishment flew through his body like a fine breeze, with each stroke, a peaceful feeling. Zalman enjoyed the weight of the roller as he moved it up and down the wall; its appearance when done would be smooth and clean. He enjoyed even the scent of the chemicals, the formaldehyde filling his lungs as he closed his eyes and breathed in. Zalman enjoyed the work.

But each day as he drove back to the shop, tucked away the cans, dappled now with clouds of color, pushing them back on the shelf until they were tight against the wall, a familiar uneasiness tugged at his heart. Outside, when he locked up the shop and walked the five long blocks home, he began to feel it more intensely. He let his feet move him forward, ignoring the pigeons pecking at a half-eaten granola bar on the sidewalk, even the next-door neighbor, an elderly Polish woman who nodded in greeting as she pulled her small cart of groceries behind her along the curb as he walked up the stairs, entered the apartment, kissed his wife's cheek, soft, cool, compliant. Even when his daughter, seated at the kitchen table, looked up from her notebooks and smiled. Zalman didn't notice any of it, and he realized then that it had been several months since he had.

When Miriam decided one afternoon in late spring that she wanted to go on a family picnic in the wonderful Central Park she had heard so much about, Zalman finally made sense of it, even if he could not yet give voice to the feeling. It had now been nearly two years since Jacob's death.

"Daddy! Come sit by me on the blanket," Debbie called out as she placed salami-and-tomato sandwiches on a navy-blue blanket that she and Miriam had spread on the grass.

Zalman put his hands in the pockets of his jacket and shook his head.

"On the dirt you want me to sit?"

Miriam laughed as she glanced at her husband's face, stern and contemplative, despite the sunny spring day. She eased herself onto the blanket.

"I think your father can just as well sit on the bench over here and eat his sandwich."

His daughter, giving up the fight, shrugged and held out one of the foil-wrapped sandwiches to him, then stretched her legs in front of her.

Zalman unwrapped the sandwich, took a bottled water from the ice case, and chewed his food thoughtfully as his wife and daughter chatted. He paid no attention to their conversation but instead let the sounds of birds chirping, the scents of roses beginning to bloom amid the shrubs, the cooling breezes, all the season wash over him as he closed his eyes. He thought about the monkeys and their antics that he would soon see at the park's zoo. It had been a long time since he had visited a zoo—on one of the excursions taken with Jacob, Esther, and, of course, young Gary. When he opened them, his eyes fell upon another family just a short distance away, under a circle of trees. A mother tending to a toddler in a stroller as the father and son were having a game of catch.

And then, as if a light had been suddenly switched on in his brain, he knew what it had all been about. He knew he missed her. He missed Esther.

Still, for days and months after the realization, Zalman was plagued by anxiety, an anxiety that affected his stomach so badly that, seeing the flushed look on his face, hearing his refusal more than once when his favorite dishes, even her special cholent—a mixture of beef, potatoes, and beans that had cooked in a large pot for eight hours—Miriam insisted that he see a doctor. No sign of ulcers, he was assured, but nevertheless Dr. Steinberg had advised, somewhat firmly, that Zalman give up smoking. Nothing good, he admonished, could come from the habit. And that same afternoon, after a lifetime of inhaling nicotine, Zalman had his last cigarette. In fact, both his wife and daughter were surprised that he never fell back into the habit, never sneaked one as he went on his daily walk each evening, never even craved it. Eventually, his smoker's cough, which had been so much a part of him, dissipated altogether, and Miriam stopped giving his tobacco-plagued shirts a second rinse in the wash. But although he received a clean bill of health, the lack of appetite, his inattentiveness, the sleepless nights, all persisted.

And while Miriam continued to prepare a full cup of coffee—black, no sugar—in the morning, and wrap her arms around him as the two got under the covers at night, all with the smile, the same smile, brightening her porcelain face, Zalman knew she was worried. At first, Miriam sympathized with his preoccupation, his sadness when he received word of Jacob's passing. Many years ago, even before they had married, he had confided in her about how Jacob had saved his life during the darkest of days and had become more than a brother to him. He told her, too, of how he had helped Jacob build the home he had always dreamed of having, of how he had moved in with the couple as they battled infertility when the home seemed as barren, as empty, as his wife's womb. And how Zalman decided to go back to the farm, back to the work of his hands, the work he loved to do, back to Miriam. She knew that his heart ached for the loss, for deserting both Jacob and Esther. But Zalman had not told her all. He could never confess how he really felt about Esther, the wife that was not his own.

Jacob had cried upon hearing the news that Zalman was leaving, he told her. They had both cried the hazy summer day he took the train to Minnesota. Still, it could not be helped. Didn't Zalman deserve a life of his own, his chance at happiness?

Zalman understood that when Miriam saw him collapse as if he were drowning in his own tears once he received the phone call about Jacob, she was frightened. She began to cry, too, as Zalman, placing the receiver down, turned to her, water seeming to gush suddenly from his eyes, a helpless stare on his face, the same look that was on his two-year-old daughter's face, a mixture of shock and sadness, the morning

Miriam had accidentally slammed the car door on her thumb. Miriam tried to comfort her husband just as she had her child, with soft words and gentle smiles, but his sorrow was not to be appeased. When she heard, finally, of the child they had lost, Miriam cried even more. It was unimaginable. He had wiped his tears, not wanting his wife and child to see him weep, and left the house.

That was when Zalman took to long walks by himself, not returning for hours at a time, and the silences had become equally long, so bad that it seemed he had lost his zest for living. He had even stopped helping Debbie with her mathematics workbook, stopped applauding when she would stand and read one of her nature poems to him, stopped insisting she resume piano lessons with a tutor. The only thing, it seemed, that had remained consistent in Zalman's life was work. The daily routine of going to the shop each day, picking up the paint cans, the brushes, the daily routine of painting. Miriam had given up arguing about his hours as she realized that the business was the one thing, the only thing, that gave him solace.

More than once she had suggested he return to the home to visit with Jacob's wife, Esther, who would surely be delighted to see Jacob's old friend again. She offered to go with him, for Miriam had never met Esther, and she was curious. She was even curious about the home. But Zalman would not hear of it. It would be too painful for the wife, for them both, feeling the emptiness of Jacob's passing. He was so adamant in his refusals that Miriam relented. And still, Zalman remained anxious, sad, and each day he disappeared a little bit more.

And so she was overwhelmed with joy when Zalman came home one evening and informed Miriam that he had changed his mind. He would visit Jacob's widow in a week's time, and maybe he would feel better too. Surely, he would.

The night before he left for the home in Brooklyn, he asked Miriam to accompany him on his evening walk. She grabbed her orange wool sweater, as the night would be a chilly one, and, telling Debbie to make sure to finish her homework, the couple slipped out the door. Miriam said nothing but could not help beaming as Zalman took her hand and the two headed down Raritan Avenue toward River Road.

"I shouldn't be too long, Miriam," he said, breaking the evening's serenity. "No more than five hours at most."

She watched as a robin swooped down from a hanging branch, landed on the sidewalk in front of them, and, just as their footsteps approached, soared up in a straight line toward the evening clouds.

"Please, Zalman, don't worry," she responded, still staring ahead as they crossed the busy street. "Take as much time as you need. I'm sure your friend, Mrs. Stein, will be so happy to see you. She'll probably want to know why you haven't come by before, especially because you and Jacob were so close."

"Yes," he answered, the sound of his voice dropping an octave. But as they walked past the dimly lit shops, the narrow delicatessen, the photography studio, the Judaica store where owners were hurriedly closing for the night, Zalman wasn't quite so sure. Would Esther be happy to see him after all these years? And surely if she missed him even a tenth of how much he missed her, wouldn't she have made an attempt to find him? Wouldn't she have reached out to him before this? He felt certain that because he was the one who had cut off communication, who couldn't bear to hear any more of Jacob's recriminations, who could no longer witness the tears of a childless woman roll down her face, that Esther was ignorant of the family he now had—his wife, the farmer's daughter, his child. He could only imagine the shock on her face when he told her that for the past two years he had been living right here, in a different state, yes, but one that was only a couple of hours away from the old Brooklyn home. And then she would laugh at the absurdity of it all and look at him with watery blue eyes, and say, "Oh, Zalman," as he took her hand.

Zalman gazed down at the fingers entwined in his as a thought occurred to him. Maybe Esther hadn't thought of him at all. Maybe, even in death, Jacob was still in control of her actions, her feelings. Seeing the familiar figure through the window, she would walk away, go up the stairs, where she would creep under the covers of their bed, the one she had shared with Jacob all those years, the door shut. Maybe she had forgotten.

He glanced at Miriam as they turned the corner on the way home. She caught his eye then and smiled. His wife had a strange capacity for reading his thoughts, and he wondered if she could read them now.

~

Zalman leaned back into the gray leather seat of the light-blue Chevy Celebrity, the car he had received as a parting gift from his father-in-law, the rabbi. After two years, the automobile still felt new, and sometimes he could swear that it even had that new-car smell. It had barely been driven since the family's cross-country journey from Minnesota. Now, except for the occasional trip to visit his wife's cousins, who lived in Queens, the car mostly sat in front of their home, Zalman moving it on Tuesdays and Thursdays only to comply with parking regulations. He could walk to the shop now and took the truck for calls to customers and, as for Debbie, well, he didn't even want to think about his only child behind the wheel right now. He should have sold the vehicle, he knew, as it would have been the practical thing to do; he might still recover a reasonable sum. Still, he couldn't imagine giving it up. He shifted the car into drive.

The Chevy purred alive, and he pulled the visor down to avoid the sun in his vision. He should have left earlier, he thought, because the sun was always a hindrance at this time of day. Again, despite it all, Miriam and Debbie popped into his mind—Miriam giving him an extra squeeze that morning as he hugged her goodbye, advising him to send her regards; Debbie's quick "Have fun, Daddy," as she slipped back into her room. How much did she know of his reasons for the journey? he wondered.

He entered onto the Belt Parkway, joining the steady stream of traffic. The distance was relatively short, but the ride was not pleasurable, with it being a Friday and, worse yet, all the family vacationers seeking that sweet spot to spend their Memorial Day weekend. He knew Esther wasn't one of them. As a teacher, she easily might have left for her brothers' homes in Florida, but he knew she'd be in the home that she had lived in with Jacob, the home of her husband's dreams.

As Zalman cruised past the tired fishers along the waterfront, the joggers, their water bottles hugging their hips, a few college students flying kites or loitering on benches beneath a violet, breezy sky, he felt his fingers gripping the wheel tighter, the image of the home taking shape in his mind. It was the Brooklyn home that was once Jacob's dream, true, but the house had been just as much his own, maybe more. The idea of it had sprung from Jacob's mind, to be sure, but it was Zalman's brain that had worked out the plans. It was Zalman who sketched the slope of the roof, angled each corner of the bedrooms, he who lovingly increased the span of the windows that looked out at a thousand days of sun and rain. It was Zalman's house from the baseboards to the moldings to the chimney, and he had a right to it as much as anyone. But what about Esther? That day in the coffee shop when he could barely look at her face. No, Zalman had no right to that house, just as he had no right to his best friend's wife.

Esther. Again, he scanned the highway for the exit, the pace of traffic slowing, then picking up once more as her face appeared before him, the gentle curve of her cheeks, the way she would sweep away the waves of her auburn hair as the strands fell against her face, and the eyes with their particular shade of stellar blue. More than that, there was an earnestness to them as they filled with tears as she poured out her sorrows to him. That moment brought him confidence that she felt the same way he did; that she loved him too; that she held back from reaching out to him out of respect, lest she disrupt his life; and that all that was needed was his return, the spark that would set her feelings aflame.

And yet, like tinnitus, an insistent buzz in the ear, he could not let go of Miriam, whose devotion had remained steadfast from the moment they met. And there was Debbie, of course, his dear child and the beacon of his future. It was because of them that he only recently revealed the tragedy experienced by Jacob and Esther—the loss of their only child. It had taken him years before he was able to truly rein in his feelings, to hide them from Miriam's discerning sight.

The sun was high in the sky now as he felt his heart beating faster. He swerved only slightly into the right lane and quickly straightened the blue Celebrity to meet the line of increasing traffic. In the same way he adjusted his thinking, not quite banishing the thoughts of his wife and daughter, but letting them rest, at least for now, in the corner of his brain.

He wasn't sure what he would do once he professed his love for Esther. But he'd never abandon them; they were as much a part of him as the blood that coursed through his veins. Yet there had always been Esther.

~

Later, it seemed almost like a lifetime, Zalman took a deep breath, felt the air spread like warm honey through his veins. Again, her image floated into his brain, consumed him. For the first time in his life, Zalman was not running away, not running to escape the Nazi terror or a shattered friendship. But now he was running *toward* something, no longer out of fear, but hope. He was ready. She was the home that he truly loved. Zalman was ready to go home.

A feeling as close to elation as Zalman had ever experienced lightened his spirit as the sun's rays peeked beyond the oncoming hill. He fumbled for his sunglasses in the glove compartment, but just as he did, he saw the exit sign, the one he needed, about to sail past his line of vision. Zalman slowed the car slightly and began the turn, a hair's breadth behind. He did not see the red truck emblazoned with the word MERCURY in his rearview mirror as it plowed into him, only the light of the sun, brilliant and gold. A light brighter than any he had ever seen before.

TWENTY-SIX

Francine, 1995

The two women seated in front of her looked like smiling Buddhas, the kind she had once seen in a picture book of China at the library. The shorter one was wearing a belted red dress with tiny white stars on it, which fell in folds as she sat, her legs crossed at the ankles, her round face framed by a halo of overly dyed reddish-brown hair. The other one was taller, skinny, and wore tan polyester pants and a matching sweater, her hair a steely gray, much like Francine's. Each woman had the same red-lipped smile stretched across her face, the same Star of David dangling between their breasts. Francine knew what the gold star meant, knew they were Jewish because, years earlier, her manager at the Kroger's, before she had gone into medical filing, had worn a similar ornament. And while there were a bunch of people Francine didn't exactly care for, the Jews weren't one of them.

"So you're from Georgia, you say?" asked the one with the dye job. "That's one place I've never been to. Must be hot there."

Francine forced a laugh.

"No, not all the time, but it can get pretty hot in the summer. Sometimes even a hundred degrees."

The women exchanged smiling glances, the gray-haired one fanning herself with one hand.

"Well, Mrs. McKee," continued the other, "you say it's just you and your husband living in the house. If you don't mind my asking, don't you think this house is a little big for only two people?"

Francine had expected the question and nodded.

"Well, it may seem so, but as I mentioned, we're both retired now, and we're moving here to be closer to my nephew and his family, who I'm sure will be visiting once in a while, and of course there are the other two boys and a grandson still back in Norcross who'll be wanting to come see us now and then," she said, adding, "Oh, I hope that's not a problem." She sat back, satisfied. Only one little lie, the one about having a nephew who lived in New York. That and the part about her sons "visiting."

The women looked at one another again.

"No, it shouldn't be, not if they're respectful of the furniture, and the grounds, and—" began the one in the dress before the one with the gray hair interrupted, "Oh, I'm sure it'll be fine, but what Esther—Mrs. Stein—is really concerned about is that you stick to the one-year lease. You see, the last tenant left suddenly, before the year was up. Nice man, very lovely family, but there was a problem." Her friend—Mrs. Stein—her smile wavering a bit, nodded her assent.

"Oh my, no! We plan to be here for at least that long, maybe even two or three years if it comes down to it. You won't have any problem with us." Francine let her southern drawl curl a little longer around the last word. She watched their faces relax somewhat, their bodies ease ever so slightly against the back of the upholstered sofa.

"Well, then," said Mrs. Stein as she rose from her seat, signaling the end of the conversation, "I think this will work out just fine," adding as the other woman followed suit, "My friend, Florrie here, will take care of the rent collection each month, and I'll be heading back to my brother's in Florida."

Before extending her hand to the two women, Francine touched the fake pearls at her neck.

"And please don't forget to visit Georgia on your way there," she said.

~

Francine had had enough. The yelling, the door slamming, all of that name-calling, was too much. If she only had the money, maybe she would take off for a little farm, somewhere with green grass and long cornstalks, and nothing but sky and the stars at night.

But instead of looking for farms in the Midwest, Francine checked out the newspaper, and sitting down with a cup of Starbucks, let her index finger slide down the listings in the realty section. She jotted down the info on house rentals that could accommodate a family of five.

She got up and surveyed the room and then looked out the double window. Standard Motel 6, standard dirty parking lot in the back. She picked up the phone and dialed the first number. No rain predicted in the forecast tomorrow, a perfect day for some house hunting. She would tell Patrick all about it after she signed the contract. He was of no use anyway.

~

It wasn't long after the family moved in that Patrick started complaining. The weather was too cold, there were bees in the backyard, and, worst of all, there was no liquor store in walking distance.

Francine sat at the kitchen table, having her coffee, black with three sugars, and watched as her husband stooped to put the drops in Kiki the Chihuahua's bulging eyes. The fourteen-year-old dog was nearly blind. Patrick, at age sixty-six, was a bit rough around the edges and mostly a pain in the you-know-what, but he did have a sweet streak when it came to his dogs, from Gracie, the German shepherd, to Mel, the fat bulldog with the ugly underbite, to Kiki, the eldest. Still, anyone who met Patrick for the first time would swear that there was nothing he loved more than a cold one followed by a nicotine drag. And maybe there was some truth to that.

She sat back, letting the hot liquid burn her tongue and slide down her throat as she mentally appraised her husband of forty years. At six foot two, Patrick was once a tall drink of water, but in the past few years, the hunch in his back had become so pronounced that now he was shorter by a couple of inches. As always, he had on a pair of buff-colored trousers and a wrinkled Braves T-shirt, a dangerous thing to wear, she thought, in Yankee territory. But Patrick didn't go out much except in the middle of the night to breathe in the cooler air, or when his body ached for another smoke.

Gracie, the German shepherd who had been lying in the corner of the kitchen, got up and stretched her haunches lazily before walking over to sniff at Francine's bare toes. She scratched the top of the animal's head, but before she could lift herself up to get the leashes, she heard the screech of the front screen door. At once, her two sons burst into the room. She wondered what they were up to now.

Francine shot up from her seat, but her husband, as usual, didn't blink an eye as he put down the bottle of eye drops and rubbed noses with Kiki.

"I thought someone was gonna order pizza," exclaimed her eldest, a thirty-eight-year-old broad-faced man with thinning hair and already an ample paunch. Probably about fifty or sixty pounds over what was healthy, over what he looked like when he was in his twenties and still handsome. She still couldn't understand why Patty, his wife, had left him and their newborn baby thirteen years ago. He grabbed a green apple from a bowl on the counter and began chomping on it.

Francine placed her hands on her hips and glowered at him like a person who was well aware of the power she had over her children.

"Albert, you are a full-grown man with a kid. Are you not old enough to order your own pizza without Mama having to do that and wipe your nose too?"

Albert shrugged and took another bite out of the apple.

"Well, I would do that, Mama, if only I knew where there was one of them New York pizza places I heard so much about. We've only been here two days, for God's sake! Where's the phone in this place anyway?"

~

It was well past midnight before Francine, still in her jeans and polo, got into bed. Albert was downstairs listening to the Stones, no doubt with young Billy by his side. And she hated to think where Elias, her youngest, was at this hour of the night. Probably somewhere in town, smoking weed. She stared out the bedroom window into the blackness, catching sight of the tip of Patrick's cigarette, its blue light floating up from the curb. How long had he been out there? Or perhaps the better question was: How much longer would he be outside? Again, she thought of going to sleep, of doing battle with her insomnia in a king-size bed that she would have all to herself, which was just the way she liked it, what with Patrick being an incorrigible snorer. Lately, it was only her recurring fears about the family's future that kept her awake.

Her thoughts settled now on the tall elderly woman with the funny name who lived next door and who would soon find out it wasn't just her and Patrick living in the home, but three others along with the animals. And if that happened, Francine mused, standing at the window as her eyelids slowly drifted downward, where on earth would they go?

~

To look at Francine, most would think that she was a woman who was tired of living, with her pale, doughy face and the rolls of fat that billowed down her hips and thighs. Her eyes, puffy, without color, suggested she had been run over by life like a steam engine, a woman whose dreams had already been spent. But Francine, at age sixty-three, did, in fact, have big dreams, dreams no one, not even Patrick, knew about.

When Francine put her head on the pillow each night, sometimes just before the first glimmer of sun, the dream would appear before her like a yellow brick road. Not some fancy island, but a farm. Broad as the eye could see with quacking white ducks and fat pink pigs and tiny peeping chicks, sleek black horses, milking cows, and dogs, not three, but a dozen of them running all over the place. It was true that she didn't know the first thing about farms, how to run one, not even how to buy one, and the only farms she had ever seen were the ones on TV and Miller's pumpkin farm, where she and the family would visit each fall when she was just a kid. Maybe it was because of all the animals roaming about, making noises at all hours of the day, or maybe it was because country life was so far removed from what she knew since she was born—the concrete cities, the screeching of tires, the stench of an open garbage can left standing too long in the heat. She knew only that she had to have a farm one day and could see herself waving the chicks in with the hem of her apron and lying on a lounger with thick pillows on a wide porch, watching a rainbow shimmer up in the sky. She wouldn't even mind getting up at five in the morning if she had a farm. She realized it was an impossible dream, something that would always remain in her head. Even so, it was hers.

~

While it was Francine's idea to move to Brooklyn, she didn't exactly love the notion of making the trip and having to deal with a bunch of Yankees who would make fun of their lack of sophistication when they called soda "pop." But the way she saw it, speaking with a Brooklyn accent and rushing all the time were not things to be proud of. Unfortunately, she didn't have a choice about the move. New York City was the place to be for steelworkers, something Albert had some training in, what with high-rises going up every month, it seemed, and the call for fearless workers who weren't afraid of heights. There weren't many buildings going up in Norcross, Georgia.

There was another reason they had moved, something she didn't want too many people to know about. The boys had gotten into trouble with the law, and some of the cops already knew their names. Albert had busted up some guy in a bar a few years back and had done some time for drag racing and sending one of his friends to the hospital after he ran into him. Elias's crimes were worse, and it all stemmed from his addictions. At one point, he was doing heroin and even robbed a grocery store because he needed to score some cocaine. He had also gotten arrested for carrying without a license. Where he got those guns she had no idea. But after rehab, he promised her that he was done with all that. That was why she didn't mind the weed so much. And now there was the problem with Albert's son, Billy. Only last year, when Billy turned thirteen, she had been called to the school on more than one occasion when the boy was caught fighting, cursing the teacher, or losing his temper in one way or another. And while boys will be boys, she thought, it wasn't a good sign.

Still, even though she thought getting away would be the best idea for them all, Francine was somewhat reluctant to come east. They had been here once before. Ten years earlier, when Albert was just getting started with his steelwork, his friend in Brooklyn had told him about a job opportunity on a high-rise with an underground parking garage they were erecting in Tribeca. Since Francine could find a job doing medical filing almost anywhere, and she figured that maybe Patrick could work in one of the Home Depots, they decided to make the move. Besides, a change of scenery might be good for Elias. So, with Albert's son Billy in tow, they made the move.

Life in the city didn't last long, though. They were there no more than a month when Albert got into another car accident that hurt someone else. Still, they couldn't take any chances. The family didn't need more trouble. It wasn't Albert's fault, anyway, she reasoned. It was just the sun. And that was when they had decided to head back to Norcross.

Francine didn't want any more trouble, but now she was worried again. There was little doubt that with the boys and the kid living there full-time, and their friends coming and going, the "old" lady—well, maybe they were the same age—knew pretty fast that there were more than just the two of them living in the house. Sometimes Francine would see the woman in front of her house, tending the flowers or looking up at the sky like she was wondering if it was going to rain. But Francine was smart enough to see behind the neighborly veneer and could tell whenever she was giving her the old snake eye.

"How y'all doin', Miss Florrie?" Francine would lean over and call from her spot on the front porch, two of the three dogs lying at her feet. The woman would nod back at her, then put her eyes on the soil again as if it were the most important thing in the world. No one could say nothing about their family, after all. On the first of the month, like clockwork, Francine would show up on Florrie's porch, envelope in hand. Each time, Florrie was surprised to see her and would look down at the white envelope when offered, not bothering to open it, then back up with her eyes on Francine before the words escaped from her lips.

"Thank you." And then like sugar, Francine would smile, turn on her Keds, and walk right back into her home. Rent paid. No questions asked.

In this way, Francine ensured that no outsiders, least of all Florrie, would be entering the home, for if they did, they were bound to find it not a little different from the house Francine saw on that first day. Just as soon as they moved themselves in, almost immediately, Francine had asked Patrick to rearrange all the furniture, which had been positioned the same way, toward the front of the home, toward the rising sun. Maybe it had been moved that way by one of the former tenants, because surely the two ladies she had met before moving in seemed too sensible. To Francine, it was ridiculous to be squinting all the time when you were watching your show. Then there was the downstairs powder room. More than once when Francine had to go, the toilet had backed up with such a stench that Patrick had to hold a hankie over his nose when he used the plunger. No point in calling a plumber, because after a couple of these bad events, he had it all fixed. Turns out Patrick was good for something.

Then there was the problem with the piano. Elias, who fancied himself somewhat of a musician since he had started guitar lessons when he was in high school, was the only one who took an interest in it. He tried playing "Ave Maria" and other songs on it, by ear, of course, and soon after, the pastel-color seat became unhinged, so that he found himself sliding all over the place every time he sat down. The well-worn booklets inside, however, remained untouched. But the worst thing was when he spilled orange juice across the piano's sleek surface, the sticky liquid sneaking between the stark white keys before puddling, finally, on the soft bench. No matter how much scrubbing Francine did, the stains remained, and the sounds that came out bore no resemblance to music at all. After that, even Elias lost interest.

But the thing that most worried Francine was that people would find out about Bull. Bull was the dog that Billy had found wandering in the back woods one day, no collar, no leash. He begged to keep him, and since they were all dog lovers, how could she say no? Billy promised to take care of the brown-and-white pit bull that looked to be about two years old. They named him Bull, an appropriate appellation for a dog with short, stubby legs planted on the floor, holding up a barrel-shaped torso.

Billy was true to his promise. Within a week, he and his pals had built a doghouse for Bull and the other dogs who, after some initial trepidation, welcomed the new creature into the home. It wasn't unusual for Francine, as she looked out the kitchen window, to see Billy and the boys out in the backyard, throwing a ball as Bull, saliva dripping from his mouth, stubby tail wagging, ran to retrieve it. Soon even Patrick, who was always suspicious when a new member was added to the group, would bend down when sitting in the old recliner and playfully pat the dog's tubular belly as the animal gurgled happily.

But one day, that all changed. Francine had been reading the morning paper at the kitchen table when a sudden sharp noise, a hurting sound like when you step on a shard of glass in your bare feet, startled her. But no, this time it was Bull, the dog, barking up a storm. Still, it didn't sound like the kind of bark he usually made when he was having fun.

Francine squinted, trying to get her eyes to focus on the scene in front of her. Billy and his friends, laughing, in a circle near a tree. Something dangling from a high branch. A rope being pulled.

"Billy! What the hell!" she screamed, as she pushed open the back screen door.

The boy turned abruptly as if he'd just been caught with his hand in the cookie jar, the three others ignoring her. Her eyes went up to a contraption they had rigged onto one of the branches of the big oak off to the side of the backyard. Hanging just out of reach was some kind of rubber toy, so bitten and torn up that it was hard to identify. Bull was barking, a mixture of anger, frustration, and fear. As always, the leash was around the dog's neck, but at the other end this time was one of Billy's friends, no older than Billy, who would wait till Bull, growling and eager, would fly straight up, making for the toy, only to pull him back at the last second, the dog's yelp shattering the air. Sometimes when he managed to snatch a piece of the rubber, he'd be rewarded with one of the chicken nuggets that they had in an open box nearby on the lawn. When Bull wasn't successful, they'd stand there, guffawing, as the dog, exhausted and panting, would quickly make another attempt. As Francine stared at the scene, it was as if a light snapped on in her head. The boys were enjoying this. She made her voice rise above the din.

"William Gerald McKee! You leave that animal be! Can't you see you're torturing him with your teasing?" Billy's face turned white as the others shifted their bodies away from her, no longer laughing, but coughing, snickering.

"Meemaw, you don't understand," Billy answered, his voice sounding more like a whimper as he looked around at the others for help. Getting none, he cleared his throat and continued, "We're not teasing him. We're *teaching* him, for our protection. It'll take time, you know. But Bull is gonna be a really good guard dog. For—for"—he stuttered—"for *protection.*" Francine could no longer contain herself.

"Y'all think I believe that bullshit? I wasn't born yesterday, you idiots! Cut that thing off the tree and do it now!" The three boys looked at Billy, whose facial muscles had begun to relax. He nodded.

The fat one passed off the dog to Billy, removed a switchblade from the pocket of his jeans, moved toward the tree, and swiftly cut the taut rope at its center, so that the ratty thing abruptly fell just as Bull's teeth swiftly latched onto it. That was when Francine saw that it wasn't a rubber bear at all, but a rhino, all torn up now, its horn hanging by a single pitiful thread. Billy himself used to teethe on it as a baby. As Billy walked the dog back into the house, without thinking, Francine extended her hand to pat its head. Bull jerked his head and snapped, just missing the tip of her index finger. He was never the same after that.

Francine had a feeling then, like a cold wind passing right through her. She was afraid that something bad was going to happen, something that would drive them away from the home, just like before. It took only two months for her to realize that she was right.

~

Elias had been gone for three days. He had gotten up one morning, dressed in his brother's brown tweed suit, which no longer fit Albert, and gone for a job interview. Instead of being his usual sullen self, sleeping most of the day and staying outside smoking weed all night, he was enthusiastic, even gave her a kiss on the cheek as she stood over a pot, cooking oatmeal. He announced that he had a job interview at the community college, not as a professor, for he hadn't even graduated from high school, but working in building maintenance. Francine stepped away from the stove and wrapped her arms around her son, feeling his bones protrude beneath the thin skin. She wondered how he was able to maintain himself, let alone a whole building, as she rubbed her face against his dark scraggly beard. Still, he could be a good worker as long as he was straight, and, at thirty-three, it was about time he had some gainful employment.

"Elias, I just know things are going to turn out great," she said, releasing him from the hug. Just the same, she kept her fingers crossed.

The entire time he was gone, Francine couldn't get her youngest son out of her mind. Thoughts of Elias consumed her in a way no one in her family could, so much so that she wasn't able to eat for the rest of the day, which was unusual for Francine, who was always hungry. She sat on the sofa in the living room, too agitated to start warming up the drumsticks for Patrick, as the setting sun covered the room in shades of orange and purple. Francine knew that mothers weren't supposed to have favorites, and yet there was always something special, it seemed, about Elias. A sweetness, a vulnerability. Unlike Albert, or anyone else for that matter, each time she came into a room, he would ask how she was feeling that day. As she lay on the couch late into the night, it was Elias who would sprint upstairs just to get an extra blanket and cover her feet. He was the same with his friends, running out on a frozen night to help a buddy who had gotten a flat tire at 2:00 a.m. But it was that same sweetness that would often get him in trouble, his inability to say no to the drugs, the need to sedate himself after each rejection. Francine sat up as she heard a sound a few feet away, but it was only the jingle of Gracie's dog tags as she scratched herself near the front door.

Later that night, after no sign of Elias, not even a phone call, Francine began to worry all over again, and this time it wasn't only about the job. He showed up briefly one evening, still wearing the brown tweed suit. His eyes were bloodshot, his cheeks sunken in. Francine took one look at him and recognized the signs. No, he hadn't been celebrating getting the job, but just the opposite. She didn't ask any questions then, and not the next day, when he would disappear for a week, leaving the crumpled suit in the garbage pail at the curb.

It was just after lunch on an afternoon when school had closed for conferences as she was pouring kibble for the dogs, all except Bull, who was now out somewhere with Billy and his friends, when she heard him come in through the back quietly. Without looking up, she knew that it was Elias. Neither of them spoke as he sat down at the kitchen table and she poured him a mugful of the coffee she had brewed a half hour earlier. He drank it in one long gulp, black. Francine dug through one of the cabinet drawers until she found an emery board, plunked herself down opposite him, and began filing her nails, which were painted a rose pink. She stole a look at her son, his hands shaking as he tried to hold the cup steady. She moved the emery board across and then back on the nail of her left ring finger as she tried to slow the beating of her heart.

"Feelin' better?" she asked finally.

He didn't answer her, but he didn't get up and leave either. She realized as she looked down the length of his body that he couldn't. He had wet himself.

"Elias," she said, putting the emery board down on the table, "let Mama help you." She walked over and put an arm around his shoulders. His shirt stank from whiskey and tobacco. There were fresh track marks on his arms. After he shrugged her off, she went upstairs.

~

The next time, the last time, Elias left, he had been gone for nearly a week and showed up one Sunday afternoon, his pupils trembling in bloodshot eyes as he shivered, wearing only a flimsy T-shirt in the forty-degree weather. Francine didn't ask questions but called on Albert, who was upstairs playing video games in the bedroom. He appeared at the head of the stairs.

"Get your brother into the shower," she said, keeping her voice low. She threw her arms around the paper-thin body—Elias was shivering now—and let her thumb slide over the grainy marks on his arm, punctured by the string of needles. He was crying—loud, sloppy sobs just like he used to when he was a baby. Then she handed him off to Albert.

She found a Reese's peanut butter cup in a drawer, unwrapped it, and took a bite, enjoying the brief pleasure it gave her. Then she glanced outside the window and saw Billy and his friends playing at the tree with the pit bull. She turned quickly away, not wanting to see more. But barely had the forbidden chocolate settled in her belly when something caught her attention.

Billy was sitting, knees up to his chest on the yellow grass, tilting his ruddy face toward the sun. The other two boys were under the tree with the dog, who was dripping saliva as, teeth bared, he made for the dangling hot dog, tied to a slim branch no less than six feet off the ground. One of them egged Bull on as the other, a rope wound around one wrist, waited just long enough for the animal to be at full height, ready to attack. With a yelp of pain, the dog was pulled back, its legs slamming to the ground.

"Here we go again," Francine murmured to herself. She heard her knees crack as she got up from the chair.

Francine felt the blood rise to her head so suddenly she thought she might faint. She screamed again. Billy jumped up, and the boys turned white, their eyes riveted. But they weren't looking at her; it was something else. Something that flew by, whether man or animal, she couldn't tell. As the rage that had blurred her eyes faded, she soon realized who or what it was. Elias, butt naked, shower water still sliding off his skin. But it wasn't that sight that caused her body to quiver; it was what she saw as she focused, the object in his hand.

"Shut up! Shut up! Shut up!" Elias was half screaming, half sobbing as he approached the group at the tree, waving the small black gun back and forth like a flag, a rallying cry. No one moved. Francine wanted to say something, but her tongue had frozen solid at the bottom of her mouth. And before she could cry out, before she could even blink, Bull was leaping up for the meat, flying, eyes blazing with a color she had never seen before. And then, just as suddenly, a blast shook the tree, the ground, and everything in it until finally an eerie silence descended over them all. And when the smoke cleared and the stench of the residue shrank from their nostrils, there was Elias, big tears running down his cheeks, the trigger of the gun dangling from his fingers. And Bull, his brown snout pressed to the ground, which quickly tinted a river of red.

Finally, after two or three minutes of silence, Albert appeared. Folding Elias against his chest and taking the gun gingerly, he led his brother into the house. Francine wasn't sure how long she had stood there, eyes closed, her hand on her forehead, when another sound, a soft one, came to her.

"Francine, we got cops."

~

Someone had heard the gunshot and notified the police. Judging by the sound of the siren, they would be at their door in minutes.

And, indeed, when Officers Kates and Ramirez showed up, they wanted to know all about it, what had disturbed the peace in such a quiet neighborhood. Francine and Patrick, who stood as tall as his hunchbacked build would allow, greeted them at the front door. Just a stupid mistake, they told the officers, just trying to get rid of some old fireworks when Patrick's cigarette went and fell out of his mouth, setting off one of the damn things. You could go check it out in the back if you want. And by the way, would either of you care for a nice cool glass of water, or maybe an Oreo cookie?

The officers declined, remaining stone-faced. Luckily, by the time they checked the yard, the boys had moved Bull deep into the woods behind the home, covering the suspicious spot with the doghouse, which was now propped just beneath the oak, from its place a few feet behind in the woods. The officers, after only a few moments, which seemed to her like an eternity, moved on with just a warning and a summons for the firecrackers.

~

It was still light out by the time the family finished packing the house up. They gathered the three dogs and, with some water and biscuits, put them into the gray van with Albert, Billy, and Elias. As Francine and Patrick checked out the living room, making sure they had left nothing behind, Francine felt a pang of regret. She had grown accustomed to sleeping on the comfortable king-size bed, looking out at the small apples dangling from the tree each morning. But she knew, too, that there was a chance the cops would find out about the accident ten years ago, how it was Albert driving his friend's tow truck with the sign MERCURY on it, how he had hit the old guy and just kept going. It all spelled nothing but trouble.

Francine felt an anger churn deep inside her, and she held back from screaming. To think that, after all these years, that accident had come back to haunt them! She'd had a bad feeling about their return, but it wasn't bad enough to stop them from leaving Norcross. And now she was going back. Francine knew that the death of a dog wasn't such a big thing, not enough to get Elias any real time. But the accident ten years ago, when Albert had borrowed his friend's tow truck just to make a few extra bucks, just might be the thing to put Albert away for years.

What if the driver had been hurt? Or worse yet, killed? Albert might not see Billy again until he was a grown man. Police had records about such things, and Francine wasn't taking any chances.

But Patrick was even angrier than she was, mad about the whole thing. Mad about the dog who had never done nothing to nobody, but mostly mad about having to move yet again, so mad that just before he closed the door, he casually dropped his cigarette, the tip still glowing, onto the carpet in front of where the TV used to be. This time, it really did light something; this time, the lie became truth.

The orange spark tested the air a bit before gaining courage, and, seconds later, the points of light grew into flames that raced in a line across the carpet toward the wall separating the living room from the kitchen, where, engulfing the wall, they shot straight up toward the white ceiling. Francine slammed the front door shut.

Francine settled into the black van next to Albert just as the tip of darkness came into view. That was when she saw her. Her arms were crossed as she stood on the corner, the old woman called Florrie who would take the check from Francine's hand precisely on the first of each month. They were breaking the lease, only by a couple of months, but so what? Francine fixed her eyes on the woman, who defiantly glared back at her, a strand of her steely gray hair waving in the wind. And in that moment, seeing her there, Francine knew that it was she who had called the police. The stuck-up bitch.

Finally, after about an hour into their travels south, Patrick turned the vehicle onto a rural road, hugging the water, opening onto a void, nothing but wide-open space in the distance.

Francine relaxed, letting her head fall back as she closed her eyes and tried to sleep. Someday, she thought, just before dozing off, someday I'm gonna get that farm.

PART V

AN OPEN DOOR

TWENTY-SEVEN

Florrie, 2010

S he could hardly be called a woman, she appeared so young. The girl was standing at the front door, her fifth and last appointment of the day. She was dressed in navy-blue tapered cotton pants and a white button-down shirt with red swirls and a raised collar. Of tall stature, like Florrie herself, she had a nervous smile plastered to her face. Florrie thought her ordinary looking at first, but then as the guest wiped a stray hair off her forehead and entered the home with the older woman following behind, Florrie noticed something about her that was indeed unusual. Her hair, a long silky copper brown, half of it fastened in the back by a turquoise tortoiseshell comb, reached down past her hips.

As Florrie examined her guest, the girl ignored her and turned her head slowly, taking in the narrow hallway with its lone bulb at the ceiling, the square-shaped living room with its sparse furnishings, the off-white leather couch, the glass-topped coffee table on which rested a slender white vase with a single purple orchid, the recessed lights, even the linear molding at the periphery of the white ceiling.

How odd, Florrie thought, that this guest was so concerned about each detail. The others, young couples with families, all prospective buyers sent by a Realtor, no longer renters, had breezed through the home, counting bedrooms, a few flushing toilets. But this woman, stopping next to the coffee table, didn't seem so eager to explore the rest of the house. Her long neck stretched as she took in each intricate detail.

"Would you like to see the kitchen and—"

The girl/woman—Florrie remembered her name, Mrs. Landau—put out the palm of her hand, stopping her in midsentence.

In other circumstances, Florrie would have considered the action quite rude, but now she simply obeyed her wish and silenced herself. The woman intrigued her. But then she made such a sudden exclamation that Florrie, in the moment, was shocked.

"A piano! Oh, I can't believe it. You have the piano!" she shouted, dropping her large round tote bag on the plush beige carpet and taking long strides toward the instrument. She stood for a minute staring at its polished black body shining beneath the overhead lights, then moved her hand toward it tentatively, almost as if she were afraid to touch it. Florrie, still riveted to the spot at the home's entrance, remained silent, her curiosity piqued.

The young woman licked her lips, a smile, a very pretty smile, suddenly overtaking her face. There was something familiar about her, Florrie thought. But, of course, it was impossible that they had ever met before. Still, the feeling scratched at the corners of her brain.

And then, as she smiled, the guest's demeanor began to change. Swiftly, she moved forward, tossed back her long hair, sat down on the piano bench, and without asking permission, opened the top to reveal the sparkling ivories that Florrie had polished only the day before, and began to play. But as the melody ascended into the air, Florrie soon realized there was something familiar about that too. Perhaps a song from her childhood, or one of the tunes she and Sid would dance to when they first married. Still, she couldn't quite place it. So she stood there, hands clasped tightly in front of her, and listened to the light but melodic tune until it ended. The girl—Mrs. Landau—sat back satisfied, finally, as if she had just completed a three-course dinner, the smile not yet faded from her face.

"That was very pretty," said Florrie. "When did you learn to play?"

The girl paused, tilted her head as if absorbed in some aura, as if she were still listening to the music, and then she turned to Florrie, and seemed to notice her for the first time.

"My father taught me when I was a little girl on the farm. We never had our own piano—pianos and farmwork don't usually go well together. But I had a friend whose home had a piano a few miles down the road, and in exchange for lessons from my father, the family would let me come and play, Katie and I learning together. Katie was a fast learner, a much better player than I was. Now my two boys are learning to play the piano at a tutor's home a few blocks from ours. We—Craig, my husband, and I—made sure they would have lessons."

"That's nice," responded Florrie. Then remembering, she said, "But that song you just played. What is its name?"

The girl nodded. "That was a favorite of my father's, a sweet romantic song. 'Clair de Lune.'"

"Oh. It was very nice."

The girl stood then, ignoring the naked keys behind her, and approached Florrie, her expression turning serious.

"'Clair de Lune,'" she repeated. "Didn't you recognize it?"

"Now that I think of it, there was something familiar about the song. But I don't know. I can't seem to place it."

The young woman was so close now that Florrie could feel her breath singe her cheeks.

"'Clair de Lune,' you played it all the time. You played it for my father."

"I played? My dear, I've never played a note in my life! Where would you ever get that idea?"

The woman stared at Florrie, perplexed, then turned her head to the mute piano and back again to Florrie. Looking closely now, Florrie noticed the color of her eyes. They were blue.

The young woman then jerked her head up defiantly. "Are you an agent?"

"What?"

"An agent. A real estate agent."

Florrie took a step back as if she'd just been assaulted. This woman must be mad, a real loony. She took a breath and gathered her nerves before speaking.

"Of course not! I'm the owner of this house, and I'm selling it myself."

"Then you must know my father. You were married to his best friend." She nearly spat the words at her.

But as soon as they were said, Florrie felt her knees grow weak, and she reached for the arm of the leather sofa to prevent herself from collapsing to the floor. She sat, but the girl remained standing.

"You're not Jacob's wife. You're not Esther."

A heavy silence like death hung over the brightly lit living room. Florrie tried to breathe again but found it nearly impossible as memories, all the sorrows of the past years, came flooding back to her in angry black waves threatening to sweep her away. Had it already been nearly ten years since 9/11 and the loss of so many innocent souls? It seemed that the world had changed then, irrevocably, and along with it, the sense of security that life had a certain predictability. But Florrie's own world had been forever changed again only a few years later when she became aware that friendship, true friendship, was a precious thing, an ephemeral thing. Her lips formed the words, but they were barely a whisper.

"You are mistaking me for my best friend."

The woman stood for a while, not moving, before finally sitting down next to Florrie. Without being prompted, Florrie continued. And

264

when before she could not find the words to speak, now she gained release in telling the story.

"She had been living near her brothers' families down in Florida for over fifteen years. She had asked me to come join her, more times than I can count, but I was never partial to that state, not with its rainy spells almost every day, the heat, and oh, those alligators! Besides, everything I've ever known is here in New York. The Big Apple is really the center of the world, with Broadway and Yankee Stadium and snow in the winters! How could I ever live in a place without *snow?*

"But Esther seemed to like it there in the warmth, being close to family, their children, now the grandchildren. She loved them all. And since Jacob passed, well, I was the only person she really had here. Me and the house."

"This house?"

"Yes, she loved this house. It had been the dream of her husband since the war to build a house. And he did just that; he built his house." Out of the corner of her eye, she saw the woman's cheek twitch. She continued.

"Time went by, though, and Esther retired from teaching, first staying in Florida during the winter months, and then for most of the year. But she would come back often to visit her old friend, and she would stay with me for weeks at a time. We were always friends, we'll always be . . ." Florrie's voice drifted off.

"And the house? She didn't stay here at her house?"

Florrie shook her head sadly.

"It's a lot, you know, the upkeep and all. It was a lot for one person to maintain, and besides, the house held too many memories—it was their first real home, where they had their child, their only child, and where he died. Right under the tree in the backyard. Esther saw the ball thrown by Jacob. She saw the whole thing . . . too many memories." She sighed.

"But now you're selling this house? This house that Esther loved so much?"

Florrie looked at her directly and shook her head.

"Oh, no! No, Esther never wanted to sell this home. Never! That's why she rented to strangers for a few years. Usually for a year at a time. And since I live just next door, I helped collect the rent, kept an eye out for problems. Some of the tenants were okay, quiet, decent people. But with each new person, the house changed a bit, the furniture, the wear and tear in the rooms, even the smells. No, the house was never the same with all those people coming and going. The last ones nearly burned the place to the ground. Even after parts of it were rebuilt, sometimes when I'm here alone, right after a heavy rain, I swear I can still smell the smoke of it all; it gets into everything, you know. Even after all these years," she added, looking up at the girl, lifting her eyebrows as if for confirmation.

"But now," the young woman repeated, "now she's decided to sell it."

Florrie spoke slowly.

"*I've* decided to sell it."

"But why? That couldn't be what Esther wants! Not after it meant so much to her! After it meant so much to Jacob! Why would you make that decision?"

Florrie looked down at her clasped hands. She was kneading the skin so much that small red marks had begun to appear across her fingers. She spoke again, this time in a deliberate, measured way.

"I'm selling the house because it is mine to sell."

A perplexed look swept across her guest's face. Florrie gazed up at her, meeting the blue eyes directly, her own face a mask of grief.

"I'm selling the home because I can't afford to keep it. I am selling it because Esther passed away."

Flecks of fire sparked in the woman's eyes and were swiftly replaced by tears. Without thinking, Florrie stood and moved to comfort her,

266

placing her arm around her shoulders, a vague memory coming to her of someone else comforting her friend many years ago. She waited until the girl's tears were spent, frightened a little at this sudden expression of sorrow from a stranger.

Mrs. Landau finally raised her head, dabbing at the wetness with the back of her hand. Florrie gazed at the broad face, the round blue eyes shielded by reddish lashes, now bright again.

"I'm sorry. This is so silly of me, really. I just didn't expect that she was—that she was gone."

Florrie patted the girl's back, and as she did so, she felt herself growing stronger, more composed.

"We didn't expect it either. None of us did. Esther died in her sleep a year and a half ago. A heart attack at only seventy-eight, they said. But what does it matter what the cause was? She's gone."

"And she willed the house to you?"

Florrie nodded.

"We were friends, friends from that first afternoon, that first afternoon I brought over my special noodle kugel. The construction of the home had just been completed. I even remember the smell of sawdust was still in the air."

She smiled weakly at the memory.

"Oh, we had our ups and downs! Sometimes we ran around like giddy teenagers, other times we were sisters in sorrow, lamenting the things we couldn't change, and there were a few years we barely spoke to each other at all. I taught her how to speak like a real New Yorker, how to bake a kugel and challah for the holidays. She offered to teach me how to play the piano—it was her passion—but I just had no interest in it. Instead, she taught me so many other things—decorating, baseball, but mostly how to be a friend. Esther was a true friend."

The girl looked at Florrie, absorbing the information, but then the atmosphere appeared to shift, each realizing once again why they were there. The young woman spoke first.

"So now you wish to sell the home."

It was more statement than question. Florrie nodded.

"Mrs. Landau, I do want to sell it, even though I have my regrets. And even though there are some more people coming to look at it today, I really might consider selling it to you since you have a connection to the home, to that piano which she loved so much. Yes, I might consider selling it to you."

A smile flashed across the young woman's face again.

"That would make me so happy! My husband and my boys would love to live here, a real family home! But first you must do me a favor. Please don't call me Mrs. Landau. My name is Deborah."

And at that moment, again something shifted in the living room with the piano, in the house.

"Zalman. You're Zalman's daughter."

"Yes, yes, I am."

Florrie looked up at the ceiling, her mind drifting past the years to the young squat man with the curly hair and blue eyes, the familiar smile in greeting, the way he tipped his cap, the man always by Jacob's side.

Florrie's mind began to gather the scattered memories, memories of the four of them going to baseball games or taking walks in the park when she would accompany the little family, Sid preferring to remain by himself indoors. Often, she now reflected as images of the past appeared, it was Zalman who sat long hours at the kitchen table after dinner, helping the boy with his multiplication tables, patiently teaching him the notes of the piano, the two side by side on the piano bench those times when Jacob would stay late at work. And it was Zalman who sat close to Esther, comforting her on the sofa when her world collapsed unexpectedly and Jacob had disappeared into a well of grief.

Zalman was more than a friend or even a brother. He had been a part of this home, just like the couple who owned it, for there was no Jacob, no Esther, without Zalman. And then one day, just like that, he was gone. Florrie never understood why, never dared ask Esther, who was mired in her own sorrow. It was at that time, too, that she and Esther had begun to drift away from each other. After that, she hadn't thought about Zalman too much, knowing only that he had returned to the Midwest to become a farmer. And only once had Esther mentioned him again, a month after Jacob's funeral, as the two were upstairs folding his suits and shoes into bags for the poor.

"I wish he could have been there."

"What?"

Esther, on her hands and knees, holding a pair of polished black tuxedo shoes, looked across the room at her friend.

"Zalman, our old friend, I wish he could have been at the funeral. I think Jacob would have wanted it."

Florrie stuffed a brown knitted sweater into a large garbage bag.

"Why didn't you ask him?"

Esther shrugged, still holding the shoes in midair.

"Oh, I wouldn't know where to begin finding him. Jacob threw away his address on the farm. And when Zalman left finally, I couldn't even call him on the telephone. Besides, I don't think at that time Jacob would have wanted me to. Later on, even though he never said anything, I believe he regretted it."

Florrie knew better than to ask any more questions. Still, she couldn't keep all her opinions to herself.

"Maybe in a few months when you are more yourself, you can try to find him. I could help you."

Esther stuffed the shoes into the bag and stood up.

"No, Florrie, I don't think so. He was Jacob's to love, not mine."

Florrie stared for several minutes at the door, which Esther slammed behind her as she left. Slowly, she began packing the rest of the pants, the shirts, and the sweaters into a bag, distracted only by the sound of Esther's sobbing down the hall.

"Did she ever mention him?"

"Mention who?"

"My father. Zalman. He spoke of Jacob often, mostly about their days together during the war. But sometimes he would speak of her too."

Florrie did not answer, but took in the girl, the whole of her now that they were both seated on the sofa. Then she heard her whisper.

"Do you think she loved him?"

Somehow, the question posed with such feeling, a mixture of earnestness and trepidation, didn't surprise Florrie.

But her own answer did.

"I think . . . well, I think a part of her did. Whether it was the love one has for a friend or a brother or even a romantic love. Yes, yes, I do think she loved him."

Deborah nodded slowly, eased back into the seat.

"My mother thought so. In fact, she really believed it. He didn't talk about her that much, but especially after Jacob's death, he spoke of their poor young boy, such a tragedy, and Esther. The way he spoke of Esther, I don't know, maybe it's how he smiled when he recalled their time together—Daddy didn't normally smile much—or the way he would sigh, as if he wanted to go back in time. Anyway, call it woman's intuition, my mother always thought there was something there. It was only recently that she confided in me that the day of the—" She stopped as a sob caught in her throat.

"The day he died in the car accident on the highway, that was the day he planned to come here. To see the house again, to see Esther. And maybe for something more. My mom never said a word of her belief to my father, only loved him, and loves him still. I guess she decided to see how the whole thing would have played out. But now we'll never know."

Florrie cleared her throat.

"My dear, he *was* here. But not for the reason you think. Oh, dear God, do you mean to say he lost his life on his way home?"

Deborah ignored her question.

270

"What are you saying? Wasn't he on his way back to tell my mother that he was leaving? That he planned on leaving her and leaving me?" Her voice rose with each word.

Florrie looked at the girl directly. She was so young.

"No, he wasn't leaving you at all. He was leaving Esther for the last time. I should know. I was sitting next to her on this very couch when he arrived because, you see, we were always together, the two of us. And when Zalman, your father, arrived unannounced, walking in without a word in that jaunty way, cap still tilted on his head, well, it was as if the years hadn't passed at all, and we were on our way to another ball game! We were shocked by his arrival, of course, and it was quite a while before any of us said a word. And then, well, we talked, the three of us barely able to catch our breaths. Mostly about the memories and the places we would go, the meals we had, the walks. And even about Gary. We could share our memories without the tears now, for the pain had been so long ago. Oh, Zalman loved that child like his own!

"And then we talked about our lives since, and how much of it was sad with so much loss. But much of it, especially for your father, was happy too. And he told us all about his life then, of his wife, the girl he had met on the farm, and mostly of his young daughter. What was her name?"

"Debbie," interrupted the girl.

Florrie smiled, her eyes crinkling. "I'm sorry. I'm getting old, I guess. Of course, Debbie. He cared only for you, you and your mother, the woman from the farm who had brought such joy, such calmness, such a sense of home to his life, he said. You two were his world, and he didn't have to share you with anyone! I think that's why he came here, to see Esther and recapture those memories one last time before going home to the woman, the child, he truly loved."

Deborah leaned forward, her eyes glistening.

"Do you mean he wasn't going to leave us?"

Florrie shook her head.

"Maybe once that would have been true. It was you and your mother he loved." She hesitated.

"And one other. Of course, he had always loved Jacob. That's why he wanted to build this house; both he and Jacob wanted it."

The room grew silent as the two remained locked in their thoughts, and then the girl brightened as she remembered something. She walked over to her large black bag, which lay slumped on the floor at the entrance, where she had first placed it. And, bringing it to the couch, she removed a giant-size document. As she began unraveling the paper, Florrie recognized it as a blueprint, a blueprint for the house. The friends had consulted it each day during the building process; it was something both the girl's father and Jacob had shown everyone proudly after the couple first moved in. Drawn in Zalman's own hand.

"Isn't it spectacular? He brought it with him when he came back to the farm, before he married my mother. I think he was so proud that he had drawn it and that he could do this for the man who saved his life. He used to call it King Solomon's castle—that's how he referred to Jacob, like wise King Solomon, a builder of castles. That's how I knew of the home. Even my boys, though they are only seven and three, love to hear that story."

Florrie stood, removed the vase with the one purple orchid from the surface of the coffee table, and, taking the blueprint from Deborah, flattened the paper across the glass as they both crouched close. Their examination of the document was almost childlike in its delight, each pointing out the width of a bedroom window, the slope of the roof, the depth of the closet in the hall, even each wide board of the front porch. All was considered, one reliving the home's past, the other imagining its future.

After about twenty minutes, Florrie began to feel her knees lock and, bracing herself against the table, slowly got up as Deborah returned the blueprint to her bag. There was no need to offer a tour of the home, Florrie reasoned to herself, since the young woman already knew each nook and cranny without ever having lived there. Florrie understood, too, why owning a home, this home for her family, meant so much to her. So instead she offered her a glass (there were still a few in the cabinet) of cool water from the tap, and suggested they go outdoors. After all, it was a lovely spring day, almost a perfect day.

They stepped onto the front porch and stood next to each other, each quietly admiring the house. It stood now, its siding repainted three times, more of a sage green, with complementary peacock-blue shutters, the wooden porch with two Adirondack chairs, double-sealed windows, white roof, brick chimney. No moat or stately balconies, but a home, a little weatherworn, with the slightest scent of burning ashes still within its walls. It was a castle.

~

A full sun was emerging from between the clouds as each took a wicker seat in the backyard, placing their glasses on the small wooden table on the deck. They each sat back, instinctively tilting their chins toward the sky, which glimmered a peaceful blue. The grass, in a multitude of greens, stretched serenely before them, faded finally in a circle of grown trees that stood stalwartly in the distance. In the back stood the colossal, tired oak, but close by in the forefront was the apple tree, which in spite of the turbulent unfolding of the years, remained stoically rooted, its thick branches curving upward, which in a few months would bear the same tiny yellow apples on each twig. Like the house itself, a promise.

It was Deborah who finally broke the silence, turning back to Florrie, her blue eyes wistful as she spoke.

"If only this house were *mine*."

Florrie looked out at the old apple tree and then at her young companion. She placed her wrinkled hand upon Deborah's young, softer one, and smiled.

"Oh, I think it already is."

ACKNOWLEDGMENTS

This book is the culmination of a long-awaited dream. From the time I was a young girl penning ambitious novels like *The Mystery of the Three Red Gowns*, through my college years and beyond as I wrote stories about my parents' devastating experiences during the Holocaust, I have wanted to become not just an author but a published author. I am grateful that I can now finally say that I am.

My list of those responsible for this is long, but at the top is my agent, Eve Attermann at William Morris, who from the start believed in my work, then helped me shape it to be something others could believe in too. Her expertise and enthusiasm have helped me believe in myself. I must thank my son, Charlie, for putting me in touch with Eve and for his constant reminder to "just keep writing." I will forever be grateful.

This book wouldn't be what it is without Carmen Johnson, senior editorial director, along with the team at Little A. She saw potential in this manuscript and helped me fulfill that potential through her astute comments, meticulous editing, and encouraging words. I am so lucky to be working with her.

I would be remiss in forgetting my friend and mentor Ben Camardi, who has encouraged me for the past ten years of my writing career. He gave me faith in myself when I most needed it.

A writer is nothing without her readers, and I am grateful to have a group of friends and relatives who, without fail, eagerly read my works and provide honest and supportive advice.

Three friends stand out in this regard. My lifelong friend, Marcie Ruderman, a brilliant editor and excellent writer, has never hesitated to read my work and provide in-depth commentary regarding the novel and its characters. From kitchen table to beach blanket, she has spent countless hours schlepping and reviewing my manuscript, and I am grateful for it all. Donna Danzig, a dear longtime friend, always steps up to read from the perspective of "an average reader." As a friend, though, there is nothing average about her, and I warmly thank her for her insightful comments and advice during our long discussions on the phone. My colleague and friend Dr. Helena Swanicke is the busiest person I know but has always been there for me with invaluable advice and encouragement.

I deeply appreciate the honest feedback on this novel from Emily Russak, Linda Herschfeld, Flo Teitelman, Jaime Wachtel, Melissa Gelfman, Susan Strumwasser, Harriet Brown, Sue Saad, Lois Zeidner, Marge Kuchinsky, Linda Lidor, and Cindy Rothenberg. Special thanks to Renee Price for her years of encouragement.

This book is about family, and it is the love of my family that inspires me every day. To Howie, Brad, and Charlie, the best sons a mother could ask for, I give my love and thanks. My deepest appreciation to Jaime and Elisha, who have become true daughters. I thank my brother, Jack, for the shared memories; and for Emily, who has become a sister. I am beyond grateful for my granddaughters, Zoey and Emmy, who give me joy every day and renewed hope for the future. Words are not enough to thank Arthur, my husband, the man who is always by my side and without whom nothing is possible.

Finally, I want to thank my dear parents, Charles and Betty Russak, who emerged from the depths of despair to provide their children with the possibility of a better world. My mother gave me the security of her abiding love, and my father showed me that with that love I could do anything—even become a published author. It is their voices and the voices of all the immigrants like them, seeking to build their own castles, that fill the pages of this book.

ABOUT THE AUTHOR

Shirley Russak Wachtel is the daughter of Holocaust survivors and was born and raised in Brooklyn, New York. She holds a doctor of letters degree from Drew University and for the past thirty years has taught English literature at Middlesex College in Edison, New Jersey. The mother of three grown sons and grandmother to two precocious grand-daughters, she currently resides in East Brunswick, New Jersey, with her husband, Arthur. For more information visit www.shirleywachtel.com.